THE ROMAN PILGRIMAGE

A Detailed Study of the Book of Romans Adopted From the Teachings of Derek Prince

George Ngondo

First Edition

BOOK HOUSE
Publishers

The Roman Pigrimage: First Edition Copyright ©2019

Unless otherwise stated, all scriptures are taken from:

1. KJV - King James Version

2. NKJV - New King James Version

3. NIV - New International Version

4. NASB - New American Standard Bible

5. Berean Study Bible

The publishers aim is to produce books that will help bring revival in the lives of Christians for the purposes of building them up into functional Christians in the kingdom of God. We encourage readers to seek the Holy Spirit for guidance as they read with reference to the word of God.

ISBN: 9781797852843

Contents

LETTER FROM THE AUTHOR...

First, I would like to thank the Almighty God and My Lord Jesus Christ for guiding me to successfully compile this book. Secondly, I would like to thank the late Derek Prince and his teachings and everyone who has played a role in making his recorded teachings available to the whole world. His was a truly rich ministry loaded with God's grace to teach the word of God.

My personal journey of salvation started with a deep desire to know God and His ways. As I prayed to God to teach me his ways, I was led to the teachings of Derek Prince who apparently had died 7 years earlier before I came to know the Lord.

As I took teaching after teaching, more and more truth was shed into my soul. I staretd using Derick Prince's sermons to prepare for my own bible study lessons for a small fellowship with some friends.

Previously, I had read the bible from Genesis through to Revelation three times but there still remained many unanswered questions in my life. As I walked through life in salvation, there were still many areas of my life in which I struggled. Deep inside me, I knew that there must be something more to salvation, that could afford me to live a victorious life.

The answer came to me when I started to study the book of Romans and I wholly laid my hands on the teachings of Derek Prince on this subject matter. Little did I know then that thorugh this study, God would deliver me from many of my weaknesses, challenges, habits and shortcommings. It took me a whole year to successfully naviagate through the book from Chapter 1 to chpater 16.

Without dout, the book of Romans is one of the hardest book to study and understand and I took one of Derek Princes advice's that 'you cannot get the full richness of this book if you read it casually.' The book of Romans, if read purposefuly and carefully, reveals deep spiritual truths about the Gospel of Christ and how we can apply it to our lives to live a victorious life.

After, I completed the study, I dicided to make a compilation of all the teachings into a book. To me, the epistle of Romans, as it is in the bible, is a compression of the full Gospel of Christ. In this book, I have expounded the epistle of Romans using Derek Princes teachings to make it easy for every Christian to read and understand. The book takes a sermon-like-form and is laden with examples and references from many parts of the bible including the new and the old testament.

This book can be richly used for personal study, for meditation, for exhotation, for sermon preparation and for bible study lessons. It provides an easy read for every Christian who yearns to live a victorious life in Christ.

If you are experienceing any great challenge in any area of your life and prayer doesn't seem to get you anywhere, maybe it is time for you to dwelve into the truth, for it is written: *"Then you will know the truth, and the truth will set you free."* (John 8:32)

In my Masters Service

George Ngondo

INTRODUCTION

Welcome to the "Roman Journey"!

You are setting out on a voyage or expedition in the realm of the spirit which will both inspire and challenge you. At times the going will be tough. It will take you through the darkest depths of human depravity and then on to the glistening heights of God's grace and glory.

The book of Romans is a unique combination of the spiritual and the intellectual, without comparison in human literature. It unfolds the most sublime spiritual truth in terms of the most flawless logic. It will not merely illuminate your spirit; it will also challenge your intellect.

For this reason, Romans will not yield its riches to careless or superficial reading. If you are to complete this pilgrimage successfully, there are two items of spiritual equipment which are essential: prayer and perseverance. Let me encourage you, therefore, with the words of the Lord to Joshua, as he prepared to enter the Promised Land: "Only be strong and very courageous."

The central theme of Romans is **'righteousness'**. It is a very important word and the Bible has a great deal to say about righteousness. God is always presented as a God of total righteousness. Speaking to the children of Israel Moses said "his way is perfect and all his works are just or righteous". (Psalm 92)

This scripture pictures the one who has grown old in the knowledge and service of the Lord and it says that his life proclaims that the Lord is righteous and there is no unrighteousness in him.

Before we go further I need to explain something about the words that we have to use. In English we have two words RIGHTEOUS and JUST which are somewhat different in their meaning but in the original languages of the Bible both the Hebrew of the Old Testament and the Greek of the New Testament there is only one word.

In Hebrew its Siddiq and in Greek it is decayeth and that one word is translated either just or righteous but there is no difference. So in a sense we have to adjust our thinking. We could make a difference between justice and righteousness. **Righteousness** we might say is moral character and **Justice** is the outworking of God's words and their application to our lives but there is no difference in the original languages.

So when we talk about RIGHTEOUSNESS we are talking about JUSTICE and vice versa.

In the book of Job 9:2, Job raises this pathetic question on *"how can a mortal man be righteous before God?"* Job was in deep agony of soul and I believe he asked that question not believing that there could be an answer to it. But God gives an answer to that question in the Epistle to the Romans, which tells us how it is possible for any person who meets God's conditions which are unfolded in Romans to be totally righteous before God.

One of the key phrases in Romans that will keep returning to is 'no condemnation'.

That is really the practical outworking of Romans. THAT YOU ARE ACCEPTED BEFORE GOD, THAT YOU ARE TOTALLY RIGHTEOUS AND THAT THERE IS NO CONDEMNATION ANYWHERE IN YOUR LIFE.

Romans also relates to the words of Jesus in the Beatitudes in **Matthew 5:6** where he says *"blessed are those who hunger and thirst for righteousness for they shall be filled they shall be abundantly satisfied."*

However, in the modern day church, righteousness is not very high in the list of the priorities of God's people. It is not always at the top of the list of many Christians when they go to church. People are mostly seeking blessing, power, healing, prosperity, spiritual gifts etc. There are not many people today who are hungry and thirsty for righteousness. I.e. people who say "unless I find righteousness, I cannot be satisfied" their whole being is a total longing for righteousness.

I pray and hope that as you go through this study, you will experience a change in your priorities. You will have a much higher value for righteousness. Other things follow righteousness. In Romans 14:17 Paul says: *"for the kingdom of God is not meat and drink; but righteousness, and peace, and joy in the Holy Ghost.*

A BRIEF OUTLINE OF ROMANS

Scholars believe that the letter was written to the saints in Rome in AD 57 either in the city of Corinth where Paul spent 3 months (Acts 20:3), or in Philippi before sending it with Phoebe (Ro 16:1) who was a deaconess in Cenchreae, a city near Corinth.

Paul was completing his third missionary journey as he anticipated a visit to Jerusalem and ultimately to Rome and even Spain (Ro 15:24, 28, 32).

There is a reference in Romans to a man named Erastus who was the administrator or the Public Works manager of the city of Corinth and quite recently archaeologists have discovered at Corinth an inscription with the name of Erastus on it crediting him with doing some public work at his own expense.

Frustrated in his former plans (Ro 1:13, 15:22), Paul wrote this letter for the purpose of instructing the saints and the church in Rome which seemed to be comprised of Gentiles and a few Jewish people who lacked proper instruction. Through this letter, Paul sort to share with them the Gospel the way it was revealed to him.

The central theme of the book of Romans is God's revelation of His righteousness. Evident in the letter is that both the Jews and Gentiles alike are sinners in need of salvation and in the person of Jesus Christ is revealed the perfect righteousness. Through the death and resurrection of Jesus Christ, provision has been made for all men and women to obtain righteousness through faith and divine power to live in accordance to this righteousness is imparted through the Holy Spirit.

We will view this letter as divided up into four main Parts:

PART 1: THE SPIRITUAL PILGRIMAGE

Consists of chapters 1 to 8 which present the analytical (methodical, logical or reasoning) and scriptural basis of the gospel.

PART 2: THE DESTINY OF ISRAEL AND THE CHURCH

Consists of chapters 9 through 11 which deal primarily with God's dealings with Israel (God's dealings with Israel are an essential part of the whole truth of the gospel). These are God's elect and what comes out of it is the ultimate deciding factor in human experience is what God has chosen. That is a very unpopular truth to the humanistic mind today and partly why Israel is not popular.

PART 3: WORKING OUT YOUR FAITH UNDER PRESSURE

Consists of chapters 12 through 15 and is an application of the preceding truths to daily living and this is characteristic of the whole New Testament. Chapter 12 starts with *"I beseech you therefore brethren that you present your bodies a living sacrifice to God."* That is the practical outworking of all the wonderful theology that has been outlaid in the previous 11 chapters.

PART 4: PERSONAL GREETINGS

Consists of chapter 16 and contains personal greetings and a benediction (Blessing) and some people again consider that irrelevant. There are many different individuals whose names are included. Probably the Holy Spirit does this to show us that personal relationships are very important to God.

PART 1 - THE SPIRITUAL PILGRIMAGE

Romans Chapters 1 to 8

This first part is a spiritual journey beginning from Romans 1 and whose destination is Romans chapter 8 which is the spirit controlled life: liberty, joy, peace, and righteousness - entered only through the door of "no condemnation" (8:1). The previous chapters 1 through 7 are stages on the way to that destination.

These chapters can only be compared to the difference between making percolated coffee and making instant coffee. To get percolated coffee, there are stages before you can get it. You roast coffee beans, grind them and then place then in a percolator before the rich aroma of coffee is attained. Every Christian needs to carefully study and meditate on Romans 1 to 7 before they can really walk into the confidence of Romans 8:1 ...*Therefore there is now no condemnation for those who are in*

Christ Jesus. However, today many Christians do not use a percolator i.e. study and meditate on Romans 1-7. They just get instant coffee. They want to arrive at the destination of 'No Condemnation' without taking the various stages of the whole journey.

A child was once asked "where does milk come from?" in a multiple choice question. The answers were supermarket, cow, and fridge. His choice was Supermarket. Why? Because the boy always heard his mother, send for milk from the supermarket.

It is a sad truth but it applies to many modern day Christians. They cling on Roman's 8:1 *"There is no condemnation to those who are in Christ Jesus"* without applying the full gospel from Chapter 1 - 7 in their lives.

In this way, this study will be like going through a percolator.

CHAPTER 1: PAUL'S INTRODUCTIONS

(Romans 1:1-32)

1.1 Paul Introduces Himself, the Gospel & the Christians at Rome

[*Romans 1:1-17*]

As is customary in writing a letter, Paul introduces himself first, and then he introduces the Gospel as the main theme of writing this letter before unveiling the addressees who were the Christians at Rome.

Rom 1:1 *Paul, a bond-servant of Christ Jesus, called as an apostle, set apart for the gospel of God,*

Rom 1:2 *which He promised beforehand through His prophets in the Holy Scriptures,*

Rom 1:3 *concerning His Son, who was born of a descendant of David according to the flesh,*

Rom 1:4 *who was declared the Son of God with power by the resurrection from the dead, according to the Spirit of holiness, Jesus Christ our Lord,*

Rom 1:5 *through whom we have received grace and apostleship to bring about the obedience of faith among all the Gentiles for His name's sake,*

Rom 1:6 *among whom you also are the called of Jesus Christ;*

Rom 1:7 *to all who are beloved of God in Rome, called as saints: Grace to you and peace from God our Father and the Lord Jesus Christ.*

Rom 1:8 First, I thank my God through Jesus Christ for you all, because your faith is being proclaimed throughout the whole world.

Rom 1:9 For God, whom I serve in my spirit in the preaching of the gospel of His Son, is my witness as to how unceasingly I make mention of you, \

Rom 1:10 always in my prayers making request, if perhaps now at last by the will of God I may succeed in coming to you.

Rom 1:11 For I long to see you so that I may impart some spiritual gift to you, that you may be established;

Rom 1:12 that is, that I may be encouraged together with you while among you, each of us by the other's faith, both yours and mine.

Rom 1:13 I do not want you to be unaware, brethren, that often I have planned to come to you (and have been prevented so far) so that I may obtain some fruit among you also, even as among the rest of the Gentiles.

Rom 1:14 I am under obligation both to Greeks and to barbarians, both to the wise and to the foolish.

*Rom 1:15*So, for my part, I am eager to preach the gospel to you also who are in Rome.

Rom 1:16 For I am not ashamed of the gospel, for it is the power of God for salvation to everyone who believes, to the Jew first and also to the Greek.

Rom 1:17 For in it the righteousness of God is revealed from faith to faith; as it is written, "But the righteous man shall live by faith." (NASV)

1.1.1 Paul Introduces Himself

(Romans 1:1, 5, 9–15)

Paul is the sole author of this epistle and he first introduces himself as a bondservant. Let us look at Paul's introduction of himself which is in verse 1 verse 5 and verses 9 through 15. Let us look at these words again so that we can have them clearly in mind.

Paul a bondservant of Christ Jesus (A bondservant is a slave. A bondservant is the translation of the Greek word doulos, which means "one who is subservient to, and entirely at the disposal of, his master; a slave.) *Called as an apostle set apart for the gospel of God* and then in verse 5 speaking about Jesus he says through whom we have received Grace and Apostleship to bring about the obedience of faith among all the Gentiles for his name's sake.

You will notice that all the Apostles in their letters always call themselves first of all a servant or a slave and then define their particular field of service which in the case of Paul was Apostleship. Then he also goes on with a further definition he says set apart to the gospel of God.

Paul had a very special and unique function in the whole history of the church. His function was to present in its entirety the gospel. So much was it his revelation that a little later on in chapter 2 verse 16 we find he actually calls it - my gospel and that is very significant.

You remember that Paul had such an abundance of revelations that to keep him humble God had to permit an angel of Satan to tame him with a thorn in the flesh (2Cor 12:7-9). I think there is no question that the revelation contained here in Romans was part of that.

There are two epistles which of which Paul is the sole author. These are Romans and Ephesians and that is not an accident because each of them contains a revelation which is uniquely the revelation of Paul.

The book of Romans is the revelation of THE GOSPEL and the book of Ephesians is the revelation of THE CHURCH. In these two areas Paul made an absolutely unique contribution to the whole Christian Church.

It is good that Paul started by calling himself a slave. Some people in the church today might describe themselves with various titles. However, in essence, every one of them is just a slave of Christ - that is, if they truly and fully submit to his rulership. Paul says first and foremost, I am a slave committed totally to the service of Jesus Christ. My particular function is an apostle and my particular area of apostleship is the revelation of the gospel.

Grace Comes Before Apostleship

Then in **verse 5** Paul says of Jesus "through him we received Grace and Apostleship". Notice that before the Apostleship comes, grace comes. Paul is very careful not at any time to glorify or overvalue himself. And he says our particular area of service 'the obedience of faith among all Gentiles'.

Elsewhere he is called the apostle of the Gentiles. In Romans 15:18 and 19, Paul speaks further about this Apostleship to the Gentiles.

"I will not presume to speak of anything except what Christ has accomplished through me resulting in the obedience of the Gentiles by word and deed in the power of signs and wonders" (Romans 15:18, 19)

So he had a special ministry to bring the Gentiles to believe in Jesus and it was by the attestation of the supernatural.

Also notice the phrase 'OBEDIENCE OF THE FAITH'. A lot of people say obedience is what matters. That is perfectly true but unless it proceeds from faith it will not work. If you try to obey God in your own strength and in your own ability, it will not work. Many Christians are trying to obey the gospel but they are not doing it out of faith and the result is frustration. So, let us bear in mind that when you emphasize obedience, that it must always proceed out of faith.

The Prosperous Journey

Then, Let us look at this one interesting fact that Paul had been praying for a long while. For a good journey to Rome the King James says that I may have a 'prosperous journey' by the will of God.

Interestingly enough in the third epistle of John verse 2, John uses the word same word when he says *"beloved I pray that above all things thou mayest prosper and be in health as thy soul prospers."*

The same word, but Let us consider for a moment what kind of a journey Paul had. It is vividly described in Acts chapters 27 and 28. He did not travel first-class. He was a prisoner in chains. The ship on which he was traveling was in an amazing storm that lasted 40 days and then 40 nights when they were without food after that it was shipwrecked on an island. And just to climax it, when he was gathering wood for a fire, a viper coiled on his hand.

The question is, did God answer Paul's prayer for a prosperous journey? The answer is yes. Amid all those challenges, Paul made it to Rome. This leads us to question, what is God's definition of prosperity? It seems God's definition of Prosperity means, 'to be able to accomplish that which you have set out to do regardless of the challenges'.

This is a very important question. There are a lot of people today who define prosperity in terms of the modern day culture – which is to live life without problems or challenges. The magnitude of our challenges may differ, but true prosperity is to wade through every storm that comes our way and accomplish that which God has assigned you to do by the grace of God. It is to be totally equipped to do the will of God.

1.1.2 The Addressee

Then we now deal with the people to whom the letter is addressed to. These are the Christians at Rome called "holy ones"— their faith a testimony to the whole Roman world. Verse: 6, 7 and 8.

6among whom you also are the called of Jesus Christ; 7to all who are beloved of God in Rome called as saints: Grace to you and peace from God our Father and the Lord Jesus Christ. 8First, I thank my God through Jesus Christ for you all, because your faith is being proclaimed throughout the whole world.

Verse 6: That word 'called' is a very important word because it is what determines whether we are Christians or not. You do not become a Christian because you decide. You become a Christian because God called you. Your role is to respond, but the initiative is not with us. It is with God. He calls us.

The word 'called' is translated as 'invited'. The church in Greek is called ecclesia. The word ecclesia is a company of people called out. It means that are we called out from the world. That is very important to remember. That is, we are not part of the world. We have been called out from the world. If you belong to the true Church of Jesus Christ, you do not belong to this world. You cannot belong in two places at the same time.

Verse 7: *"to all who are beloved of God in Rome"* It is important to remember that God loves the people he calls. That is good news, because God called us because he loved us. *"He loved us before the foundation of the world"*. He had made all these important decisions before time ever began but it is only when we hear his call that we begin to enter into the experience.

You should always reminisce how and when God called you, when you just obeyed the voice or the nudge. When God calls us and we do not respond, we could never count on God calling us again. Thank God you made that decision. This is a very solemn and very serious thought. We should never trifle with the call of God.

Today, I believe that, God desires to save every one dwelling in this world. He has a set and appointed time for calling each one of us individually. The difference is how we respond to that small inner voice, when He comes calling. There is no guarantee that He will call you again if you do not respond to that first call.

So Paul says that these Christians in Rome are called by God because they are loved by God. God's call is the outworking of his love. He reaches out his hand and says "if you will take my hand, I will lift you out of that mess you are in and I will place you on a rock beside me.

Then Paul goes on in **verse 7:** *"called as Saints"* You will notice that a little earlier, he said 'called as an apostle' of himself. What he says is that those Christians are called 'to be Saints' or 'holy ones'. You see, when God calls you something, you are what he calls you. You may not feel like it. People may not see you that way. But what God calls you, is what you are going to be. When you are called 'holy ones', you are going to end up as a holy one. You might as well start quickly because God means business.

Then he gives this beautiful familiar New Testament greeting: grace to you and peace from God our Father and the Lord Jesus Christ. What a beautiful greeting. It would be interesting to notice how many times in the first eight chapters of Romans Paul uses the name Jesus, the word Christ or Messiah and the word Lord. It is 32 times. That is why Romans is so powerful because it centres, on the centre - which is Jesus.

Whenever we get off the centre, the power begins to leak out and we have to resort to human energy human or methods.

When our main desire is to present and uplift the Lord Jesus, the Holy Spirit says "I will give you all the help you need". Notice the order Grace and peace. In the New Covenant we have Grace before Peace and grace is what we cannot earn. Grace is the free unmerited favour of God. We did not earn it. We cannot deserve it. We just receive it. So before we get peace we need to remember that GRACE COMES BEFORE PEACE.

Then in **verse 8** Paul says *"I thank my God through Jesus Christ for you all"* it is very important to notice that Paul almost invariably began his epistles by thanking God for the people to whom he was writing to. That is a very important principle. If you cannot thank God for somebody, do not pray for them because your prayer will be illegitimate.

One more thing about these Christians in Rome he says *"I thank God because your faith is being proclaimed throughout the whole world"*. Of course Rome, as the name indicates, was the great capital city of the Roman Empire which dominated a big area of the world at that time. So whatever happened in Rome would affect the whole of the Roman Empire.

One of the principles of Paul in his mission was get to the main cities. He never went to little villages unlike some modern missionaries. He did not start out in the jungle. The place where things happen is the city. If you reach a city then, you reach the places around it because the things will go out from the city.

If you study Paul's methods, it was always to strike at the heart or at the main city - wherever it is.

Now, Paul had not been to Rome but he had a lot of friends in Rome and he was proud of the fact that the whole Empire was talking about these Christians at Rome. How did they achieve that? I guess that the most important instrument that the early Christians had was their personal testimony.

Jesus said "you shall receive power after the Holy Spirit has come upon you and you shall be my witnesses." Here were people from all sorts of different backgrounds, nationality or social background, saying the same thing - this person Jesus has changed my life. And everybody started to want to know - who is Jesus?

And they got the amazing answer. He was a carpenter's son, who was crucified some years ago, but that was not the only answer. They also got the answer that - he rose from the dead on the third day.

Of all the various spiritual instruments available to the early church, the most effective single instrument was personal testimony. *"They overcame him by the blood of the lamb and the word of their testimony"* (Revelation 12:11)

In Matthew 10:33-35 Jesus says: *"But whosoever shall deny me before men, him will I also deny before my Father which is in heaven."* Our personal testimony is the greatest way to spread the Gospel. When you get the opportunity to testify, do it. Do not hesitate.

1.1.3 Paul Introduces the Gospel

Let us look first of all at Romans 1 verses 2 through 4.

Verse 1 ends with the words "the gospel" of God and then concerning this gospel Paul says *"which God promised beforehand through his prophets in the Holy Scriptures".* You find that Paul is always very careful to make sure that no one thinks he has improvised this gospel. He invariably emphasizes that the whole concept and the coming of the gospel was clearly predicted in the Old Testament Scriptures. He says all we are doing is fulfilling what the Scriptures have said. That is very important especially when dealing with the Jewish people.

The Gospel was promised through the prophets. In writing this letter, Paul also had in mind, the Jews in Rome who were privy to what was written by the prophets of the old about the messiah. Many Jews, have never known a Bible with a New Testament and to Christians we have never known the Bible without one.

Paul was fighting this separation of the old and the new. He said everything we are preaching in the new has its origin in the old. If you really want to be able to reach the Jewish people you have to come to the place where you can show them directly, that out of their own scriptures, a gospel of the circumcision and a gospel of the un-circumcision. This is the circumcision of the Jewish people and the un-circumcision of the Gentiles.

It is not a different message but it is a different approach. If you go amongst other people who have never heard the Gospel, it is very easy to preach Jesus to them. But to go to the Jewish people you have to show them that this is what was promised right from Genesis onwards. Paul was very careful never to open up to the possible accusation that he was improvising something.

The very essence of the gospel

Verse 3: *"Concerning his son who was born of the seed of David according to the flesh;*

Remember that Christ is the Greek word for which the Hebrew word is Mushiya or Messiah. So when we talk about Jesus Christ, we are actually saying Jesus the Messiah. So the gospel centres on one person - Jesus and this is what Paul says about him:

Verse 4: *"who was declared with power to be the Son of God by the resurrection from the dead according to the Spirit of Holiness Jesus Christ our Lord."*

He was the son of God and he was also the son of David. He had a human nature and he had a divine nature. He was declared or separated out as the Son of God by a mighty act of power which was the resurrection from the dead according to the spirit of holiness.

Paul wrote in Greek but there are many evidences he thought in Hebrew. Sometimes if you are not aware of the Hebrew phrases you will not understand this. Hebrew does not talk about the 'Holy Spirit' it speaks about the 'Spirit of holiness'.

So when Paul says the spirit of holiness he is saying the Holy Spirit, the power that raised the dead body of Jesus from the tomb.

What did the Holy Spirit do by that? He declared Jesus to be the son of God. He is separating him out from all other men who had ever died and been buried as the Son of God.

As the spirit of holiness, he bore testimony to Jesus perfect holiness. If there had been anything unholy in the life of Jesus at any point, he would never have been resurrected. But the resurrection attested that he really was what he claimed to be - the Son of God. And it attested his perfect stainless holiness.

You see, God reversed the decision of two courts:
- a Jewish Court and
- a Roman Court

They had sentenced Jesus to death and insisted that he was to be buried. It is a strange thing the unbelievers had much more faith in the resurrection than the believers. You will notice that the enemies of Jesus were really anxious in case he should arise. So after his death and burial the Jewish leaders went to Pilate and said: now we know that deceiver said that he would rise on the third day. So we do not want that to happen. So would you give us a Guard to protect the tomb and Pilate said you can have your guard and you can take the seal and seal the tomb, so that the stone could never be moved without the seal being broke.

So these two courts in a sense did their all to have Jesus stay in the tomb. But on the third day God reversed their decisions. That is the highest court in the universe and brought Jesus out from the tomb on the third day.

Bear in mind that the gospel centres in the DEATH, BURIAL and RESURRECTION of Jesus. If we ever get away from those three central historical facts we are not dealing with the gospel.

There is a whole lot of teaching today that does not contain the gospel. The gospel consists of these simple historical facts. It is unlike other religions which just have sacred books that present intellectual truth. The gospel relates to human history. It is either true or its false. It must be one or the other.

God impacted human history with Jesus and he is made something available to us, which is both attested by history and confirmed in our personal experience. That is the gospel.

Just notice that the gospel centres in three historical facts: the death, burial and resurrection of Jesus. The more we can focus our testimony and our teaching on those the more effective it will be. It is not primarily a matter of emotion. It is plain facts.

Attempts to stir people emotionally will produce a temporary response which does not last. What we have got to do is to communicate to people's minds and spirits these three glorious facts:

1. Jesus died for our sins
2. He was buried
3. He rose again the third day.

Let us look also at 1stCorinthians 15 which is the well-known glorious resurrection chapter and Paul says in the first eight verses: *"1 Moreover, brethren, I declare unto you the gospel which I preached unto you, which also ye have received, and wherein ye stand; 2 By which also ye are saved, if ye keep in memory what I preached unto you, unless ye have believed in vain. 3 For I delivered unto you first of all that which I also received, how that Christ died for our sins according to the scriptures; 4 And that he was buried, and that he rose again the third day according to the scriptures: 5 And that he was seen of Cephas, then of the twelve: 6 After that, he was seen of above five hundred brethren at once; of whom the greater part remain unto this present, but some are fallen asleep. 7 After that, he was seen of James; then of all the apostles. 8 And last of all he was seen of me also, as of one born out of due time. (1Cor 15:1-8)*

Paul here goes further and attests to the fact that after Jesus died, buried and was raised and was seen by many disciples aside from him. Paul makes sure that he gives his personal testimony that he also saw the risen Jesus.

Going back to Romans 1:15-17: Paul sums up the gospel and he gives one good reason why neither he nor we should ever be ashamed of it. It is because - IT IS THE POWER OF GOD TO SALVATION. If we are ever prone to be ashamed of the gospel it is because we have lost sight of the fact that it is the power of God to salvation.

No one today is ever ashamed of power least of all of the power of God. It is the power of God not for destruction but to salvation. For total deliverance for human personality: spirit, soul and body for those who believe. The key word is believe and then Paul says it is to the Jew first and also to the Greek. Historically the gospel was presented first to the Jewish people and then to the Gentile world.

Then Paul further sums it up in verse 17 *"for in it the righteousness of God is revealed from faith to faith as it is written but the righteous man shall live by faith"*

So the essence of this is to believe. It is the power of God to those who believe and it invokes righteousness. Here Paul emphasizes that through the gospel, God has revealed a way by which man can become righteous in the sight of God. He quotes from the Old Testament from the Prophet Habakkuk 2:4 *...But the righteous will live by his faith* - to prove that what he is saying is not an improvisation of his own but something that was determined and prophesied by the prophets of God many years ago.

So the key blessing of the gospel is that it brings us righteousness. A righteousness which God accepts and we shall see, as we go on, that it is only on the basis of this righteousness that we can receive any of the other blessings of God. In Romans 5, Paul speaks about the gift of righteousness and then in Romans 6 he speaks about the gift of eternal life the order cannot be reversed.

We will not qualify to receive the gift of eternal life unless God had reckoned us righteous. A righteous God could not bestow his gifts on unrighteous men and women. The first problem was to resolve the issue of righteousness. Remember the question of job: that "how can a mortal man be righteous before God" - the answer is through believing the gospel.

When we use the word faith we need to be on our guard against a misunderstanding that has arisen in the church over the centuries both in Hebrew and in Greek. The word for faith primarily describes character and then what you believe.

So to reduce the gospel just to it theological proposition is to rob it of its truth. The word means initially faithfulness or commitment. So the gospel is the power of God only to those who out of commitment to God believe what he declares. Remove commitment and you have a kind of desiccated theological faith that does not produce the results that God has promised.

You cannot be a believer in the biblical sense without being personally committed to God through Jesus Christ. Commitment is the basis.

1.2 God's Wrath Against Sinful Humanity

[*Romans 1:18 – 32*]

Now, Paul goes on in the next half of this chapter with the opposite side of the coin. He has talked about the revelation of God's righteousness. Now he talks about the revelation of God's wrath and both are contained in the gospel because when we look at what happened to Jesus on the cross we need to bear in mind that he endured the wrath of God.

Why?

Because he became the sin offering; he took our sin. He took the judgment for our sin, he paid the penalty. And once he became sin, the total wrath of God was poured out upon him on the cross. So if you ever think that the gospel is simply a sentimental Father Christmas message, you have got to see the other side of it. It also revealed the wrath of God against all sin.

If anybody could have commanded sin to God, it would have been Jesus but when he became sin, God disowned him. God abandoned him and the wrath of God was poured on him.

So do not imagine dear brothers and sisters, that there is any way you will ever get God to condone your sin. He will deal with it. He will forgive it. But He will never tolerate it.

Now Let us look at the description of God's wrath against the whole human race. This is a very important part of this first chapter because a lot of people somehow think how God could punish harmless innocent people. That is not God's problem because there are no harmless or innocent people. God's problem is how he can forgive sinners. That is the problem which is resolved in Romans.

In these following verses God, makes the sin and accountability of the whole human race abundantly clear.

Rom 1:18 *"For the wrath of God is revealed from heaven against all ungodliness and unrighteousness of men who suppress the truth in unrighteousness."* the problem was that God had made the truth available to humanity but they chose to suppress it because it did not suit them.

Rom 1:19 *because that which is known about God or may be known of God is evident within them for God made it evident to them*

Rom 1:20 *For since the creation of the world his invisible attributes, his eternal power and divine nature have been clearly seen being understood through what has been made so that is the human race are without excuse.*

Notice that Paul says that through creation God has made the truth about himself available to all men everywhere.

Two particular aspects of the truth are: God's eternal power and His divine nature. His divine nature means that it reveals a being: who is totally greater than men and one who is all powerful.

Now how does this revelation come? This is a vital issue. It is one of the simplest pieces of reasoning which Paul has given to us. He says that which is evident of God, which may be known of God is evident to them or within them, for God made it evident to them.

There is a combination of two things: What is external and what is within and it is the combination of those two things that constitute the revelation.

First of all there is the order of the universe and particularly the heavenly bodies with their manifest beauty and order and system and,

Then and this is what is unique about man of all creatures on earth. There is within man what can be called a logical, mathematical faculty that can appreciate the logic and the mathematic of creation. Cows do not have that faculty neither do lions or snakes or any other beast. There is only one creature on the face of earth today that has that faculty and it is man. Therefore man is uniquely accountable for what is revealed to him of the nature of God because there is something in him that can appreciate it. Astronomers can calculate where every major star was three thousand years ago. No other animal on earth can do that. We have the ability to see that the whole thing was designed by a person, who has a faculty like ours but much greater than ours.

Ludwig Wittgenstein a philosopher said we could not say of an illogical universe what it will look like. That is exactly what Paul is saying. He says, the very fact we can describe the universe and use categories and terms that imply continuity and system and design means that is the kind of universe we live in.

Now people who do not believe in God habitually talk about the laws of nature. But really that is a contradiction, because in our human experience we do not know of any law that was not made by a lawmaker. For every law that is made there is a lawmaker that makes it.

The principle of proper explanation is to proceed from the known to the unknown. But when we talk about a law that was not made by anybody, we are proceeding from the unknown. It is an invalid method of explanation.

So Paul is saying that there are two things together which constitute a sufficient revelation of God. The order and the design and the harmony of the universe, but that is not enough because that would not constitute a revelation to a cow, but it does constitute a revelation to a being who has within himself the same kind of logical and mathematical faculty that can relate to that.

Therefore man has a unique responsibility. That he alone as far as, all creatures on earth are concerned, is able to appreciate, from creation, the nature of God.

Now Paul is very emphatic about that. We know today, that there are millions of people who deny this. Paul very bluntly calls them fools.

We hear a lot about evolution but I want to point out to you that there is another side which is devolution. A lot of things are not evolving but they are devolving. It is illogical to talk about evolution as if it was the only possibility. The fact of the matter is that, there is greater evidence for devolution than evolution in the world today particularly in the human race.

Rom 1:21 *"for though even though they knew God they did not honor him as God* (more literally they did not glorify him as God) *or give him thanks, but became futile in their thoughts and their foolish heart was darkened."*

It is very important to notice the first two downward steps of humanity. It is very important to notice that Paul is not talking about things they DID. Rather he is talking about things they did not do. Bear in mind that you can be just as guilty for the things you do not do as for the things you do.

The first two things they did not do are:

- They did not glorify God
- They did not give him thanks.

Dear brothers and sisters on the basis of observation of many different Christians, the moment you cease to glorify God and give him thanks, you have started on a slippery downward path and if you are there at this particular moment, then you had better repent because Paul describes this path as it goes on a downward trend and the end is a horrible.

Question: How should we Glorify God? Giving Glory to God is an attitude. It is not in singing 'we give you Glory Lord'. It is an attitude of reverence, fear and awe towards the most high every moment of our lives.

1.2.1 Consequences of Failing to Glorify God

What were the first two results of failing to glorify God and failing to give him thanks?

Rom 1:22 *Professing to be wise they became fools*

The first result was to become foolish. The word professing means to keep on saying the same thing again and again. They kept on talking about how wise they were and all the time they were getting more and more foolish. The second result:

Rom 1:23 *they exchanged the glory of the incorruptible God for an image in the form of corruptible man and birds and four-footed animals and crawling creatures.*

The first great sin is the breaking of the first commandment: You shall have no other God beside me. There are no words to describe the awfulness of idolatry. Can you even begin to picture the insult offered to the great eternal God to depict him in those forms. Notice the downward trend of the futile mind: first it is flying creatures, then its animals and finally its reptiles. It is always a downward trend. It is never upward.

Once you have taken those first two steps on the downward path, you are going to go on going downwards unless you repent.

1.2.2 God's Judgment on the Human Race

Now Let us go to God's judgment on the human race for these things. Three times in this passage Paul uses the phrase 'God Gave Them Up'. What a terrible phrase. I pray that God will never give you up.

There is a phrase in the Prophet Hosea about the tribe of Ephraim. It says "Ephraim is joined to idols leave him alone". That is the worst that God can ever say about you. Notice it was because of idolatry.

Now, the first thing to which God gave them up was **lust** and **defilement** verses 24 and 25 following:

Rom 1:24 *"therefore God gave them over in the lusts of their hearts to impurity that their bodies might be dishonored among them,*

Rom 1:25 *for they exchanged the truth of God for a lie and worshiped and served the creature rather than the Creator, who is blessed forever."*

They changed God's likeness into something vile and degrading. God had given them a form which was made in the likeness of God, but because they distorted the likeness of God and defiled it, God said alright, I will let you defile your own bodies through lust and impurity.

But that is only the first. The next 'God gave them up' is in verse 26

Rom 1:26 *"for this reason God gave them over to degrading passions for their women exchanged the natural function for that which is unnatural.*

Rom 1:27 *In the same way also the men abandoned the natural function of the woman and burned in their desire towards one another men with men committing indecent acts and receiving in their own persons the due penalty of their error"*

What Paul is describing here is homosexuality. It is the next step down. It is interesting that these first judgments affected their bodies. We will also see that the final judgment affected their minds.

It is interesting that Paul says the women led the way in homosexuality. As far as Greece is concerned that is historically correct. On the island of Lesbos there was a Greek poet named Saffle about the ninth or eighth century before Christ who was what we call a lesbian. That is where the word comes from. She wrote poetry glorifying this form a relationship in a sense. Very beautiful poetry but so corrupt. It is rather remarkable that sometimes very excellent art forms are used to glorify the most ungodly things and thereafter the men followed the pattern of the women. This is something that is rather common.

It says *"they received in themselves or in their own persons the penalty of their error"*. There could be many expressions of that penalty and probably STD's and AIDS are some of them. Paul says in 1st Corinthians 6:17 *"every person who practices immorality sins against his own body"*. We can therefore conclude that you cannot practice immorality without doing some kind of damage to your body.

Can we also say that immorality is the common cause of the majority of life threatening sicknesses? An unclean spirit gets an opening to come in. In ministering deliverance, this should not be left out.

Then the third 'God gave them up' is in verses 28 through to 30. These are terrible verses. You can never read them without feeling a sense of anguish. We cannot fail to acknowledge their absolute accuracy. One thing about the Lord is that He tells it like it is.

Rom 1:28 *"just as they did not see fit to acknowledge God any longer, God gave them over."*

Let us pause there for a moment. They did not want to retain God in their knowledge. This is the diagnosis of the problem that is universal in the world today. Why did they not want to retain the knowledge of God? Because they knew if they did, they would be accountable to him. Each one would have to give an account of himself to God.

In humanism, one thing that they passionately oppose is the idea that they are subject to God and that they have to give an account to God on everything they do. The proponents of the theory of evolution do not believe in creation because they do not want to be answerable or accountable to God. That is the real basic motive.

"Just as they did not like to retain God in their knowledge God gave them over to a depraved mind, so that they do what ought not to be done." What can be more terrible than a depraved mind? The previous two cases which

God gave them over to were physical problems. But now their whole mind is corrupt. They became filled with all unrighteousness.

This list contains 21 things. It comprises the outlook of people who refuse to acknowledge God, glorify Him and be thankful to him.

Rom 1:29 *"Being filled with all unrighteousness, fornication, wickedness, covetousness, maliciousness; full of envy, murder, debate, deceit, malignity; whisperers [gossipers],*

Rom 1:30 *Backbiters, haters of God, despiteful, proud, boasters, inventors of evil things, disobedient to parents,*

Rom 1:31 *without understanding, covenant breakers [untrustworthy], without natural affection, implacable, unmerciful:*

Notice where gossips appear in that list? That is important because gossiping is the church-going sin. They are put among murderers, haters of God etc.

Untrustworthy means people that you cannot make a covenant with. That is perhaps the most conspicuous feature of our age. People are no longer willing to make covenants. Nations break treaties, governments break promises and men and women break their marriage vows to one another. The deepest problem of our society is that: men and women are not willing to make covenants. Then Finally;

Rom 1:32 *"although they know the ordinance of God that those who practice such things are worthy of death they not only do the same but also give hearty approval to those who practice them."*

It is true that people who are in this kind of thing approve one another. I think they feel they would be lonely if they stood on their own. So anybody who is as wicked as they are, they endorse.

In 2nd Timothy 3, you will find a historical parallel, where Paul says what man will become in the last time. He describes nearly all these things:

1 But mark this: There will be terrible times in the last days. 2People will be lovers of themselves, lovers of money, boastful, proud, abusive, disobedient to their parents, ungrateful, unholy, 3without love, unforgiving, slanderous, without self-control, brutal, not lovers of the good, 4treacherous, rash, conceited, lovers of pleasure rather than lovers of God— 5having a form of godliness but denying its power. Have nothing to do with such people. (2 Timothy 3:1-5)

Now, Romans is the logic and 2 Timothy 3: 1 – 5, is the historic outworking of that.

So we need to bear that in mind that it is being worked out. It is vital to remember that this is Corruption and Corruption is irreversible. The result of man's sin is corruption in every area of his being. Corruption cannot be reversed in any area of life.

So God's program is to make a new creation i.e. to start over. Those who do not enter into the new creation must endure the inevitable progress of corruption in their life.

Chapter 2: GOD'S JUDGMENTS, THE JEWS & THE LAW

(Romans 2:1-29)

2.1 Increased Moral Knowledge Increases Responsibility

[*Romans 2: 1-12*]

This chapter deals with people who have been guilty of all the things of which the whole human race has been guilty of. Nonetheless, because they have acquired some religious knowledge, they begin to feel that they are better than the others and in a different class because of the fact that they know what is right and what is wrong.

In essence Paul simply points out that, far from making them better this knowledge merely increases their responsibility. They are all the more accountable for the fact that they know more.

We need to remember that Paul was writing 19 centuries or more ago and so he addressed his remarks primarily to his own Jewish people. At that time, the Jewish people were the ones who had the advantage over the other nations. That is, they had as Paul says 'the oracles of the Word of God'. They knew God's standards of right and wrong which most other nations did not know. But Paul says; far from making them better, that simply made them even more accountable for the wrong that they did.

It is important to understand that after 19 centuries, in certain sense the shoe is on the other foot. Now, it is no longer so much that the Jews that have the knowledge, it is the Gentiles i.e. the professing Christians.

Many of us because of our parental background have the knowledge of God from childhood. So in respect of what we know we are now in the place of the Jews. 19 centuries ago Paul, does not exonerate the Jews.

But today, it places upon us the same kind of responsibility that was upon the Jewish people at that time. It is very clear from the state of the church today, that multitudes of Christians are content with knowing more than other people but are not able to apply it.

That was precisely the problem of the Jews in Paul's day. Let us face the fact that we are in the same position as the Jews of the first century. We are the ones who have the most to account for.

Let us read the first 16 verses of Romans 2.

Rom 2:1 Therefore you have no excuse, every one of you who passes judgment, for in that which you judge another, you condemn yourself; for you who judge practice the same things.

Every time Paul says therefore you need to pick up your ears and ask, why he says therefore. You need to find out what it is there for. This therefore is there because chapter 1 has concluded that all humanity is guilty. He is talking about people who judge others because they know more but in essence they are in the same category. So that is why the therefore is there.

Rom 2:2 And we know that the judgment of God rightly falls upon those who practice such things.

Rom 2:3 But do you suppose this, O man, when you pass judgment on those who practice such things and do the same yourself, that you will escape the judgment of God?

Rom 2:4 Or do you think lightly of the riches of His kindness and tolerance and patience, not knowing that the kindness of God leads you to repentance?

Rom 2:5 But because of your stubbornness and unrepentant heart you are storing up wrath for yourself in the day of wrath and revelation of the righteous judgment of God,

Pause and consider this statement for a moment. It is indeed a terrible thing to be storing up wrath for yourself.

Rom 2:6 who will render to each person according to his deeds:

Rom 2:7 to those who by perseverance in doing good seek for glory and honor and immortality, eternal life;

Rom 2:8 but to those who are selfishly ambitious and do not obey the truth, but obey unrighteousness, wrath and indignation.

Rom 2:9 There will be tribulation and distress for every soul of man who does evil, of the Jew first and also of the Greek,

Rom 2:10 but glory and honor and peace to everyone who does good, to the Jew first and also to the Greek.

Rom 2:11 for there is no partiality with God.

Rom 2:12 For all who have sinned without the Law will also perish without the Law, and all who have sinned under the Law will be judged by the Law; …

Rom 2:16 on the day when, according to my gospel, God will judge the secrets of men through Christ Jesus.

Now, as usual Paul is pretty intense and it takes a good deal of care to find out precisely what he is saying. In these passages, Paul has outlined five main principles of God's Judgment.

2.2.   The Five Main Principles of God's Judgment

2.2.1 According to Truth

The first principle of God's judgment is found in verse 2. It says *"the judgment of God rightly falls upon those who practice such things."*

The literal text here is that the judgment of God is according to truth upon those who practice such things. So the first principle is that the judgment of God is according to truth. It is according to the truth of God's Word. This is very important. In John 17:17 Jesus speaking to the Father says "thy word is the truth" - God's Word is the truth.

Again Jesus himself said in John 12:47- 48 while warning the people of his day that they would one day face judgment according to the words that he had spoken to them.

John 12 47 and 48 Jesus is speaking: *"if anyone hears my sayings and does not keep them I do not judge him for I did not come to judge the world but to save the world he who rejects me and does not receive my sayings has one who judges him. The word I spoke is what will judge him at that day."*

So we need a bear in mind that as we read the scriptures, we are already facing our judge and that is why Paul said in 1st Corinthians 11: *"we should judge ourselves that we should not be judged by God."* If we read the Word of God and we apply it in our lives and repent and bring our lives in line with the word of God we have judged ourselves.

For this is the standard of divine judgment and if we do that God will not judge us.

We really have just two options: either we can judge ourselves according to the Word of God and bring our lives in line with the word of God or we can refuse to do that and then God will have to judge us according to His word.

One of the greatest mercies of God is that he has given us, through the Bible, God's standards for judgment that we may apply them to ourselves. And as Paul indicates, in this particular chapter, the person to apply the standard to you is not your brother nor your neighbor but yourself.

2.2.2 According To His Deeds

The second principle of God's judgment is stated in *verse 6* where Paul says *"God will render to every man according to his deeds."* All through the Bible, it is emphasized that God's judgment will be based on our deeds i.e. on what we do. We will not be judged by the claims we have made or even the prayers we have prayed. We will be judged by what we have actually done.

1st Peter 1:17, emphasizes this in very clear language. *"If you address as father the one who impartially judges according to each man's work* (these words are addressed to Christians. Notice if we call God our Father, we need to bear in mind that he impartially judges according to each person's work. Then it says and this is a remarkable statement which most Christians would not be very ready to receive.) It says *"Then conduct yourselves in fear during the time of your stay upon earth."*

That is not said in many places today, but there is a sense in which we should live in the fear of God knowing that one day we are going to account to God for the lives we have lived.

But making it clear that its Christians he is speaking to, Peter continues in the next verse 18: *"knowing that you were not redeemed with perishable things like silver or gold from your futile way of life but with precious blood as of a lamb unblemished and spotless blood of Christ"*

One reason why we need to walk so carefully with God is because of the tremendous price that he paid to redeem us, which is the blood of his own son Jesus. That is the value that God set upon us. The more you value something the more careful you are about that thing. So God has a very careful scrutiny upon the lives of each one of his redeemed children because of the price he paid to redeem us.

If you walk into a cheap store and buy a cheap piece of jewelry. You are really not too concerned if you lose it. But if your spouse has bought you a really beautiful and rather costly ring or whatever it might be, you are going to be very careful about what happens to that ring. And not merely because of its value, but because of the one who gave it to you.

So Peter is saying we need to be very careful about the lives we lead because of the tremendous investment that God has made in each one of us. And he emphasizes that God is going to judge us by what we do.

Bear that in mind you will not be judged by your denomination. You will be judged by what you have done. You will not be able to walk up to God and say I am a Methodist or am Anglican or a Pentecost. The point is how you have lived your life.

2.2.3 God is impartial

The third principle of judgment is stated in verse 11. *"There is no partiality with God."* God is impartial. That word partiality in the old King James is "there is no respect of persons with God".

The word 'person' in Greek is the word 'face' but it means the outward appearance of a person.

God is not interested in the part you play. God is interested in what you really are. So nobody's going to be judged because of their role in life. The general will be judged just the same way as the private in the Army. The preacher will be judged just the same way as the newest convert. The wealthy man will be judged just the same way as the beggar in the street. There is no looking at people's external appearance and judging them on that basis.

In the Epistle of James, James rebukes the Christians of his time because he said: *"you make a difference between the rich man who come in fine clothes and the poor man who just has nothing to commend himself."*

You are looking at the outward part. Peter and James and Paul say: God looks at what is inside.

2.2.4 By or Without the Law

The Fourth Principle of God's Judgment is stated in verse 12 and it is very important for us today. *"For all who sinned without the law will also perish without the law and all have sinned under the law will be judged by the law"*

Between Adam and Moses, there was no law. Those who lived in that period did not have the law. E.g. Cain sinned without the law just like Sodom and Gomorrah, they sinned without the law.

Then the law came through Moses. Those who lived after Moses was given the law, and before Jesus came, lived under the law and will be judged according to the law.

Afterwards, Jesus came. But Jesus did not come to abolish the Law, but to fulfill the law (Matthew 5:17) and the fulfillment of the law is LOVE (Romans 13:10): *"Love does no wrong to its neighbor. Therefore love is the fulfillment of the Law"*

Therefore, we who live under the law of love will be judged according how much love we gave to our neighbor. Did you repay evil for evil? Or did you persevere in doing good to others even though they did not deserve it? We will be judged according to the light that we have. If we have had the full light of the law, we will be judged by that, but if we have not had that light we will be judged by the light that we do have.

Question: Has there ever been a generation of Christians in the history of the church that has had greater light available to them than this generation?

Today, we have as many Bibles as we can afford to buy. Bible Commentaries, Interpretive books, devotionals etc. We can go to conferences and meetings. We can switch on the radio and TV and hear the preacher and that is wonderful. Thank God for it all. Thank God for the Liberty that makes this possible. But bear in mind that this carries with it a tremendous responsibility. We are going to have to answer to God for the measure of light that is available to us in our day. I honestly tremble when I think of what that entails for me personally.

2.2.5 According to Motives

The fifth principle of Gods Judgment is in verse 16: *"In the day when God will judge the secrets of men, by Christ Jesus, according to my Gospel"*. God is going to judge our deeds. Not merely the outward deeds, but he is going to judge the motives and intentions behind those deeds.

Three people may do something that seems outwardly the same but their motives may be quite different. For example, three peoples might make a generous contribution to some Christian cause:

    a.   One might do it out of a sincere heart of love for the Lord and his people and,

    b.   The second might do it to impress his fellow church members and,

    c.   The third might do it with the motive to receive a blessing from God.

The outward act is the same. The amount is the same but the motives are totally different. God looks at the motives. Let us look at a passage in 1st Corinthians 4:5:

"Therefore do not go on passing judgment before the time but wait until the Lord comes who will both bring to light the things hidden in the darkness and disclose the motives of men's hearts and then each man's praise will come to him from God."

Many times we are warned against judging one another. The particular reason given here is that we do not have all the facts because we only see the outward acts. But God looks on the inner thoughts and motives of the heart and God takes those into account when he judges.

2.3.   God Will Render to Every Man According to His Deeds

Now let us go back to Romans 2:6 for a moment. I want us to deal with one other rather difficult topic. God says He *"will render to every man according to his deeds"* and then he speaks of two different kinds of people: Those whom God accepts and those whom God rejects. And they are described in the next verses.

He says in verse 7: *to those who by perseverance in doing good seek for glory and honor and immortality, eternal life;* in verse *8: but to those who are selfishly ambitious and do not obey the truth, but obey unrighteousness, wrath and indignation.*

The essence of the problem is being self-centered. It is a conspicuous feature of people who are under the power of Satan. They are almost invariably extremely self-centered.

So there are the two kinds of people.

 a) Those who by perseverance in doing good seek for glory and honor and immortality will receive eternal life and,

 b) Those who are selfishly ambitious and refuse the truth of God by whatever means it may be revealed to them but prefer unrighteousness, God will give wrath and indignation.

Bear in mind that Paul addressed this letter to the saints in Rome. To those who are called. This is not for outsiders – the non-believers. It is those who Romans 1:5-6 ...*among all the Gentiles for His name's sake, among whom you also are the called of Jesus Christ;*

To assess the total judgment of God is beyond the capacity of any of us. But those who are described as receiving eternal life have two features:

 a) First of all they persevere in doing good,

 b) Secondly they seek for glory, honor and immortality, eternal life

The word seek indicates faith. They believe that God will reward them according to their response to him and according to what they have done. Those are the two basic requirements to be accepted by God in any age or any generation - before the gospel or during the gospel.

The two basic requirements are doing good and applying what you believe. And without faith it is impossible to believe God. There are many different ways in which faith expresses itself in different ages and generations.

Some examples of people who did not come to God on the basis of the gospel, but who fall into this category of persevering in doing well and seeking for God's glory and honor.

Luke 11: 31 – 32: Jesus is rebuking the men of his generation and he says:

31"*The Queen of the South* (That is the Queen of Sheba) *will rise up with the men of this generation at the judgment and condemn them, because she came from the ends of the earth to hear the wisdom of Solomon; and behold, something greater than Solomon is here.* **32**"*The men of Nineveh will stand up with this generation at the judgment and condemn it, because they repented at the preaching of Jonah; and behold, something greater than Jonah is here.*

Now, it appears that those two classes of persons: The Queen of Sheba and the men of Nineveh are not going to be resurrected with the resurrection of Christians because they are going to stand up in the same resurrection with the people whom God has rejected but they will be accepted on the basis of what they did according to the light available to them. They responded in faith to God with their actions.

So those are the two categories of people those who by what they do, they express their faith in God and those who reject the truth of God and prefer unrighteousness.

In case you should immediately start and try to work out exactly who belongs in which category, Romans 11:33 should serve as a warning:

Oh, the depth of the riches both of the wisdom and knowledge of God! How unsearchable are His judgments and unfathomable His ways! (Rom 11:33)

So be warned. Do not take the office of judge. It does not belong to you. There is only one judge and that is God and we are specifically told that his judgments are unsearchable. You cannot search out the judgments of God.

You have to take the stand of Abraham who said *"shall not the judge of all the earth do right"*

It is a sad thing that today; many Christians think that it is their responsibility to know exactly who is going to heaven.

2.4 The Question of Conscience

[Romans 2:13 - 3:20]

Now we are going to look at the question of conscience which is a rather difficult one to deal with. Sometimes, some of the things Paul says are not altogether easy to understand or to interpret.

We will read verses 13 - 15 and then verses 26 – 27 which give us a picture of how God deals with people who do not have a revelation of him in the word.

Rom 2:13 *"For not the hearers of the law are just before God, but the doers of the law will be justified"*.

Paul is taking about the Law of Moses as the great pattern of law. That is the perfect law or the God given law. Now, there are only two possible ways of achieving righteousness. These are:

- By keeping rules and
- The other is by trusting God in faith

The natural instinct of every human being when confronted with the issue of righteousness is to start to think in terms of rules.

Many people see righteousness as keeping a set of rules: I do not get drunk, I do not Smoke, I am not a hypocrite, I do not commit adultery, I do not fornicate, I go to church every Sunday, I pay my tithe, I do not do this, I do not do that etc. They pull out their list of little rules which they keep. Everybody has a list that is tailored to his or her own life.

That is natural with all human beings when the issue of righteousness is raised. To think in terms of keeping rules. What Paul says applies not only to the Law of Moses, but to every set of rules by which people might seek to make themselves righteous.

However, it is not possible to achieve righteousness by keeping any set of rules. Christianity is not a set of rules. We do not achieve righteousness with God by keeping a set of rules, but rules have a place in life. So Paul is saying: It is not the people, who hear the law, whether it is the Law of Moses or any other Law, it is the people who apply it who will be justified.

Notice, it is not the hearers who are just or righteous, but those who apply it will be justified. It does not say that they will become righteous. It says God will reckon righteousness to them. None of us can be just unless we are justified by God.

Paul goes on and deals with the issue of conscience.

Rom 2:14 *"for when the Gentiles who do not have the law do instinctively or by nature the things of the law, these not having the law are law to themselves"* i.e. they do not have any direct revelation of God's law but there is something inside them which does the same for them as the Law would do.

Rom 2:15 *"in that they show the work of the Law written in their hearts, their conscience bearing witness and their thoughts alternately accusing or else defending them,*

What is written in their hearts is not the law; it is the working of the law. We have in every one of us, something that works like a law, to achieve the same results as achieved by the law, which is not to make us righteous, but to bring us to the point where we see that we need God's mercy to be made righteous. That is absolutely different.

Then it speaks about conscience, which is the function in man which produces this consciousness or awareness that tells us - do not tell a lie.

Then Paul pictures a kind of court scene going on inside us. One of our thoughts says: well that is true, I did lie and the other says no it was not really a lie. It was just a little exaggeration. Paul pictures this kind of court scene going on inside us. Have you experienced that inside yourself? that is what Paul is talking about. Paul is saying that conscience is doing for people, the same thing that the law does. Not making them righteous, but showing them that they need God's mercy. And that is the work of the law – to show us that we need God's mercy.

One common thing about people who have had no contact with God is that they have a set of rules which they call traditional norms, which are actually Laws which govern them. You will hear them say: in our tradition, children have unquestionable loyalty to the parents, fathers are the final authority, girls stay virgins until marriage, improper behavior is punished etc.

Most of them have a deep sense of obligation to their norms. What Paul is picturing is a kind of a law court inside our consciousness and our conscience is the prosecutor.

So Paul gives us this very vivid picture of the internal court scene that is going on inside us and he says people who do not have the law or any law can have conscience produce in them the same effects that the law produces which is not to make them righteous.

Now Let us look at verses 26 and 27

Rom 2:26 *"If therefore the uncircumcised man the* (non-religious man) *keeps the requirements of the law will not his un-circumcision be regarded as circumcision."*

Rom 2:27 *And shall not uncircumcision which is by nature, if it fulfil the law, judge thee, who by the letter and circumcision dost transgress the law?*

If therefore the uncircumcised man makes the correct response to legitimate requirements, will not his un-circumcision be regarded as circumcision? That is, if he was physically un-circumcised yet he keeps the law, will he not judge you?

Paul is talking to the Jews who had the letter of the law handed to them and consider un-circumcision as a transgression of the law. So what Paul is saying is this, it is not the outward observance of rituals or norms or ceremonies. It is the inner response of your heart that determines how God looks at you.

He says very correctly that there are a lot of instances in which the religious man has the wrong response and the non-religious man has the right response.

Remember the parable of the Good Samaritan in Luke 10:25-37? What Paul is saying is that, it is not always the people with all the religious talk who can deliver. God is interested in the people who deliver and not in the people who talk.

2.5 The Jew is Condemned by the Law

[Romans 2:17-29]

Then, Paul homes-in on his fellow Jews and he gives a number of specific examples of the ways in which they break the law although they boast about the law and he says:

Rom 2:17 But if you bear the name "Jew" and rely upon the Law and boast in God,

This has not changed the least bit in Israel. Twenty centuries have changed nothing in this situation. It is precisely as Paul describes it. It is not only Jews who act that way. Born again Christians also boast in God today.

Rom 2:18 and know His will and approve the things that are essential, being instructed out of the Law,

Rom 2:19 and are confident that you yourself are a guide to the blind, a light to those who are in darkness,

Rom 2:20 a corrector of the foolish, a teacher of the immature, having in the Law the embodiment of knowledge and of the truth,

How would you describe such a person in one word - **arrogant?** Nothing creates pride more easily than religious knowledge. Many of us are in danger of becoming proud because we have knowledge.

Ask youself this, do you think at this present time that the world out there is saying this of the church. Do not you think that it applies exactly to us who call ourselves Christians? You see the boot is in the other foot. Because we are busy doing the things that we tell other's not to do. How many times have we seen headlines all around the world talking about the scandals taking place in the church?

What Paul is saying is up-to-date. This is not just something from the past or just religious theory. This is reality and we just need to put ourselves in the place of the people to whom Paul was writing to. This can be said legitimately of us today.

Rom 2:21 you, therefore, who teach another, do you not teach yourself? You who preach that one shall not steal, do you steal?

Rom 2:22 You who say that one should not commit adultery, do you commit adultery? You who abhor idols, do you rob temples?

A little boy receives instructions from the father. When the farther goes away, he wants to do exactly the opposite of those instructions. What goes on in that little mind? That is true of religion too. Preaching against things ultimately makes people want to do them. The Bible is so accurate and so up-to-date. You who abhor idols do you rob temples – Malachi 3: 7 says:

from the days of your fathers you have turned aside from my statutes and have not kept them. Return to me and I will return to you says the Lord of Hosts but you say how shall we return what do we have to do and then God says will a man rob God yet you are robbing me. But you say how have we robbed thee? in tithes and offerings. (Malachi 3: 7). I suppose it is much worse to steal from God than it is to steal from your fellow human beings.

Rom 2:23 You who boast in the Law, through your breaking the Law, do you dishonor God?

Rom 2:24 For "The name of God is blasphemed among the gentiles because of you," just as it is written.

Rom 2:25 For indeed circumcision is of value if you practice the Law; but if you are a transgressor of the Law, your circumcision has become uncircumcision.

Now that is God's attitude towards external ordinances, Let us just look at it again in verses 28 and 29

Rom 2:28 "for he is not a Jew who is one outwardly neither is circumcision that which is outward in the flesh

Rom 2:29 but he is a Jew who is one inwardly and circumcision is that which is the heart by the spirit the Holy Spirit not by the letter and his praise is not from men but from God."

Paul is saying whatever you do outwardly is not what really matters. What really matters is your heart relationship to God. The word Jew is taken from the name Yehuda or Judah and the meaning of Yehuda is praise. So Paul says you are only a real Jew i.e. a real Yehuda, which is the Hebrew word for it, if your praise comes from God.

Paul is not saying in these scriptures everybody who believes in God is a Jew. Some people interpret this wrongly. We are members of the body of Christ in which both Jew and non-Jew come together and form one body. But being a Christian does not make us Jews. What Paul is doing is not increasing the number of people who are entitled to be called Jew. He is restricting it to those who fulfill the inward conditions.

Now this is so important because our attitude towards the Jewish people is very very important.

Let us turn to a similar passage in Romans Chapter 9. Here we are dealing with God's choice or God's election. Paul is speaking about the unfaithfulness of many of the Jewish people and he says this with great grief in verse 6-8:

But it is not as though the Word of God has failed for they are not all Israel who are descended from Israel. Nor because they are his decendants are they all Abraham's children. On the Contrary, it is through Issack that that youir offspring will be reckoned. In other words, it is not children by physical descent who are God's children, but it is the children of promise who are regarded as Abraham's offspring.(Romans 9:6-8)

The vital qualification for being accepted as a true Jew or as true Israel is not the outward ordinances but it is embracing by faith the promise of God and without turning.

We will find that again in Galatians 6:15-16. Again it is the same principle. *It is not the outward but it is the inward for neither is circumcision anything nor un-circumcision but a new creature and those who will walk by this rule peace and mercy be upon them and upon the Israel of God. (Galatians 6:15,16)*

Now there are both Gentiles and Jews who walk according to this rule. The new creation is the Gentiles who have been born again by faith in Jesus. They have this inner transformation which comes from the new birth. Then he says and upon the Israel of God.

Now habitually Christians use that phrase to refer to the church, but that is not legitimate. The Israel of God is that section of Israel which has embraced the promise, acknowledged Jesus as the Messiah and entered into the blessings of the New Covenant.

So here, Paul talks about Gentile believers as those who walk according to this rule and Jewish believers as the Israel of God.

The word Jew and the word Israel are applied to all who fulfill the qualifications of having descended from Abraham Isaac and Jacob, but here Paul is pointing out that it is not the outward but it is the inward.

In Christian terminology, it is not the fact that you were baptized. The question is what has happened inside you. That is where God looks - that is the important issue. However in dealing with religious people this truth is unpopular. It is unpopular with many professing Christians. It is unpopular with Jews but it is the truth and we need to give heed to it.

CHAPTER 3: THE WHOLE WORLD IS ACCOUNTABLE TO GOD

(Romans 3:1-31)

Now we are going to move into chapter three but we are going to continue the same theme which is: The knowledge of what is right or the knowledge of God's laws does not by itself make us righteous. On the contrary it increases our responsibility and again in the first verses of chapter 3 Paul applies this to his own Jewish people and he says:

3.1 God Remains Faithful

Rom 3:1 What advantage has the Jew or what is the benefit of circumcision?

You might say, well if circumcision does not make us be accepted by God, then why did God impose all these ordinances upon the Jews. What is the benefit?

Rom 3:2 Great in every respect. First of all, that they were entrusted with the oracles of God.

That is the Jewish people. However, today it is the Christians who are entrusted with the full oracles of God. It is the Christians who have available to them the full Word of God.

Rom 3:3 What then? If some did not believe, their unbelief will not nullify the faithfulness of God, will it?

The word faith does not merely cover what we believe intellectually. It covers our personal commitment to God. And so rather than saying unbelief, here it is better to say unfaithfulness. Their unfaithfulness or the unfaithfulness of some of the Jewish people did not nullify God's faithfulness. God remained faithful even when Israel were unfaithful. That is what Paul is saying.

So he says: shall their unfaithfulness nullify the faithfulness of God?

Then the next words in this translation are, may it never be. The Old King James version says God forbid! It means - how could you think of such a thing.

Rom 3:4 May it never be! Rather, (It means that it is something unthinkable. How would you dare to mention such a thing or suggest such a thing?) *let God be found true, though every man be found a liar, as it is written, "That you may be justified in your words, and prevail when you are judged."*

Now, that is quoted from Psalm 51 which is David's great prayer of repentance after he was convicted of the sin of murder and adultery. And the words that preceded are these: *Against thee only have I sinned and done this evil in thy sight.*

Now those are amazing words because David had murdered a man and taken his wife. You would say that David had sinned against the man (Uriah) and he had sinned against Uriah's wife. But at this moment of tremendous agony, David says: *against thee, thee only have I sinned and done this evil in thy sight.*

There comes a point, which only the Holy Spirit can bring us to, when we realize that no matter how much our sins and our evil doing may affect other people, the terrible thing about them, is how they affect God.

Charles Finney said we have not come to true repentance when we simply look at the consequences of our sins. True repentance is getting a vision of what our sins have done to God. It is sad to see that there is very little of such repentance in the modern church and the results are evident. So David had this terrible inner revelation of how his sin affected the Almighty God. The agony that it caused the heart of God. The man whom God had chosen to be king had betrayed God betrayed his trust.

And then he says in the light of that, God whatever you say is true and when you enter into judgment with us your truth prevails. It is very important that we somehow come to that place where we acknowledge that what God says is right. That what he says is always true. He is never wrong.

How many times are we tempted to think that God did not really do the right thing in a certain situation. You feel that you are not sure that you can trust the way God is handling the situation. It really takes a deep dealing of the Holy Spirit to bring us to that place.

Revelation 4:11 in the old King James says - *for thy pleasure everything is and was created.* In essence, God created them that way, because He wanted them that way. The best reason for anything is that God wants it that way. There is no higher reason that we can ever get.

We need to come to the place of bowing before God, his judgments, his ways, his will; saying God everything you say and do is totally perfect.

Moses said to Israel: *His way is perfect and all his works are righteous.* God has never done anything unrighteous. I hope that will be the result of studying Romans. We will get a new picture of the total righteousness of God and for that we have to humble ourselves.

We may not have committed precisely the sins that David committed, but in every one of us there are those things which were horrible in the sight of God. We need to come to the place where by the revelation of the Holy Spirit, we see what our sins have done to God. God sometimes has to take us by a hard route - but that is the place that Paul is talking about here in this passage.

Then he goes on and very frequently in Romans, Paul imagines an objection against his teaching, he states the objection and then answers it. It is a typically Jewish way of thinking.

Many successful lawyers are Jewish because it is right there in the Jewish mind - from their background – this way of balancing one thing with another. One thing about Jewish people is – if you ask them a question, they will usually answer with a question.

You will notice when you study the teaching of Jesus that he was a real Jew. Almost invariably when he was faced with a question he answered with a question. E.g. What should we do about divorce? Have not you ever read and so on?

So here Paul is anticipating the objections of his fellow Jews, and every one of these objections are still made even today by the Jewish people who are confronted with the gospel.

So he says:

Rom 3:5 *But if our unrighteousness demonstrates the righteousness of God, what shall we say? The God who inflicts wrath is not unrighteous, is He? (I am speaking in human terms.)*

Rom 3:6 *May it never be! For otherwise, how will God judge the world?*

Paul imagines somebody saying: Well, what you are telling us is that the more unfaithful we are the more glory God receives for His faithfulness. So if we want to give glory to God, Let us go on being unfaithful. That is the objection and this is his answer: God Forbid!

Then he returns to the same theme in verse 7 and 8:

Rom 3:7 *Someone might argue, "If my falsehood enhances God's truthfulness and so increases his glory, why am I still condemned as a sinner?"*

Rom 3:8 Why not say—as some slanderously claim that we say—"Let us do evil that good may result"? Their condemnation is just!

That is a perversion of the truth of the gospel. In the Middle East, it is a common misrepresentation both for Jews and for Muslims that the Christian faith is about doing what you want and getting away with it. Paul deals with it and says – their condemnation is just. I am not going to waste time on people who think like that. They deserve the condemnation, because they have heard the truth and deliberately rejected it.

3.2 No One is Righteous

Rom 3:9 What then? Are we better than they? Not at all; for we have already charged that both Jews and Greeks are all under sin;

We are all guilty of sin whether we are Jews or whether we are Gentiles. We all have this in common. We are all sinners.

This is true for most born again Christians as it is for the Jewish people today - to see that they are sinners. You will be amazed how hard it is for them to see their sin.

Then Paul comes out with this whole series of scriptures taken from the Old Testament. Each of which affirms the sinfulness of all men but particularly the Jews. Paul knew what he was dealing with. He knew his own people.

So he comes out now with a whole series of quotations from the Old Testament. All proving that we are all guilty before God.

Beginning Verse 10:

Rom 3:10 as it is written, "there is none righteous, not even one;

Rom 3:11 there is none who understands, there is none who seeks for God;

Rom 3:12 all have turned aside, together they have become useless; there is none who does good, there is not even one."

Rom 3:13 "their throat is an open grave, with their tongues they keep deceiving," "the poison of asps is under their lips";

Rom 3:14 "whose mouth is full of cursing and bitterness";

Rom 3:15 "their feet are swift to shed blood,

Rom 3:16 destruction and misery are in their paths,

Rom 3:17 and the path of peace they have not known."

Rom 3:18 "there is no fear of god before their eyes."

It would be good to turn to one of the two passages in the Old Testament where those words are found - Psalm 14 and Psalm 53.

When a scripture is recorded more than once, we need to take heed to it. God, by the Holy Spirit caused that statement to be recorded twice in case anybody might miss it.

The fool hath said in his heart, There is no God. They are corrupt, they have done abominable works, there is none that doeth good. (Psalm 14:1)

Notice that believing wrong, leads you to live wrong. You cannot believe wrong and live right and you cannot believe right and live wrong. Our living is the product of our believing. When they said there is no God, they open and expose themselves to all forms of evil.

The Lord looked down from heaven upon the children of men, to see if there were any that did understand, and seek God. (Psalm 14:2)

The sons of men are the total human race. I want to point out to you that there is no one in his natural fallen condition who seeks after God. It is not in the human heart to do it. One thing is that - if you believe that you are a sinner, you make progress much faster than those (very religious men) who do not believe that they are sinners.

If you acknowledge that you are indeed a sinner, God puts in your heart the desire to seek the truth. I have realized that I am looking for the truth because God put that in my heart. By myself, I am not capable. Therefore I cannot take credit for that. In whatever circumstance that you are seeking the truth, remember that it is God who puts that in you. Never take credit for it. Left to yourself, you do not understand, neither do you seek God.

They are all gone aside, they are all together become filthy: there is none that doeth good, no, not one. (Psalm 14:3)

Not even one. That is so emphatic !

Let us return once more to Romans chapter 3 and we read these passages again. They are all taken from the Psalms and from the prophets.

Romans 3: 13-18

> **13** *"Their throats are open graves; their tongues practice deceit.""The poison of vipers is on their lips."*
>
> **14** *"Their mouths are full of cursing and bitterness."*
>
> **15** *"Their feet are swift to shed blood;*
>
> **16** *ruin and misery mark their ways,*
>
> **17** *and the way of peace they do not know."*
>
> **18** *"There is no fear of God before their eyes."*

As we contemplate that list for a moment, lets ask the question - What area of the human personality is most emphasized and dealt with first? It is the MOUTH. The first four statements are about what we do with our mouth. James said the tongue is an unruly evil. No one can control his own tongue.

So Paul quotes from the Psalms and from the prophets and he goes on.

Rom 3:19: *Now we know that whatever the law says, it says to those who are under the law, so that every mouth may be silenced and the whole world held accountable to God.*

That is very important. It is addressed primarily to the Jewish people. It says it is of no good you are pointing your finger at the Gentiles and saying this is what they have done. This is your own book. It was given to you first. It applies to you then to other people. Your own book tells you that there is none who does good and not even one.

That is the destination that Paul has brought us to. The whole world is accountable to God both Jews and Gentiles. Both religious people and non-religious people areall accountable to God.

Then he goes on to say that keeping rules or the law does not change the fact that we are still accountable to God.

All are corrupt, all have gone astray and so he comes to this great summation and he is worked hard to get here in verse 20:

Rom 3:20 Therefore no one will be declared righteous in God's sight by the works of the law; rather, through the law we become conscious of our sin.

It applies to the Law of Moses and also it applies to every other kind of law. No one will ever be justified in the sight of God by keeping rules.

Protestants, Baptists, Pentecost's, Catholics etc. all have a set of rules but no one will ever be justified or reckoned righteous in the sight of God by keeping their rules. What we have done is, we have switched from the Law of Moses which was a perfect law. Which was given by God and we have turned to our own laws.

Laws are important for any group of people. A group of people need laws to keep them under control. But by keeping those laws, it does not make you righteous.The main issue in the New Testament is whether we are made righteous by keeping laws or by faith. Many Christians have never really given any serious consideration to this truth.

But if you have been made just by faith, you probably will keep at least all the relevant laws. If you cannot get through this, you will never complete this pilgrimage. This is the first stage in understanding the Gospel. If you do not see this clearly and embrace it, and realize how true and how relevant it is, you cannot go any further. You will keep slipping back into the same problems.

Legalism is the greatest single problem of the Christian Church. Legalism also is the cause of much of the sin in the church, because a lot of sincere and honest men have embraced this set of do's and do not's. Do not commit adultery, do not lust, do not do this or do not go there etc. They focus their attention on keeping the rules and instead become enslaved by them.

The way to be pure is not to keep resisting lust. Because the more you resist lust, the more it dominates your thinking. There is a totally different way of becoming righteous - which is a righteousness of God which is by faith of Jesus Christ.

Therefore, by the keeping of rules no flesh or no human being will be justified or be reckoned righteous in God's sight. Then he says - for through the law comes the knowledge of sin. That is a startling statement for religious people.

So many Christians find it very hard to comprehend why Paul says that the law is what causes us to recognize sin. Then they wonder, why did God give the law, if all it can do is make us aware that we are sinners? That it cannot make us righteous.

3.3 Purposes for Which the Law Was Given

We are going to devote the next part of this study to the purposes for which the law was given. If we do not deal with this, there will be very many unanswered questions in your mind and you will never really be able to give attention to the positive which Paul is building up to.

3.3.1 The Law reveals God's righteousness

First, the law (Torah in Hebrew) uniquely reveals God's righteousness, holiness, wisdom and justice. It is a unique revelation as nothing else can be set beside it. When you want to talk about holiness, the place to go is the tabernacle of Moses. The tabernacle of Moses is the most challenging and compelling call to holiness. It is unique. There is nothing else anywhere in the world that has the same challenge to holiness and righteousness and justice as the law.

3.3.2　To show men the reality and power of sin

The second purpose of the law is to expose sin. First the diagnosis and then the medicine. Psychologically, this is very true. It is of no use to explain to people, God's Way of salvation, if they have not realized that they have the disease of sin. A person has to first be convinced that he is a sinner before he will recognize and receive God's plan of salvation.

God does not offer us the plan of salvation until he has shown us how desperately we need it. That we are sick with an incurable disease called sin and that there is only one remedy.

Romans 3:20 insunuates that by the works of the law no flesh will be justified or achieve righteousness in God's sight. For through the law comes the knowledge of sin.

That is the first purpose for which God gave the law to show us the disease of sin. The law is God's diagnostic tool to make us aware of the condition of sin which prevails in our lives. Apart from the Bible and books based on the Bible, there is not any book in the world that reveals the nature of sin. This is one of the priceless benefits of the Bible.

Philosophers of old like Plato were really interested in the issue of righteousness. Plato called it excellence or virtue and his conclusion was that knowledge is a virtue. He worked this thing out. He did not come to it lightly and he said "if people know what is right they will do it". But that is contrary to the human spirit. We are continually confronted by people who know what is right and yet they do not do right. People who know what is wrong and do it and people who also know that doing wrong will cost them dearly yet still they do it.

Only the Bible diagnoses this force within us, called sin, which causes us to do things against our own best interests even when we know that what we are doing is not right. So knowledge by itself is not the solution. The solution consists of knowledge and its application. The Gospel helps us with the application of the knowledge. Therefore the solution is the Gospel

Let us read a few other passages on this theme from Romans 7. We will be dealing with this chapter in detail a little later on.

What shall we say then? Is the Law sin? May it never be! On the contrary, I would not have come to know sin except through the Law; for I would not have known about coveting if the Law had not said, "YOUSHALL NOT COVET." (Romans 7:7)

So how did he come to know about sin? – It is through the law.

Again in verses 12 and 13;

So then, the Law is holy, and the commandment is holy and righteous and good. (Romans 7:12)

Paul is very careful to point out there is nothing wrong with the law. The fault is not in the law.

Therefore did that which is good become a cause of death for me? May it never be! Rather it was sin, in order that it might be shown to be sin by effecting my death through that which is good, so that through the commandment sin would become utterly sinful. (Romans 7:13)

The purpose of the law is to bring sin into the open. The total sinfulness of sin and to show all its ugliness i.e. in all its real colors and there is no other source of this revelation but the Bible.

3.3.3   To show that men cannot achieve righteousness by own effort

The third purpose of the law is to show men that they are unable to achieve righteousness by their own efforts and Paul gives us his own experience again in the 7th chapter of Romans verse 18 to 23.

For I know that nothing good dwells in me, that is, in my flesh; (The word flesh is sometimes used in the technical meaning. It does not mean the physical body but it means the nature which we have inherited by descent from Adam. The old Adamic nature) *for the willing is present in me, but the doing of the good is not.* (Romans 7:18). Can you identify with these words? (Rom 7:18).

For the good that I want, I do not do, but I practice the very evil that I do not want. (Rom 7:19).

But if I am doing the very thing I do not want, I am no longer the one doing it, but sin which dwells in me. (Rom 7:20).

See what sin has done. This shows that there is a power at work in us which works contrary to our own sincere will and intention.

Find then the principle that evil is present in me, the one who wants to do good. (Romans 7:21).

For I joyfully concur with the law of God in the inner man, (Romans 7:22).

but I see a different law in the members of my body, waging war against the law of my mind and making me a prisoner of the law of sin which is in my members. (Romans 7:23).

This is a typical case of a prisoner-of-war. Someone who is been taken captive. Someone who has been put in a prison and is made to fight against the side that he is on. So that is Paul's description of his own experience and this is true for everyone.

The more religious knowledge you acquire, instead of getting better you steadily get worse and the harder you try to be good, the quicker you get worse until you start thinking - this thing does not work. Why? Because you have had the diagnosis but you have not received the remedy.

We can never get out of this prisoner-of-war scenario. All we have to do is to continue fighting against our captor - 'the body of sin' - through the grace provided to us by our Lord Jesus Christ.

The Lord says in Revelation 3:21: *To the one who is victorious, I will grant the right to sit with Me on My throne, just as I overcame and sat down with My Father on His throne.*

3.3.4   To foretell and for show the Savior

The fourth purpose of the law is to foretell and for show the Savior, the Messiah. In this context Paul calls the law a tutor.

Let us turn for a moment to Galatians 3:24: *Therefore the law has become our tutor to lead us to Christ the Messiah that we may be justified by faith*

The word that is translated tutor, is actually the word from which we get the English word pedagogue (instructor) and it was used to describe a senior slave in the household of a wealthy man whose job was to give the wealthy man's children the first basic instructions in right and wrong. And then when they became old enough, to lead them every day to the school or to the tutor who is going to teach them. So this man was not the teacher but he was the one who took them to the teacher.

And Paul says that is what the law did for the Jews. It gave them the first principles of right and wrong but it could not teach us the whole thing. It became our slave to lead us to the Messiah who would teach us.

So the purpose of the law was to direct Israel to the Messiah. To reveal him and foreshow him and this it did in two ways: by foretelling and by foreshadowing. There are many prophecies in the law that clearly predicts the Messiah.

Let us look at one Deuteronomy chapter 18:18, 19. Here, the Lord is speaking to Moses and he says:

'I will raise up a prophet from among their countrymen like you, and I will put My words in his mouth, and he shall speak to them all that I command him. (Deut 18:18)

'It shall come about that whoever will not listen to My words which he shall speak in My name, I Myself will require it of him. (Deut 18:19)

So there is a clear prediction that God was going to raise up to Israel from amongst their own brothers a prophet who would be like Moses. This prophet was to have unique authority because he was going to tell them all that God commanded and if they did not listen, God would require it of them. All the apostles of the New Testament unanimously concur that this promise of the prophet like Moses was fulfilled in Jesus.

So there was a foretelling of the Messiah but the Messiah was also foreshadowed in the law in many of its ordinances and sacrifices.

In fact every sacrifice in the law in some way or another foreshadows Jesus. There is not a single sacrifice that does not tell us something about Jesus. For example the Passover lamb which was slain in Egypt and whose blood protected the Israelite households from the wrath and judgment of God which came upon the Egyptians who were not protected. This is perhaps as clear a picture of Jesus the Lamb of God as you can find anywhere in the Bible. Let us look at two passages in the New Testament in which this picture of the passover lamb is applied to Jesus.

The first is in John 1. The introduction of John the Baptist, who was sent to prepare the way for the Messiah. Verse 29 says - *the next day John the Baptist saw Jesus coming to him and saying behold the Lamb of God who takes away the sin of the world.* He was the one who fulfilled the passover of a lamb.

Then very specifically in 1st Cor 5:7, Paul applies this to Jesus. He says and he is referring now to the ordinance of the passover in which every Jewish home had to be purged of leaven. He says - *cleanse out the old leaven that you may be a new lump just as you are in fact unleavened for Christ our Passover also has been sacrificed.*

So here Paul states specifically that Christ was the true Passover lamb and of course we bear in mind that his sacrifice or his death took place at the Passover season. So the law pointed those who were under it - the true solution the Messiah who was to come.

3.3.5   To keep Israel as a separate nation to which Messiah could come

Then the fifth reason for the law which is not always understood especially by Gentiles is to keep Israel as a separate nation to which Messiah could come. They were kept in custody or shut up and Paul says this again in Galatians 3:

But before faith came, we were kept in custody under the law, being shut up to the faith which was later to be revealed. (Galatians 3:23)

So the Jews were shut up by the law in a special situation to keep them ready for the Messiah. Let look at the words of Balaam. A prophecy concerning Israel in Numbers 23, is his prophetic vision of Israel:

"As I see him from the top of the rocks, And I look at him from the hills; Behold,   a   people who dwells   apart, And will not be reckoned among the nations. (Numbers 23:9)

The word nation is the word for Gentiles. So even after they were dispersed driven out of their own land for 2,000 years that prophecy has been fulfilled concerning the Jewish people.

A people who dwells apart who shall not be reckoned amongst the nations. It is one of the most remarkable facts of history that that Jewish nation could be dispersed from their own land in the year 70 AD and 19 centuries later after having spent nearly 2,000 years amongst at least 100 other nations could still be a separate identifiable people.

If you scattered Britons or Americans or Kenyans amongst the other nations and came back at the end a hundred years, you would not probably find a single Briton or Ameriocan or Kenyan. It is unique and it is true only of Israel and the thing that kept them separate primarily was the Law of Moses. One particular ordinance has been the Sabbath which has always separated them from other people and they kept that at a tremendous personal cost and sacrifice to themselves.

You see God, had to have a people to whom the Messiah could come. There is hardly anyone in other nations who does not have an ancestor three generations back who was an idol worshiper. God could never have sent his son to such a nation because if he had obeyed his parents he would have been worshipping a false god. God had to prepare a nation very carefully and especially to whom he could send his son - who could obey his parents and keep the ordinance of his nation and still be faithful to God his father. It is a tremendous miracle in a way that God was able to do that.

3.3.6   To provide humanity with a pattern of a nation governed by just laws

Then the sixth reason for the law was to provide humanity with a pattern of a nation governed by just laws. Let us look just for a moment in Nehemiah chapter 9:13 – 14.

This is part of a tremendous prayer which he was praying after the return from the Babylonian exile. They rehearse all the acts of God on behalf of Israel.

> *"Then You came down on Mount Sinai, And spoke with them from heaven; You gave them just ordinances and true laws, Good statutes and commandments.*
>
> *"So You made known to them Your holy sabbath, And laid down for them commandments,*   *statutes*   *and*   *law,*
> *Through Your servant Moses. (Nehemiah 9:13-14)*

That is a true statement. Basically in our world today nearly all the nations that have a code of law that preserves human integrity and morality can trace those laws back to the law of Moses.

So the law established a pattern to which all other nations could look to see what it would be like to be a nation governed by just laws.

3.3.7   To provide endless material for spiritual meditation

Finally and this is very important and it is not usually taken into account. The six purpose of the law was to provide inexhaustible material for spiritual meditation. When you look at the opening words of Psalm 1. The first three verses tell it all:

blessed is the man who walketh not in the counsel of the ungodly nor standeth in the way of sinners nor sitteth in the seat of the scornful but his delight is in the law of the Lord and in his law doth he meditate day and night

What is the result?

He shall be like a tree planted by the rivers of water that bringeth forth his fruit in season. His leaf also shall not wither and whatsoever he doeth shall prosper. (Psalm 1: 1-3)

Do you want to be successful? the key is what you meditated on. The successful man meditates on the law day and night and that is the key to his success.

Therefore, in Summary these are the purposes for which the law was given.

1. First of all to show men the reality and power of sin. There is nothing else in human experience that can diagnose sin but the law.
2. Second to show men they are unable to achieve righteousness by their own efforts.
3. To foreshadow the Savior the Messiah and foretelling him in prophecy
4. To keep Israel as a separate nation to which the Messiah could come and the words that Paul uses are – Keep Israel in custody or shut up a nation.
5. To provide humanity with a pattern of a nation that is governed by just laws.
6. To provide inexhaustible material for spiritual meditation.

If you read almost any of the five books of Moses (Genesis, Exodus, Leviticus, Numbers, Deuteronomy), you will find inexhaustible lessons to guide you and guard you and warn you.

3.4 God's Solution to man

[*Romans 3:21-26*]

Paul now reveal's God's solution to man.

Romans verse 20 is some kind of a milestone. It tells us that we have come so far in this pilgrimage and therefore, by the works of the law no flesh will be justified in God's sight for through the law comes the knowledge of sin.

Beginning in verse 21, Paul begins to reveal God's solution. In his great wisdom God did not offer the solution until He had shown the problem. Paul here has in great detail and very systematically outlined the whole problem and he has shown us that the law is not the solution. He now unfolds God's solution to us as we read verses 21 through 26.

Rom 3:21 *But now apart from the Law the righteousness of God has been manifested, being witnessed by the Law and the Prophets,*

Paul is being very careful to say that I am not innovating this. It is all contained in the Old Testament. He is explaining what was implied in the law and the prophets.

Rom 3:22 *even the righteousness of God through faith in Jesus Christ for all those who believe; for there is no distinction;*

Again the message here is that there is no way to righteousness except by faith in Jesus the Messiah. Christ is Greek translation for Messiah which is Hebrew for the saviour. This righteousness which is by faith is offered to all those who believe the word. There is no difference or distinction as to who believes.

There is no distinction whether we have the law, or we are religious. There may be many differences i.e. different races, different colors, different cultures, different languages, different religions, but there is one thing that we all have in common. That we are all guilty of sin and that we are all accountable to God in respect to sinfulness. In that respect there is no distinction between the Jew or Gentile, Protestant or Catholic, black or white, we are all the same.

Rom 3:23 for all have sinned and fall short of the glory of God,

The word sin here means - to miss them mark or to come short of the mark. There are a number of words in the Bible for wrongdoing and each one is very specific e.g. **Transgression** means walking across a line that is marked. Transgression is disobeying a known commandment.

Now the Jews were guilty of transgression. In most cases, the Gentiles were not guilty of transgression because they did not have a known commandment. So they were different in that respect. But in respect to sin, which is coming short of the purposes for which we were created, the gentiles have also sinned. We were all created for the glory of God.

Another word is **iniquity**. A better translation for iniquity is rebellion. That is another aspect of wrongdoing. Rebellion is in the heart of every one of us. But rebellion is primarily an attitude and not an act. We will deal with rebellion in Romans chapter 6. That is where the old rebel is dealt with.

Sinner: All people are sinners. We are not cleaner than the others on the account that we have the law. A preacher once said: 'A person has no right to exist who does not exist for the glory of God'.

The only justification for existing in God's universe is to give him glory. You cannot go to church and sing 'we give you glory lord' and think that you have given glory to God. That is lip service. To glorify God means to begin to live the purpose for which God created you for. If it is to show mercy, then begin showing mercy, if it is to sing, then sing for him, if it is to teach, then teach, if it is to shepherd, then shepherd.

If you were called to be a shepherd and instead you chose to sing, which is not bad at all, you still have fallen short of the purpose which God created you and subsequently failed to glorify God. And that is accounted for you as sin. Sin is coming short of the purpose for which we have been created.

Therefore, we are all alike in that respect. We have sinned and in sinning we have come short of the glory of God. We have missed the purpose for which we have been created. That is why, sinners always in some respect, are frustrated because they are not living the purpose for which they were created.

It can be likened to buying a Mercedes Benz saloon car and use it to move furniture. It will not do it so well. Or if you buy a truck and use it as a taxi - you will have problems. The reason is that it was created for another purpose and now it is being misused. That is true of every sinner.

Now we come to the solution:

Rom 3:24 *being justified as a gift by His grace through the redemption which is in Christ Jesus;*

We are only justified when we respond.

Justified means I am acquitted. My case has been tried before the court of heaven and they have handed down a verdict - not guilty. It is wonderful because there is no higher court than the court of heaven. When heaven says you are not guilty, it does not matter what your neighbors say. It does not matter what other people think about you. You are not guilty - that is part of being justified.

It also means being reckoned righteous. God reckons righteousness to you on the basis of your faith. And as a result of that, something happens inside of you. God calls things as they are. Whatever God calls, that is what it is. It may not be obvious immediately, but the change process begins. So God chooses to call us righteous and when he calls us righteous, we become righteous.

The other translation means I am just as if I have never sinned. Why? Because, I have been reckoned righteous, with the righteousness of God. Not my own righteousness, not by my best efforts but by faith I have received as a gift, the righteousness of God.

If you do not receive it as a gift, my dear brethren, you will never get it. You cannot work for it. You cannot earn it.

God said in Isaiah 64:6: *all your righteousness's are like filthy rags*. He did not say all your sins. He said the best that you can do in the sight of God is like a filthy rags. And those filthy rags will never get you to heaven.

Isaiah 61:10 describes what it is like to be justified or to be reckoned righteous.

> *I will rejoice greatly in the LORD,*
> *My soul will exult in my God;*
> *For He has clothed me with garments of salvation,*
> *He has wrapped me with a robe of righteousness,*
> *As a bridegroom decks himself with a garland,*
> *And as a bride adorns herself with her jewels.*

A lot of people know what it is to be saved, but many who are saved do not know what it is to be justified. First of all he clothes you with a garment of salvation. That is a wonderful kind of undergarment, but then he wraps you around with a robe of righteousness. He totally covers you with a robe of his righteousness. And it does not matter from what angle the devil looks at you; all he can see is the righteousness of God. He has nothing he can say against you and that is justification.

It is grieving to see so many Christians who do not really get excited about their faith. Today, it is common to see many unhappy faces in the church. They sing praises to the Lord, pray and so forth but they do not show it in their demeanor. Simply because they do not look like it. Many Christians have never really grasped this truth. They have no comprehension that God has covered them with a robe of his righteousness and that they have to greatly rejoice in the Lord.

King David knew it! That is why he danced the way he did for the Lord.

If you do not show it in your demeanor, conduct, character or attitude, then what it means in actual fact is that you do not really believe what you are saying. Only the Holy Spirit can make it real to you.

We receive righteousness as a gift (Bear that in mind) by His grace and grace is the supernatural working of God which does things for us that we do not deserve. Grace cannot be earned. Grace starts when you have come to the end of your abilities.

Being justified as a gift by His grace through the **redemption** *which is in Christ Jesus.* That word redemption in the Greek version of the Old Testament is used for the 'mercy seat' and they are in the tabernacle of Moses.

God provided a mercy seat which was exactly the same dimensions as the Ark, which covered the broken law and which was the place where God manifested himself and spoke and which was overshadowed by the cherubs of glory. As long as the Ark was uncovered you did not have access to go on. But when the Ark is covered by the mercy seat then God can draw near to you and you can draw near to him. And he can speak to you. That is, you have access into the immediate presence of Almighty God because of the mercy seat. And the mercy seat is the sacrifice of Jesus, his shed blood -that is the only basis of access to a righteous God.

Rom 3:25 whom God displayed publicly as a propitiation in His blood through faith. This was to demonstrate His righteousness, because in the forbearance of God He passed over the sins previously committed;

Propitiation = Appeasement, Conciliation

So God displayed to the whole universe, the one soul, sufficient propitiation, for all the sins we have all committed. This is demonstrated by the life laid down and the shed blood of Jesus. God did not do it secretly. He did not do it in a corner but He did it very publicly.

Then it goes on to say that this was to demonstrate His righteousness i.e God's righteousness, because in the Forbearance (tolerance) of God he passed over the sins previously committed.

You see, we have a mystery, that under the Law of Moses and for nearly fifteen centuries, Israel were continually remembering their sins. Take just one ordinance, the day of Atonement once every year. They made a remembrance of their sins. But no sacrifice that they brought did away with those sins. The sacrifices of the law merely covered those sins until the next sacrifice was due. But when Jesus came, the writer of Hebrews says; *he put away sin by the sacrifice of himself.* He did not just cover sin he disposed of sin, he removed it.

So in this demonstration God vindicated or justified his righteousness. That for fifteen centuries, He had passed over sins which had never been properly atoned for. God knew what he was going to do. He did it in faith on the basis of the assurance that Jesus would ultimately provide the all sufficient sacrifice. Everything that God did in respect of Calvary, he did in faith. Jesus died in faith.

Rom 3:26 for the demonstration, I say, of His righteousness at the present time, so that He would be just and the justifier of the one who has faith in Jesus.

That is the core of theme Romans. That God can be just and justify the sinner. How could God pass over sin without compromising his own righteousness? The answer is Romans 3:26. That is the key descriptive verse that God might be perfectly righteous and still forgive sinners.

God's problem is not punishing sinners. God's problem is forgiving sinners. And he is the only one who could provide a solution. The solution is contained in this verse.

3.5 Outcome of God's Solution

Now we come to the effect of receiving this propitiation as we read verses 27 and 28:

Rom 3:27 *Where then is boasting? It is excluded. By what kind of law? Of works? No, but by a law of faith.*

Rom 3:28 *For we maintain that a man is justified by faith apart from works of the Law.*

We pointed out in chapter 2 that religious knowledge produces pride. The more religious people know, the prouder they get and pride is an abomination to God. So he is got to do away with Pride. He does it by this law of faith which leaves us nothing to boast about.

We cannot claim anything we did not do for ourselves. God did it all. All we can do is receive by faith the free gift of righteousness which God offers us.

Let us look at the Islam as an example. What is the attraction? It is a religion of works. Why do people like a religion of works? because it gives them something to boast about. It suits human pride. That is not the only example. It is also true of Orthodox Jews and it is true of a lot of professing Christians who have not realized that we have nothing to boast on God. God did it all and all we can do is receive by faith what God has done. Boasting and pride are incompatible with faith.

Habakkuk 2: 4 says : *Behold, his soul which is lifted up is not upright in him: but the just shall live by his faith.*

Faith and pride are incompatible. This is very important to remember because a lot of people are in danger of getting proud when we do some little thing for God. We get some success in our ministry and we think there we are - the man with all the answers. That is terribly dangerous. There should be no room for pride. It is totally excluded.

It is very interesting that in the course of his earthly ministry, Jesus dealt with two persons whom he especially praised for their faith.

The interesting thing about them is that neither of them was Jewish. One was the Roman centurion: he said I am not worthy that you should come under my roof. Just say the word and Jesus said: I tell you I have not found faith like that in all of Israel. What went with his faith? Its humility. The centurion said… 'I am not worthy'.

The other one is the woman who had a demon-possessed daughter in Matthew 15:22-28.

21Then Jesus left Galilee and went north to the region of Tyre and Sidon.

22A Gentile woman who lived there came to him, pleading, "Have mercy on me, O Lord, Son of David! For my daughter is possessed by a demon that torments her severely."

23But Jesus gave her no reply, not even a word. Then his disciples urged him to send her away. "Tell her to go away," they said. "She is bothering us with all her begging."

24Then Jesus said to the woman, "I was sent only to help God's lost sheep — the people of Israel."

25But she came and worshiped him, pleading again, "Lord, help me!"

26Jesus responded, "It is not right to take food from the children and throw it to the dogs."

27She replied, "That is true, Lord, but even dogs are allowed to eat the scraps that fall beneath their masters' table."

28"Dear woman," Jesus said to her, "your faith is great. Your request is granted." And her daughter was instantly healed.

Jesus really tested her humility when he said that it is not right to take the children's bread and throw it to the little dogs. Jesus in essence called her a dog. That is an insult in the many parts of the world. In the Middle East, to be called a dog is the worst of all insults. He was putting her in her place. He was saying I am committed by covenant to Israel. I made a covenant with them through Moses. That I would be their healer but I have no covenant with you. So you are just a little dog.

You see, when God seems to be hard, He is most merciful. Then when she persisted, and said *"That is true, Lord, but even dogs are allowed to eat the scraps that fall beneath their masters' table."* Jesus said to the woman great is your faith. Help yourself and take what you want.

What was the conspicuous thing about her character? She was a humble person. Therefore, let us be careful that we do not become proud because, pride and faith cannot coexist.

Rom 3:29 *Or is God the God of Jews only? Is He not the God of Gentiles also? Yes, of Gentiles also,*

One of the claim of Judaism is that God, is the God of Jews only.

Rom 3:30 *since indeed God who will justify the circumcised by faith and the uncircumcised through faith is one.*

But God is one. The basic requirement is faith. Faith may be expressed by circumcision or it may operate without circumcision, but whatever way it comes, its faith and faith alone is the basis of justification. Circumcision without faith will not justify a man. And then he finishes with this very important verse.

Rom 3:31 *Do we then nullify the Law through faith? May it never be! On the contrary, we establish the Law.*

It is very important to see that faith in Jesus and the New Testament does not set aside the Law of Moses. Romans 7:14 says: *We know that the Law is spiritual; but I am carnal, sold as a slave to sin.*

CHAPTER 4: JUSTIFICATION BY FAITH

(Romans 4:1 - 4:25)

We have covered a lot of ground but we still have a rather difficult road to cover before we get to our destination in Chapter 8. In the previous section and towards the end of chapter 3, we looked at God's provision for man's problems. Up to that point Paul had simply been unfolding the problems.

But in the latter part of Romans chapter 3 beginning with verse 20 and onwards, Paul unfolds God's final (total and all sufficient) sacrifice, which is through faith in the atoning death and the shed blood of our Lord Jesus Christ.

Now, Romans chapter 4 Paul looks at two of the great fathers of Israel i.e. Abraham and David and Paul proves from the scripture that each of them was not justified by works but by faith.

He focuses mainly on Abraham who is the father of all who believe. But he also quotes from many psalms of David.

4.1 Abraham Justified by Faith

Rom 4:1 what then shall we say that Abraham, our forefather according to the flesh, has found?

This is a very important question for all of us - for Jews and Gentiles. How did Abraham achieve righteousness with God?

Rom 4:2 for if Abraham was justified by works, he has something to boast about, but not before God

Rom 4:3 for what does the Scripture say? "Abraham believed god, and it was credited to him as righteousness."

Rom 4:4 now to the one who works, his wage is not credited as a favor, but as what is due.

Rom 4:5 But to the one who does not work, but believes in Him who justifies the ungodly, his faith is credited as righteousness,

Now, here is one of the most important passages from the Old Testament - Genesis 15:6

Abraham had been having a conversation with the Lord about the fact that the Lord had made a great promise to him about him having an heir. Abraham had no heir, and there follows this conversation between the Lord and Abraham.

And He took him outside and said, "Now look toward the heavens, and count the stars, if you are able to count them." And He said to him, "So shall your descendants be." (That was the promise) Then he believed in the LORD; and He reckoned it to him as righteousness. (Genesis 15: 5-6)

Abraham at that point did absolutely nothing but believe. Paul and also James in his epistle, points out that, that was how Abraham achieved righteousness. He did not earn it. It was not on the basis of what he had done, but it was credited to his faith.

And Paul says in Romans 4 verse 5, *"But to the one who does not work but believes in him who justifies the ungodly his faith is reckoned as righteousness."*

That is a very powerful verse. It points out that if you want to receive righteousness by faith from God in the same way as Abraham did, you just need to believe. There is no other way.

What is the first thing you have to do? You have got to stop doing anything. You have got to come to the end of all that you can do to earn

God's favor. You have to do nothing but believe. This is the pattern and example of Abraham.

Now at this point, Abraham's faith was accounted to him for righteousness. It does not mean that Abraham never made any mistakes. After that, we find if we look in the following chapters that Abraham made some serious mistakes. In Genesis 16, we read how he and Sarah took the initiative out of God's hands and decided they had better get a child by Hagar.

I want to point out to you in that in the life of faith we should never take the initiative. That is a basic principle. The initiative must always come from God. This is the pattern of Jesus. He said *'the son does not do anything except what he sees the father doing'*. (John 5:19).

The only safe basis for living the life of faith is consistently letting God take the initiative. Each time we do what Abraham did and take the initiative out of God's hands we end up in trouble.

Then in Genesis 20, Abraham told a lie about Sarah and permitted her to be taken in by a Gentile king (Abimelech king of Gerar) which was not good behavior. That is not the way a husband ought to behave. We are told that Sarah was a model wife. She totally submitted to him and that is remarkable. She submitted in faith and God intervened.

What I want to point out is that, God did not approve those two aspects of Abraham's conduct but his faith was still reckoned to him as righteousness. This is tremendously important for us because the moment we truly put our faith in the atoning death of Jesus, and believe that, on that basis, righteousness is reckoned to us, we are reckoned righteous. That does not mean that we will never make mistakes. Our faith will still be reckoned to us as righteousness as long as we go on believing. The real danger is when we give up our faith.

Let us turn to a passage in Luke chapter 22 which is very significant. This is a scene at the last Supper and the Lord Jesus has been warning his disciples that they are going to betray him, flee from him and desert him i.e. Simon Peter in particular. But all of them say 'this could never happen Lord' and in verses 31 and 32 Jesus says this to Peter: *"Simon, Simon, behold, Satan has demanded permission to sift you like wheat;* (Luke 22:31)

That is a remarkable statement. Apparently Satan went to God and said let me get at those apostles the way he did with Job. Then he says specifically to Peter: *but I have prayed for you, that your faith may not fail; and you, when once you have turned again, strengthen your brothers."* (Luke 22:32)

Jesus did not pray for Peter not to deny him. In the circumstances it was inevitable that Peter would deny him. Taking into account Peter's character at that point and the tremendous onslaught of the forces of darkness that was to come against him shortly, it was inevitable that Peter would deny Jesus. What Jesus said in essence is that:

'Peter you are going to make a terrible mistake. You are going to feel terribly ashamed. You are going to feel the bottom has dropped out of your life. But do not give up believing. If you can hold on to your faith, I will see you through and the subsequent course of events. '

To each one of us, we may be facing tremendous tests and temptations. Some of which you did not expect and at a certain point, you may feel that you failed God and the bottom has dropped out of your life. What can I do? What you can do is to go on believing? Do not give up your faith because God will see you through if you do not abandon your faith. That is the one critical mistake you must not make.

As long as we continue to sincerely believe in Jesus and accept the righteousness that God offers us and on the basis of that faith, there is no guarantee that we will not mistakes. There is no guarantee that we will not get into problems. There is no guarantee that we will not fail. I do not have any guarantee from God that I cannot fall into some snare of Satan tomorrow but God will get me out provided I go on the believing.

There are many Christians who do things that are regrettable but God says as long as you keep on believing, your faith will be reckoned to you as righteousness and on that basis I will see you through. You may not know how, it may seem impossible but do not give up your faith.

Verses 6 through 8

Here is where Paul brings in David and he says:

Rom 4:6 *just as David also speaks of the blessing on the man to whom God credits righteousness apart from works:*

(This is from psalm 32: 1-2)

Rom 4:7 *"Blessed are those whose lawless deeds have been forgiven, and whose sins have been covered.*

Rom 4: 8 *"Blessed is the man whose sin the lord will not take into account."*

Notice that David says here that there are three things included in this blessing: our lawless deeds have been forgiven, our sins have been a covered and God no longer takes our sin into the account. God does not any longer keep a reckoning of our sins.

Now Paul returns to Abraham after that little digression about David and he deals with this very important question relating to circumcision which was;

Did Abraham have to be circumcised before his faith was reckoned as righteousness?

This is a vital question for all who come from a Jewish background. But it goes beyond that because there are other external ordinances of faith and many people compare baptism to circumcision.

We could say; is my faith reckoned to me as righteousness before I am baptized? The answer is yes. If you sincerely believe and you intend to obey, your faith is reckoned to you as righteousness from the moment you believe. Afterwards, baptism in a certain sense is a seal of the righteousness which you already have by faith, and also to receive the Holy Spirit. (Acts 2:38)

There is a difference between John's baptism and Jesus baptism. The people whom John baptized were baptized because they were sinners, who had confessed their sin. In Christian baptism we are united with Jesus in burial and resurrection. We are baptized because we have been made righteous. It is the fulfillment of our righteousness. Remember, Jesus was baptized that he might fulfill all righteousness (Mathew 3:15) and when you and I are made righteous by faith in Him then we fulfill our righteousness by the external act of baptism.

Now Let us look at what Paul says in Romans 4 verse 9:

4.2   Abraham's Decendants

Rom 4:9 Is this blessing then upon the circumcised or upon un-circumcised also for we say faith was reckoned to Abraham as righteousness?

Rom 4:10 How was it reckoned? While he was circumcised or uncircumcised? Not once circumcised but while uncircumcised.

This is an extremely important point. Abraham did not go through circumcision before Genesis chapter 17. But his faith was reckoned to him as righteousness in Genesis chapter 15. And there was a considerable period of time between those two chapters.

Rom 4:11 And he received the sign of circumcision, a seal of the righteousness of the faith which he had yet being uncircumcised: that he might be the father of all them that believe, though they be not circumcised; that righteousness might be imputed unto them also:

That is, the father of all people from a non-Jewish background, and the father of circumcision to those who, not only out of the circumcision, also follow in the steps of the faith of our father Abraham.

The point here is that God had promised Abraham that he would be a father of a multitude of nations. Not just of one nation Israel but of all nations and that in due course people from every nation on earth would become spiritual descendants of Abraham through faith.

The point is that we do not have to be circumcised to become descendants of Abraham. We are descendants of Abraham by faith alone. So Abraham becomes the father of two different kinds of people:

1. First - those who are circumcised on the basis of faith (bear in mind that our circumcision is of no benefit. The vital deciding factor is faith) and then
2. Second, he becomes the father of those who exercise faith as Abraham did without being circumcised. That is all believers from a non-Jewish background.

So in this way, the promise of God to Abraham was fulfilled before circumcision was introduced.

Then Paul goes on to say concerning Abraham that he is the father of circumcision, not merely to those who are circumcised but to those who also follow in the steps of the faith of our father Abraham which he had while he was uncircumcised.

Therefore, it is not enough for a Jew to be circumcised to become a descendant of Abraham. According to this, no one is a true descendant of Abraham unless he walks in the steps of the faith of our father Abraham. The essential condition is faith and God reaches people in two different ways:

1. He reaches the circumcision on the basis of the faith which caused them to be circumcised and

2. He reaches the uncircumcised, i.e. the rest of the world basically without demanding circumcision on the basis of their faith.

So this is the pattern which Abraham established. We are all descendants of Abraham according to scripture, through faith in Jesus Christ, the seed of Abraham, and this is extremely important to us. It takes us beyond simply the issue of circumcision. It makes it very clear to us that it is faith and faith alone that makes us sons of God and sons of Abraham and that this faith does not depend on some external ordinance. This is really the basic issue that we are saved by faith alone. Not by faith plus something else.

Always be on your guard against people who want you to add something to faith. That is unscriptural. The only condition to be a descendant of Abraham is faith. God insists upon this and he will not waive this condition. He will be very tolerant in other areas. He will allow for many differences but He will not change that condition.

We need to emphasize once more, the vital importance of faith. Jesus said to Peter, *'I pray that your faith may not fail'* because that is the basic requirement of belonging to God and of being a child of Abraham.

4.3   Abraham – The Pattern to all who believe

Paul says in verse 12 that:

Rom 4:12 *and the father of circumcision to those who not only are of the circumcision, but who also follow in the steps of the faith of our father Abraham which he had while uncircumcised*

So Abraham is more than just a figure. He is a pattern. He went ahead and he laid out the way. To be truly his descendants we have to walk in that pathway. We have to follow in his steps. We will just briefly list the steps of the faith of Abraham:

Abraham did five things

1. He accepted God's promise by faith alone without evidence.
2. He recognized he was incapable of producing the promised result.
3. He focused without wavering on the promise and this was reckoned to him as righteousness and as a result.
4. He and Sarah both received supernatural life in their bodies and,
5. Thus the promise was fulfilled and God was glorified.

So those are the steps of the faith of our father Abraham.

That is what Abraham left us as a pattern. This is the pathway of faith which is set before every one of us. It is not some external ordinance, but it is a life time walk of faith following in the footsteps of Abraham. We have to do as Abraham did. We have to accept God's promise just the way it is. We have to reckon that we are incapable of producing what God has promised in our lives. We have to focus on the promise and not on our own ability or inability. Then we will receive the supernatural grace and power of God released in our lives through our faith and in this way the promise of God will be fulfilled in our lives.

4.4 Abraham Receives the Promise

Now let us look at how Paul fills this out by reading on from verse 13.

Rom 4:13 For the promise, that he should be the heir of the world, was not to Abraham, or to his seed, through the law, but through the righteousness of faith.

Rom 4:14 For if they which are of the law be heirs, faith is made void, and the promise made of none effect:

What Paul is saying is that God made this initial promise solely on the basis of Abraham's faith. It would have been totally unfair and inconsistent later on to add as a further condition that you have to keep the law. Paul points out that the law was actually given 430 years later. It was never a condition of entering into the promise that God had made to Abraham.

In fact what he points out is, and this is a very remarkable statement, but it is also very true:

Rom 4:15 *Because the law worketh wrath: for where no law is, there is no transgression.*

That is worth meditating upon for a little while. Let us take an example of a young boy who when he is left alone in the house by his parents turns the house upside down. When the parents come back, they do not get angry with the boy but tell him categorically that he should never repeat that again. Then on another occasion, the parents leave the boy alone and the boy turns the house upside down as before. When the parents come back home they become very angry with the boy and punish him.

Why were the parents angry the last time and not the first time? Because when there is a law, the breaking of it produces wrath. But when there is no law, there is not that reaction of wrath. When the law is imposed and it is broken the reaction of the one who made the law is wrath and anger. That is a lesson to parents. Do not make too many laws for your children. The more laws you make the more the more angry you are likely to get with your children. Try and keep them as few and simple as possible.

We have a very incorrect picture of what the law does. We have a somewhat skewed idea that the law will get people closer to God. The truth is that it will not. That is very important because a lot of people trying to get close to God by making all sorts of laws for themselves and actually what happens is they get further away from God.

The law does not bring us close to God. Centuries of religious tradition somehow has persuaded many that the law was going to do us good.

Rom 4:16 *For this reason it is by faith, in order that it may be in accordance with grace, so that the promise will be guaranteed to all the descendants, not only to those who are of the Law, but also to those who are of the faith of Abraham, who is the father of us all,*

The only way we can receive grace is by faith. Ephesians 2:8 really says it all: *by grace you are saved through faith and that not of yourselves it is the gift of God not of works lest anybody should boast.*

This is to guard us against pride. Religious legalism invariably produces pride in the people who practice it. God does not like pride at all. The first sin in the history of the universe was pride. In our churches today, we tend to get angry with adultery and fornication and drunkenness etc. which is very right. I am not suggesting that we should tolerate those things but we tolerate a whole lot of pride and that is a much more serious sin than all the others.

God wanted to make sure that no one would be excluded from this promise and so it had to be by faith that it might be by grace. None of us can ever earn righteousness from God. We either receive it as a gift by faith or we do not get it. There is no alternative way to be reckoned righteous with God.

Then Paul goes on again quoting from Genesis 17:4.

Rom 4:17 *as it is written, "A father of many nations have I made you") in the presence of Him whom he believed, even God, who gives life to the dead and calls into being that which does not exist.*

God called Abraham a father of many nations when he did not have a child in his own body. This is very important to understand. When God calls out something; that is what it is. You may not see the evidence when God calls you a saint. You may not feel like it, but it is not in feeling. It is faith.

When God called Gideon a mighty man of Valor, what did he feel like? He felt like a timid coward. But later he did become a mighty man of Valor. God's calling comes before the reality because it is always on the basis of faith. *It is not of him who runs or of him who wills but of God who shows mercy.* (Romans 9:16)

Rom 4:18 *in hope against hope he believed, so that he might become a father of many nations according to that which had been spoken, "So shall your descendants be."*

Abraham hoped, yet he had no hope. Have you ever hoped and yet you feel that there is no hope but you go on believing. Whatever you do, do not stop believing. So Abraham, in hope against hope believed in order that he might become a father of many nations according to that which had been spoken.

Rom 4:19 *Without becoming weak in faith he contemplated his own body, now as good as dead since he was about a hundred years old, and the deadness of Sarah's womb;*

That faith is realistic faith. He tells it like it is. My body is dead but that does not make any difference to God's promise. I do not try to somehow persuade myself that there is a little life still left in my body. That would not be faith. From the look of things, there is no hope in the natural. There is no way this could come about. Abraham accepted the fact that not only was his own body as good as dead but Sarah's womb was also in a similar state.

This is how Abraham thinks; there is no way in the natural that we could ever have a child of our own. But I still believe what God said. It is much better to face the fact that the situation is desperate but there is only one person who can help you and that is God. That is faith.

Rom 4:20 yet, with respect to the promise of God, he did not waver in unbelief but grew strong in faith, giving glory to God in respect to the promise of God

Rom 4:21 and being fully assured that what God had promised, He was able also to perform.

Abraham was made strong by faith. He received strength in his physical body through faith and Sara received strength. Her womb was quickened. She became alive again in that respect. This was not a temporary change in Abraham because after his wife Sarah died, he married again and he had five more children. That was a permanent miracle. It was not bad going for a man who was a hundred years old. Who in hope and against hope believed God with respect to the promise of God and did not waver in unbelief.

Remember what James says in his epistle about people who waver. *For let not that man think that he will receive anything of the Lord. He is a double-minded man unstable in all his ways.* (James 1:7-8)

Abraham was made strong by faith giving glory to God.

Now Romans 3:23 says *For all have sinned and come short of the glory of God.* What is the real serious aspect of our sin? It is not what it does to us but the fact that it robs God of His Glory. That is the real terrible fact about sin.

Now, because we have robbed God of his glory, is there any way that we can ever give him back the glory which we robbed Him? The answer is yes. We can give back the Glory we have robbed God by faith.

How did Abraham give glory to God? It was not by his efforts but by believing God. So God has provided a way by which we can give back to him the glory that our sin deprived him, by believing him. When you believe God and his promises are worked out in your life, then that gives Him glory. That is the only way we have.

4.5   Three Facts About Grace

Now, let us focus a little bit on grace. Generally speaking many people know very little about grace. Their idea of grace is some kind of a modified religious effort. Let us look at these three facts about grace:

1. **Grace begins where human ability ends.**

   As long as you can do it yourself, you do not need God's grace. When you come to the point where you know you cannot do it, but God wants you to do it, then you move out by faith into the realm of grace. Many Christians are afraid to do what God tells them to do because they feel that they cannot do it. In a certain sense God never tells us to do something we can do. God's is always moving us out beyond our own ability into the realm of grace by faith.

2. **It is received only by Faith.**

   For by grace are ye saved through faith; and that not of yourselves: it is the gift of God: (Ephesians 2:28)

   Every time your faith is challenged, you can react in either one of the two ways: 'Oh God, are you asking that of me?' or 'Oh thank you God', I can see that you want my faith to be strengthened. You want me to receive more of your grace. I accept this. '

   Every major step of progress that you will ever make in the Christian life will be made in response to a challenge. This is the way to grow. Every time you run away from a challenge, you are diminishing your spiritual stature but every time you accept a challenge you are growing in spiritual stature.

   In Hebrew 10: 38, the writer quotes Habakkuk 2:4 and *says the righteous man will live by his faith but if he draws back my soul shall have no pleasure in him.* That is God speaking. In the course of the Christian life, there are brothers and sisters who come to a point where they are afraid to go forward in faith. Where they feel that God is presenting them with a challenge that they are not prepared to accept and from that time onwards they begin to die spiritually.

It is written that 'the just will live by faith'. The only way you can have a life is by faith. The more God requires you to operate in faith, the more life you will have. If you want to play it safe and say 'God I do not want to take any risks' you are shutting yourself off from divine life. It does not mean that you will be a lost soul, but that you will not know fullness of divine life which God plans for you in this world. Do not be afraid of the challenge of faith.

We are living in a world today which desperately needs the word of God. But it is not going to get any easier to bring the Word of God to the nations. In Matthew 24:14 Jesus said: 'this gospel of the kingdom shall be proclaimed in all the world, to all the nations and then the end will come'. The end will come when the church has done its job. At the same time in the preceding verses Jesus warned us of persecution, false prophets, famines and abounding lawlessness. He did not say the world situation is going to get easier. In fact he made it very clear that the world's situation is going to get harder. That is the opportunity to stretch your faith and that is the challenge.

Now everyone has to make a personal decision but remember that if you take the cowardly way, you will wither. If you move forward in faith, you may stagger. You may fail but sooner or later God will see you through.

3. **The result of Grace always Glorifies God**

In whom ye also trusted, after that ye heard the word of truth, the gospel of your salvation: in whom also after that ye believed, ye were sealed with that Holy Spirit of promise, which is the earnest of our inheritance until the redemption of the purchased possession, unto the praise of his glory. (Eph 1:13-14)

Abraham was made strong by faith giving glory to God. (Rom 4:20). When you move from faith (believing God) to grace, the result is Glory to God.

Now we come to the application at the close of this fourth chapter.

Rom 4:22 Therefore It was also credited to him as righteousness.

Rom 4:23 Now not for his sake only was it written that it was credited to him,

Rom 4:24 but for our sake also, to whom it will be credited, as those who believe in Him who raised Jesus our Lord from the dead,

Rom 4:25 He who was delivered over because of our transgressions, and was raised because of our justification (our acquittal)

Righteousness will be reckoned to those who believe in Him who raised Jesus our Lord from the dead. What are we required to believe in order to receive righteousness by God? We are required to believe that the Lord delivered up Jesus our Savior, our substitute, to the punishment of death because of our sins. But that on the third day he raised him up again that we might receive righteousness.

The key to this is identification. When you grasp that it is the key that unlocks what happened at the cross. On the cross there was a two-way identification:

1. First of all Jesus identified with us. He took the sinner's place. He became the last Adam. He exhausted the whole evil inheritance that has come upon the whole Adamic race and when he was buried that whole inheritance was terminated.

2. Then he rose again on the third day, the head of a new race. We have to realize and reckon that he was our representative. So when God vindicated his righteousness by the resurrection on the third day that was our righteousness that was vindicated. We were reckoned with him in death, reckoned with him in burial and reckoned with him in resurrection also.

That is what we have to believe. The key word is identification. When Jesus died, I died. When he was buried, I was buried. When he rose, I rose. By believing that, I receive righteousness by faith from God.

CHAPTER 5: RESULTS OF JUSTIFICATION BY FAITH

(Romans 5:1 - 5:21)

In Romans chapter four, we focused mainly on the example and the pattern of Abraham and his faith. We also saw the conditions that Abraham had to fulfill in order to become the father of a great multitude of nations. We have also seen the conditions that we have to fulfill in order to qualify to be reckoned as the descendants of Abraham.

Now, moving on to chapter five and we will headline the first study as:

5.1 The Five Experiential Results Of Being Justified By Faith

We pointed out earlier that the gospel is anchored in history and in human experience. It is not just an abstract or intellectual set of theories. It is tied to history and human experience. It is tied to history because it is based and centers on three historical facts that: That Jesus died, and that he was buried, and that he rose again on the third day.

If those facts are not true, then gospel is not true. And if it is true, then the Gospel is true. The Gospel is anchored to human experience because when we believe it and act on it, it produces results in our experience.

So now we are going to look at the results or experience of being justified by faith. What happens in us when we meet these conditions to have righteousness reckoned to us by faith?

Let us just give the alternative interpretations. To be justified means we are acquitted, we are not guilty, we are reckoned righteous. We are made righteous just as if we never sinned.

What does it feel like or what happens to us when we are justified?

Paul deals with this question in the beginning of chapter 5.

Rom 5:1 *Therefore, having been justified by faith, we have peace with God through our Lord Jesus Christ*

Rom 5:2 *through whom also we have obtained our introduction by faith into this grace in which we stand; and we exult in hope of the glory of God.*

Here are the first three experiential results of being justified by faith.

5.1.1   We Have Peace with God

First of all we have peace with God for the first time in our lives. We in harmony with God our Creator and in a certain sense because we are in harmony with the creator, we are also in harmony with the creation. Many of us have had that experience after we have met the Lord and received righteousness by faith. Everything looks different. Not everybody has a dramatic experience but you get peace with the environment, peace with creation and God.

In my personal experience, I used to fear death but after salvation that fear disappeared. Forces that frightened you now no longer frighten you. Everything suddenly becomes different.

You have peace because your bill has been paid. Your peace is a complete. For the first time you are a complete person. Every part of you is in harmony with every other part of you.

5.1.2   Justification by faith gives us access into God's grace

The second experiential result is in verse 2. *Through whom (That is Jesus) also we have obtained (accessed) our introduction by faith into this grace in which we stand.*

Being justified by faith gives us access into grace which upholds us. We can stand in this grace we are no longer carried to and fro. We are no longer the plaything of forces, but we are standing firm in the grace of God. God's grace is upon us and whenever you hear the word grace it is probably good to think of it in terms of favor or charity.

The Greek word for grace Charris from which we get charisma. All these words basically mean beauty, elegance, charm. We may not think about it like that. But somebody said that beauty is in the eye of the beholder. When God looks at us with favor, we become beautiful. We are in this marvelous condition of having God's favor upon us. I feel so strengthened when I recognize that in any situation, if I am walking in the will of God, God's favor is on me.

The Book of Proverbs says that God's favor is like a cloud of rain. The Book of Psalms says that God encompasses the righteous about with favor like a shield. So we are protected on every side by the grace or the favor of God as we walk along. We are under this beautiful cloud of the latter rain and every now and then the cloud bursts and precipitates some of the latter rain upon us.

If you could think of grace in terms of beauty, you will see, one of the things that is absent in living a religious life. I do not think that is God's will. God wants us to be beautiful and simple like little children. God says: he will beautify the meek with his salvation. The beauty that comes upon us is his favor.

5.1.3   We Exult In Hope Of the Glory Of God

The third result which is stated at the end of verse two is that we exult in hope of the glory of God. We now have hope at the end of the tunnel. It may be a long dark tunnel but there is light at the end of it. We know that ultimately we are going to share God's glory in eternity forever.

In Colossians 1:27 Paul says: *To me it was granted that I should make known among the Gentiles the unsearchable riches of Christ which is Christ in you the hope of glory.*

Once Christ comes in you, you have a hope of glory. Hope is a very important part of salvation.

Romans 8:24, which we will come to later, says: *For in hope we have been saved, but hope that is seen is not hope; for who hopes for what he already sees?*

We are saved by hope. Hope is called in 1st Thess. 5:8 a helmet of salvation. It is the protection of the mind. When I was saved, although God did a wonderful change in me, I still had a tremendous mental struggle for a good many years. When we first get into salvation, we may go through various struggles. However, eventually when we receive deliverance from our struggles, we find that there is protection provided in the scriptures - THE HELMET OF HOPE - A quiet and serene confidence of expectation of good. And we exult in that hope. It means we get so happy we have to tell other people about it and we get excited.

Those are the first three experiential results of being justified by faith. Now we come to fourth experiential result of being justified by faith. It is another kind of exalting. Verses 3, 4 and 5:

Rom 5:3 *And not only this, but we also exult in our tribulations, knowing that tribulation brings about perseverance;*

Rom 5:4 *And perseverance character and character hope;*

Rom 5:5 *and hope does not disappoint, because the love of God has been poured out within our hearts through the Holy Spirit who was given to us.*

5.1.4   We Exalt In Tribulation

The fourth result is exalting in tribulation, pressures, tests, trials and problems. How many people go that far? You will not only exult in hope of the glory of God but also you will exult in trials and testing. Paul gives us reasons why we should be happy when we are tested.

Let us turn for a moment to James. James and Romans are just two opposite sides of the same truth.

> James 1: 2-4 says: <u>2</u> *consider it all joy, my brethren, when you encounter various trials,*

> James says joy and Paul says exult. Both give essentially the same reason, that the testing of your faith produces endurance. The only way you can learn endurance is by enduring. There is no other way.

> <u>3</u> *knowing that the testing of your faith produces endurance.* <u>4</u> *And let endurance have its perfect result, so that you may be perfect and complete, lacking in nothing.*

That is exciting is not it? Would you not wish to be perfect and complete lacking in nothing? There is only one way to it and that is the tribulation route. It is the testing. It is enduring. Testing that will bring you through to the place where you will be perfect and complete lacking nothing.

If you want to achieve that goal, then you have to take that route. You do not have to arrange the tests - God will take care of that.

In Romans 5, Paul says that we exult in our tribulations knowing that tribulation brings about perseverance and that is the same word that in James is translated endurance. Endurance is an essential part of

Christian experience. If you do not acquire endurance there are a whole lot of things in the Christian life you will never attain.

Rom 5:4 *and perseverance, proven character; and proven character, hope;*

We do not know what a person is like until we have seen him go through trials. There is no way of knowing in advance what kind of a person you are dealing with until you have seen the person go through trials.

Trials produce proven character and proven character produces hope. It is always exciting to see how God gets you out of the trials. Ultimately, when you get out, it might seem that God was a little slow in doing it, but he would do it anyway.

So when you have been through a whole series of tests and the next test comes, you do not get depressed. You do not wring your hands and say what is happening now? You should say: It would be interesting to see how God gets me out of this. That is hope. But you do not get that kind of hope without the testing.

Now we come to one of the most glorious statements in Romans. **Verse 5** says:

Rom 5:5 *and hope does not disappoint, because the love of God has been poured out within our hearts through the Holy Spirit who was given to us.*

What is the final basis of our hope? It is the love of God poured out in our hearts. That is a tremendous declaration. It does not say some of God's love has been poured out in our hearts. It says the entire love of God that is poured out into our hearts through the Holy Spirit.

After you have been baptized in the Holy Spirit, you do not need to pray for love but rather, by going through these steps, **love or agape love** becomes available to you. Something about love that escapes the notice of many is that it is the strongest thing in the universe. God's love is stronger than anything else.

In the Song of Solomon 8:6, it says love is as strong as death and death is irresistible. No one can resist death but when Jesus died and rose from the dead, he proved that love is stronger than death. So love is the strongest force in the whole universe. Never underestimate its strength.

Let us look for a moment the famous a LOVE chapter: 1st Corinthians 13. From verse 4 and following, Paul describes what love is:

4Love is patient, love is kind and is not jealous; love does not brag and is not arrogant, 5does not act unbecomingly; it does not seek its own, is not provoked, does not take into account a wrong suffered, 6does not rejoice in unrighteousness, but rejoices with the truth; 7bears all things, believes all things, hopes all things, endures all things. 8Love never fails; but if there are gifts of prophecy, they will be done away; if there are tongues, they will cease; if there is knowledge, it will be done away. 9For we know in part and we prophesy in part; 10but when the perfect comes, the partial will be done away. (1 Corinthians 13: 4-10)

Here is the key. Love bears all things, believes all things, hopes all things and endures all things. That is the love which is shed abroad into our hearts which gives us hope. That is the ultimate source of both endurance and hope. It is God's love in our hearts. Nothing can wear out the love of God. Nothing can crush the love of God.

Let us turn back to Romans chapter 5 and look at the description of the love of God which is found in verses 6 through to verse 10.

The love of God is expressed in Christ and in Christ death on our behalf. Bear in mind that is the expression of the total love of the Godhead (Father Son and Holy Spirit) beginning in verse 6:

Rom 5:6 For while we were still helpless, at the right time Christ died for the ungodly.

Rom 5:7 For one will hardly die for a righteous man; though perhaps for the good man someone would dare even to die.

Rom 5:8 *But God demonstrates His own love toward us, in that while we were yet sinners, Christ died for us.*

Rom 5:9 *Much more then, having now been justified by His blood, we shall be saved from the wrath of God through Him.*

Rom 5:10 *For if while we were enemies we were reconciled to God through the death of His Son, much more, having been reconciled, we shall be saved by His life.*

Now in this scripture, Paul uses four different descriptive words to describe what we were like at the time Jesus died for us. This gives us a measure of the love of God.

1. In verse 6 he says; we were **helpless**. We could do nothing to help ourselves. There was no response that we could make that would change the situation.
2. At the end of verse 6 he says; that we were **ungodly**.
3. In verse 8 he says; God demonstrates his own love toward us in that while we were yet **sinners** Christ died for us and;
4. In verse 10 he says; while we were **enemies.**

That is the full measure of the love of God. That Christ died for us while we were still helpless, ungodly, sinners and enemies of God. That is what is referred to as agape Love i.e. divine love and it is unconditional. It makes no demands. Christ did not say to his disciples that; if you do this or if you will do that, then I will pay the penalty for your sins. He did it all simply out of his own spontaneous will. He was under no pressure. He was under no obligation. He owed us nothing and that is the love that Paul is talking about here.

It demands no response, it makes no conditions, it simply love. And in the last resort, it is irresistible. It is the strongest force in the whole universe. When we have finished with all our displays of power and cleverness and expertise, the strongest thing that we will ever have is the measure of God's love within us. Love is never defeated and love never gives up. Love bears all things, believes all things, hopes all things, and endures all things.

Sometimes we tend to think of love as something rather weak and sentimental. We think that people who talk about love are weak people. That is a total misconception. On the contrary, the love of God is the strongest thing in the universe. God does not say: well I will give you a little measure of my love today and if you do better, I will give you some more tomorrow.

When he baptizes us in the Holy Spirit, he just pours out the whole thing. In John 3: 34-35, it says that God does not give the spirit by measure. He does not measure out a ration say this is how much you have earned and this is what I will give you. He just dumps the whole thing out upon us.

As a man, I would not have done the same. I would have made some conditions or some demands for you to receive the full measure. I would have probably said: well, if you straighten out a little bit, I will give you this much.

Probably I could have been saved a while back had anyone talked to me about the love of God. Maybe the brethren thought that I was too bad. I am glad that God did not think that I was too bad.

5.1.5 Exulting In God

The fifth and final experiential outworking of being justified by faith is **exulting in God** which is in verse 11. This is the climax.

Rom 5:11 *And not only this, but we also exult in God through our Lord Jesus Christ, through whom we have now received the reconciliation.*

How much exalting do you do? Do you do as much exalting as Paul talks about in this verse?

The climax is rejoicing and exalting is (not in what we have experienced, not in a gift received, not in a blessing) but in God himself. That is what David may have had in mind in Psalm 43.

Let us read Psalm 43 for a moment and see what David said. David was in a situation where he was really depressed. He just did not feel things were going right.

He says in Psalm 43:2 at the end: *why do I go mourning because of the oppression of the enemy?* And he answered his own question. That is the reason that most times we go mourning – the enemy. What was the remedy? He cried out to God in verse

3 *O send out Your light and Your truth, let them lead me; Let them bring me to Your holy hill And to Your dwelling places.* **4** *Then I will go to the altar of God, To God my exceeding joy; and upon the lyre I shall praise You, O God, my God. (Psalm 43:3-4)*

What was David's joy? It was God himself. That was the supreme joy of David's life. When he was depressed and cast down and did not know where to turn, he said I will go to the altar, the place of sacrifice. He said I will lay my life upon the altar of God. I will give myself. I will abandon myself to him without reservation and I will know him as my exceeding joy. That is the goal of the Christian life.

As we go on into this study of Romans, we will find that at the end of chapter 8, which is where we are headed, that the destination is none other than God himself.

Here we get just a little glimpse. It is like being on a mountaintop, and knowing that you have not arrived, but you can see your destination briefly for a moment. We see just in the distance our destination, a glistening mountain peak which is **God Himself** - our joy.

5.2   The Comparison between Adam and Jesus

Now, we are going to move on to the second half of Romans chapter 5. This here is an intense and concentrated piece of reasoning you will find anywhere in the Bible.

Rom 5:12 *Therefore just as through one man sin entered into the world, and death through sin, and so death spread to all men, because all sinned.*

Rom 5:13 *for until the Law sin was in the world, but sin is not imputed when there is no law.*

Rom 5:14 *Nevertheless death reigned from Adam until Moses, even over those who had not sinned in the likeness of the offense of Adam, who is a type of Him who was to come* (that is Jesus).

First of all Let us notice that Paul points out two time periods there which succeed one another.

The first is from Adam to Moses, when there was no God given law for the human race. God had given Adam just one commandment. But he did not give him a law and from the time of Adam his transgression onwards there was no God given law on earth until Moses.

Then we come to the time of the coming of Jesus and in John 1:17 it says that the law was given through Moses - a very important statement. The whole law, the entire law, the complete system, came at one time through one man – Moses.

It says: *the law was given through Moses but grace and truth came by Jesus Christ. (John 1:17)*

It is always important to bear in mind when you study about the law that it was only given to one very small section of the human race, maybe about 3 million people, at a certain point in history. Furthermore, it could only be fully carried out in one place geographically. And that was the land of Israel because much of the law entailed doing things that could only be done in Israel. A specific section of the human race, but the most important section of the human race because the whole purpose of redemption depended on that little nation called Israel.

Now Paul says that Jesus was the outworking of a pattern that was given even initially in Adam. Adam received one commandment, in a garden, with everything his heart could ever but desire but he disobeyed it. Jesus received the commandment from the father to lay down his life for the world and in a garden Gethsemane he accepted that commandment and obeyed it.

So there is a close parallel between Adam and Jesus. In order to understand this parallel more fully, Let us turn for a moment to 1st Corinthians 15:45 and 47. This is the chapter that deals with the resurrection but we will not go into that in detail.

*So also it is written, "The first MAN, Adam, **became a living soul.**" The last Adam became **a life-giving spirit**.* (1 Corinthians 15:45)

This is the contrast between first and last Adam. Between a living soul and life-giving spirit and then in verse 47;

The first man is from the earth, earthy; the second man is from heaven. (1 Corinthians 15:47)

Here, Paul gives two titles to Jesus. He calls him first of all the last Adam and then the second man.

People often refer to Jesus as the second Adam. That is not correct. Paul is saying say's. He is first of all

- The last Adam and then
- The second man.

When Jesus died on the cross, he died as the last Adam and in him the whole evil inheritance of the entire Adamic race was exhausted. When he died, it died and when he was buried, it was buried. He finished it.

This complemented even the evil of the generations to come because it says in Hebrews 9:14: ... *through the Eternal Spirit that he offered himself without spot to God.*

So through the Eternal Holy Spirit, which goes beyond time, he complemented in himself, the awful inheritance that came upon the entire Adamic race. It was put away completely. Then when he rose from the dead he was the second man i.e. the head of a totally new race - the Emmanuel race, the God-man race.

We arose out of the death of sin and the curse of Adam to become members of a new race of which Jesus is the head.

This is stated in Colossians 1:15-18: *He Jesus is also the head of the body the church and he is the beginning, the firstborn from the dead. So that he himself might come to have first place in everything.*

So Jesus is the head of the body which is the church and he is the firstborn from the dead. He is the first one to rise in resurrection into a totally new kind of life. That kind of life that had never existed before. Jesus rose from the dead with resurrection life. He rose as the head of the body and he was begotten out of death. In a natural birth, normally the first part of the body that emerges is the head. When the head emerges we know the body will follow and in this birth Jesus, the head emerged first, and his resurrection is the guarantee of our resurrection.

So he is first of all, a new creation and the last Adam. He had to deal once and for all with the whole evil inheritance. Then he had to arise from the dead, the second man, and the head of an entirely new race which had never existed before.

So that is the essence of the comparison between Adam and Jesus. Now we come to the details. This comparison has two aspects: there are aspects in which Jesus was like Adam and there are aspects in which Jesus was unlike Adam.

5.2.1   The aspects in which Jesus was like Adam

Romans 5: 18 -19

Rom 5:18 *So then as through one transgression there resulted condemnation to all men, even so through one act of righteousness there resulted justification of life to all men.*

The first comparison is this: Adam by one act of disobedience brought condemnation on the whole race descended from him. He received the command and disobeyed it. Sin entered and death followed. Since then, sin and death have been passed upon all of Adam's descendants including every one of us.

But Jesus, through one act of righteousness, obtained the possibility of justification of life for all men. The one act of righteousness was the sacrifice of himself upon the cross. That word: **'act of righteousness'** is important because we will meet it again in Romans 8:4 where it says the righteous requirements of the law can be fulfilled in us. Just take a note of that word. It is also used in Revelation 19:8 where it says *'the fine linen is the righteous acts of the saints'*.

So the word means, a righteous act that fulfills a requirement of God. By his sacrifice on the cross, by that one righteous act, Jesus fulfilled the requirement of God and made possible for justification of life.

To be justified means acquitted, not guilty, reckoned righteous or made righteous. Just as if I had never sinned. Jesus by his sacrifice made that possible and because he made it possible for us to be reckoned righteous, he made it possible for us to receive life. It is very important to see that, all through Romans, that God never bestows life or any blessing on the unrighteous. The first requirement in redemption is that we have to be made righteous. After that God can pour his blessings upon us. A righteous God will never pour his blessings on the unrighteous. So righteousness is the first issue and that is why it is the central theme of Romans.

Rom 5:19 *For as through the one man's disobedience the many were made sinners, even so through the obedience of the One the many will be made righteous.*

Here is the next point of similarity: By Adams one act of disobedience, all of his descendants became sinners but by Jesus's one act of obedience, all those who believe in him are made righteous.

This comparison is important because the people who became sinners as a result of Adam's sin including you and me, were not just sinners by label, they were sinners by nature and by act. And so correspondingly, when we are made righteous through faith in Jesus, God not only puts a new label on us. He takes away the label sinner and puts on the label righteous but to add on that, we are made righteous by nature and by act.

Just as Adams disobedience made us all sinners by nature, in exactly the same way Christ's obedience makes us all righteous by nature.

5.2.2   The Aspects in which Jesus was unlike Adam

In verses 15, 16 and 17, each of them contains a difference.

But the free gift is not like the transgression. For if by the transgression of the one the many died, much more did the grace of God and the gift by the grace of the one Man, Jesus Christ, abound to the many. (Rom 5:15)

So Paul says here that there is a great difference, because Adam's one disobedience brought consequences upon all of us and all of us added our own acts of disobedience. On the contrary when it comes to Jesus, Jesus one act of obedience, brought justification to us and we had nothing to add of our own. It was totally Jesus.

So whereas Adams guilt was compounded by our own guilt, Jesus righteousness is unique and we can add nothing to it. That is the first point of comparison.

Then secondly is in verse 16:

The gift is not like that which came through the one who sinned; for on the one hand the judgment arose from one transgression resulting in condemnation, but on the other hand the free gift arose from many transgressions resulting in justification (Rom 5:16)

The point of difference there is that, Adams one act of disobedience, brought condemnation on the whole human race, but Jesus sacrifice and his act of righteousness made it possible for us to be justified from countless acts of disobedience.

In the case of Adam, just one act of disobedience brought disaster on all of us. In the case of Jesus, one act of righteousness, made it possible for all of us to be forgiven countless acts of disobedience.

Then in verse 17, the third point of difference is:

For if by the transgression of the one, death reigned through the one, much more those who receive the abundance of grace and of the gift of righteousness will reign in life through the One, Jesus Christ. (Rom 5:17)

This verse is so packed with meaning. Through Adam's one act of disobedience, death reigned over the whole race and we are all subject to death. What it says is that, when Jesus came, he came to those who sat in the region and shadow of death. That is where the whole human race was sitting with no way of escape.

Then it says in the gospel *'on them light has arisen'* - a totally sovereign act of God. We who were sitting in that region of the shadow of death could do absolutely nothing to bring the light. We had no claims upon the light. It was the sovereign mercy and grace of God that would cause the light to shine.

So death reigned as a king and as a tyrant over the whole human race. But for those of us who receive the abundance (more than enough, more than sufficient) of grace, we also receive the gift of righteousness. This kind of righteousness is a gift. You can only receive it by faith.

You cannot work for it because you will never qualify for it. It can only come by faith.

When we receive this abundance of grace and the gift of righteousness, we are delivered from the kingdom of Satan. We are carried over into the kingdom of God. But Jesus is very different from the devil. The devil is a tyrant who rules over everybody and he does not share his reign with anybody. But Jesus the King invites us to reign with him and bear in mind it is not in the next world that we are talking about. It is reigning here in this life - right now in this world. We are called to share the throne with Jesus.

This is the wonderful truth. Ephesians 2 in verse 4 and following it says: *4 But God, being rich in mercy, because of His great love with which He loved us, 5 even when we were dead in our transgressions, made us alive together with Christ (by grace you have been saved), 6 and raised us up with Him, and seated us with Him in the heavenly places in Christ Jesus, (Ephesians 2: 4-6)*

Notice every one of those verbs is in the past tense. They are not future because of our identification with Jesus is that God made us alive with him. God has **resurrected** us with him and has **enthroned** us within him. We are identified with him in everything that followed his death. We were buried with him by baptism, and then we are made alive with him, we are resurrected and then we are enthroned with him. Jesus says come sit with me and share the throne with me. That is what the abundance of grace means.

The book of Job says that God takes the poor from the dunghill and sets them on high with the princes of his people. God picked me up when I was on the dunghill, the ash heap; he took me, delivered me, redeemed me and asked me to sit with him on the throne. Is not that great?

There is no way to describe that kind of grace.

Rom 5:20 *The Law came in so that the transgression would increase; but where sin increased, grace abounded all the more,*

This is going to surprise you but we will come back to that in Romans chapter 7. The law was brought in to make us more conscious of our sinfulness but where sin increased grace abounded all the more.

Rom 5:21 *so that, as sin reigned in death, even so grace would reign through righteousness to eternal life through Jesus Christ our Lord.*

Turning in reference, to Colossians 1 we read. *For He rescued us from the domain of darkness* (where we were), *and transferred us to the kingdom of His beloved Son, in whom we have redemption, the forgiveness of sins.* *(Colossians 1: 13-14)*

That is what Redemption does. It takes us out of the domain of darkness, from out of the kingdom of Satan and transfers us into the kingdom of God and sets us on the throne with our Lord Jesus Christ. We are to reign with him in life and that surely is abundance of grace.

CHAPTER 6: GOD'S SOLUTION FOR THE OLD MAN

(Romans 6:1 - 6:23)

In the second half of Romans chapter 5, we dealt with a very elaborate and complicated comparison between Adam and Jesus. We will now go to something a little simpler but very drastic in Romans chapter 6.

6.1   Understanding the Old Man

The old man is the old Adamic nature which we all inherited. God has no plan B for our old man. He does not send him to church or to Sunday school. He does not teach him to memorize Scripture. He has sentenced him to death and there is no alternative. We have already dealt with the forgiveness of our past sins in Romans 3 and that is very wonderful, but that is not all that we need.

To many Christians, going to church is like a ritual. We go in to speak the same old phrases like "pardon us miserable offenders etc." Perhaps, repeating these rituals make us feel less guilty or less miserable when we come out of church. This is probably the most that religion can do for us. We are never quite sure whether our sins are fully forgiven.

Perhaps one of the functions of religion is to make you feel guilty and many people think that they have achieved something tremendous if they could walk out of church feeling less guilty. They do not know if there is anything beyond that.

But the embarrassing thing is that we walk out of church, knowing fully well that in the following week, we were going to go on committing the same sins. The question is, do I please God by confessing sins that I am going to go on committing or do I provoke him?

The answer to that question is here in Romans 6. It is one thing to have our past sins forgiven, but that is not all because inside every one of us, without exception as descendants of Adam, there dwells a rebel even if our past sins have been forgiven. That old rebel inside us is going to go on committing the same kind of sins unless he is dealt with.

It is a significant fact of history that Adam never got any children until he was a rebel. So every descendant of Adam is born out of rebellion (iniquity). Every one of us has a rebel. Sometimes he is very noticeable and he can be seen in all our attitudes and actions. Sometimes he is concealed - he can be very religious, very polite, very nice, but he is still in the heart, a total rebel.

God will make no peace with that rebel. He has sentenced him to death. The good news is that through the mercy of God, the execution took place more than 20 centuries ago when Jesus died on the cross. That is the way out and that is the solution from God.

But for a little while we will look at what the Bible says about this Adamic nature in each one of us. It is called **the old man** (The Old Self). It traces us directly back to Adam the first man. It is also called the carnal nature. It is also called the flesh. It is also called the body of sin and it is called the body of the flesh.

The Bible uses certain words in a special technical way. Almost any system of communication has certain technical words it uses. Electronics has certain technical words. If you want to understand electronics, you have got to learn the correct use of those technical words.

In the same way, there are a few technical words in the Bible. Perhaps the most important one is the one we are talking about - The flesh, the body, the body of sin etc. it does not mean our physical body.

However, in other places the flesh means the actual physical body. But in many instances it does not mean that. It means the nature that we inherited with our body by descent from Adam and only the context can show you which way to translate it.

E.g. Romans 7:5 says...'for while we were in the flesh' that does not mean when we were alive in this body. It means before we came to know the Lord.

Romans 7:18... 'I know that nothing good dwells in me that is in my flesh'

Romans 7:25... Thanks be to God through Jesus Christ our Lord! So then, on the one hand I myself with my mind am serving the law of God, but on the other, with my flesh the law of sin.

None of those places does it mean the physical body. It means the old Adamic nature.

Then take the word body in Romans 8:10... 'if Christ is in you though the body is dead because of sin yet the Spirit is alive because of righteousness'. When Christ comes into us we do not actually die physically but the old body of sin, the old Adamic nature is sentenced to death.

Then the body of sin in Romans 6:6... 'Knowing this that our old self or our old man was crucified with him that our body of sin might be done away with. When you are saved you do not cease to have a body but the body of sin is put out of action. It is rendered unable to function any longer.

Colossians 2:11 speaks about the body of the flesh just to make this clear.

It says... and in Him you were also circumcised with a circumcision made without hands, in the removal of the body of the flesh by the circumcision of Christ. (Colossians 2:11)

Well we do not lose our physical body by this experience but the body of the flesh. The old sinful Adamic rebellious nature is dealt with. It is put out of operation.

6.2   Dead to Sin, Alive to God

Going back to the beginning of Romans chapter 6, Paul starts this chapter by imagining an objection that would be made. Perhaps he was addressing a Jewish objection. It seems that these are just the typical objections that a Jew who pinned his faith to keeping the Law of Moses would make.

At the end of chapter 5, Paul says in verse 20: *where sin increased grace abounded all the more.* So the more sin emerged and manifested itself the greater the grace of God. Now the objection he made at the beginning of verse one chapter 6 (bear in mind that the chapter divisions were not there in the original text. They were put in by the translators.)

Rom 6:1 *What shall we say then? Are we to continue in sin so that grace may increase?*

An objector may say "ok so if that is the way, then the more we sin the more grace we get, so the way to continue in grace is to keep on sinning" That is the objection Paul Imagines.

Rom 6:2 *May it never be! How shall we who died to sin still live in it?*

Then Paul interjects and says; by no means can this be. Now the essence of what Paul is saying is this: if you talk that way, you have no understanding of how the grace of God works because the grace of God does not leave us alive in sin. When we enter into the grace of God, a dramatic experience takes place. We become dead to sin that we may live to righteousness in the grace of God. So what Paul is saying is that it is a contradiction to talk about living in sin and in the grace of God.

God does not give grace to people who live in sin. The condition on which we receive God's grace is that we cease to live in sin. This is extremely important because there are multitudes of Christians who talk about the grace of God, but do not understand what it means to be in the grace of God. You cannot live in sin and be in the grace of God. They are two mutually exclusive alternatives. If you are in the grace of God you are not living in sin. If you are living in sin, you are not in the grace of God. So you have to choose.

The grace of God is free but it is not cheap. There are vital radical conditions attached to the grace of God and if you do not meet those conditions, you cannot talk about being under the grace of God.

Now Paul backs this up by an argument from the significance of Christian baptism. Amongst most evangelicals (Pentecostals, Baptists etc.) the importance and the significance of baptism is greatly underrated. It is much more important than most people who practice baptism imagine.

Nobody can claim salvation through faith in Jesus without being baptized. Jesus said that *'he that believeth and is baptized shall be saved'*. There are lots of people who say they believe but have not been baptized yet. That is between God and them. But please do not trespass on the grace of God. Paul assumes that every Christian he is writing to has been baptized.

Both the baptism in the Holy Spirit and Baptism in the water has a tremendous life-changing experience. It is not just a little ceremony that you go through to join a congregation. After one receives Christ, baptism is an urgent matter. It should be done immediately. There should be no casual attitude to baptism. It is vital and it is crucial. It is not just a ceremony. Most Christians have not grasped the significance of baptism.

Rom 6:3 *Or do you not know that all of us who have been baptized into Christ Jesus have been baptized into His death?*

That is the point. Notice also that you are baptized into Christ Jesus. You are not baptized into a Baptist Church or a Pentecostal church or

Africa Inland Mission etc. The only thing into which you are baptized is Jesus Christ himself.

Rom 6:4 *Therefore we have been buried with Him through baptism into death, so that as Christ was raised from the dead through the glory of the Father, so we too might walk in newness of life.*

We have been buried with Christ in that watery grave that we might be resurrected as Jesus was resurrected. Not in his own strength but in the supernatural power of the Holy Spirit - the Glory of God that brought him out of the tomb.

When we get baptized in water, what we are saying in essence is "God from this moment onwards, I am not going to live in my own strength. I have died and the power that is going to keep me going from this moment onwards is the supernatural power of your Holy Spirit. I am going to walk in a supernatural walk of life.

Rom 6:5 *For if we have become united with Him in the likeness of His death, certainly we shall also be in the likeness of His resurrection,*

When he speaks about you being united with him in the likeness of his death, what is Paul speaking about? If we have been baptized, we shall also be in the likeness of his resurrection. If you have not been baptized, you are taking a risk because the promise is to those who have been united with him through baptism.

Rom 6:6 *knowing this, that our old self was crucified with Him, in order that our body of sin might be done away with, so that we would no longer be slaves to sin;*

Rom 6:7 *for he who has died is freed from sin.*

Let us look further into this mystery of identification. It is the key that opens up all the riches of the cross. We do not just contemplate Jesus on the cross. We say; when he died, I died because he took my place.

He was my representative. He was the last Adam. The total evil inheritance that was due to me and all the descendants of Adam came upon him.

Now if I want to be identified with him and go all the way with him. What do I have to do? What is the key step? If we have been buried with him through baptism into his death that is where we join the procession.

That is the act of our will and obedience by which we declare our identification with him for the rest of the journey. Because when we are buried with him, then we have got the right to enter into everything that followed his burial. He was made alive, he was resurrected, and he was enthroned.

If you want to go up, you have got to go down first to the basement (through baptism). After that you decide which floor you want to go. It is a tragedy that so many Christians just press M for mezzanine floor and get off there. After baptism we are entitled to go anywhere we ask the elevator to take us.

So here's the truth. Let us look for a moment in Colossians 2:10-12

> *And in Him you have been made complete, and He is the head over all rule and authority; and in Him you were also circumcised with a circumcision made without hands, in the removal of the body of the flesh by the circumcision of Christ; (Colossians 2:10-11)*

That is not removing your physical body but that is getting rid of that old Adamic rebel that has dominated us for so long. And then verse 12:

> *Having been buried with Him in baptism, in which you were also raised up with Him through faith in the working of God, who raised Him from the dead. (Colossians 2:12)*

Baptism is the key point of uniting us with Jesus. In some countries which are not Christian, people do not really mind very much if you say I am a believer in Jesus. But if you go out and get baptized, the whole world explodes and who makes it explode? Satan. Because he knows that is the point at which you have got out of his cross and passed through the water.

Going back to Romans 6:6 Paul is saying: don't you remember you were baptized. Do not you know what that meant? You were buried with him and you finished the old life. So you cannot talk about living any longer in sin when you have been baptized.

6.3   The Rebel

In the section 6.2, we looked at Paul's answer to the suggestion that we might go on living in sin in order that grace might abound and Paul refuted that suggested objection by saying that it is impossible to live in sin and be in the grace of God because in order to be in the grace of God, we have to be identified with Jesus in death, burial and resurrection. And when we are identified with him in his death - that is the end of sin, we have died to sin.

So it is illogical from then on to talk about living in sin. The objection of this imaginary objector is based on a misunderstanding of what it is to be in the grace of God. To be in the grace of God you have to be identified with Jesus. You have to pass with him through death into resurrection. The death is a death to sin. From then on it is unscriptural and illogical to talk about living in sin.

And so we looked at God's dealings with what is called the old man. The flesh, the body, the body of sin, the body of the flesh - all those are different phrases used to describe, not our physical body, but the old Adamic nature which we have inherited from Adam. And every one has by nature a rebel inside us.

Even the sweetest little baby, that cute little daughter of yours who is just two years old - inside her, there is a rebel. Little children most often than not often tend to do things which they are told not to do. That is just an early manifestation of that rebel. He or she may be a genuinely tender loving little child but she or he has the same problem. The boys rebel shows and the girls rebel does not show except in unguarded moments.

Have you ever had that unguarded moment when the rebel suddenly pops out?

We are going to dwell a little, on this subject because, in many cases where the gospel is preached, salvation is presented as an escape from sin and forgiveness and a new life. But in many cases nothing is done with the rebel. He is left to hide under a coating of religion and religious language.

There are many nations which claim to be predominantly Christian and some with even over 80% of their population who claim to be Christians. If there are really these many worthy or born-again Christians in these nations, the world would be totally different. The problem is that many of these Christians have got the language and they may be quite sincere, but have stopped short of making Jesus the Lord of their lives.

Someone testified that she received Jesus as Savior when she was still a girl, but she said it was many years later before she confessed him as Lord. That does not make sense because Paul says in Romans 10:10 that if you want to be saved you have to confess with your mouth that Jesus is Lord and believe in your heart that God has raised him from the dead. There is no salvation that stopped short of acknowledging the lordship of Jesus. It is a false salvation. There is a great deal of false conversion in the so-called Protestant, Charismatic and Episcopal world today.

A lot of people in church today are not saved. What they really have is a form of religion. All they have is a label. Salvation is a lot more than changing labels. That is, you sit there in church and you have got a sinner's label pinned on the back of your jacket. Then you go forward and say a little prayer and you come back and somebody pins 'saved' on the back of your jacket. That is not it. There is a lot more to it than that. You have got to deal with this rebel inside you. He is a very slippery character. He is very cunning and he has a lot of ways of evading execution.

There was certain preacher who had a dream. In the dream he saw a typical street meeting with a ring of people standing around a man at the center of the ring who was preaching. He looked and listened and what the man was preaching saying was very good, but he did not like the way the preacher looked. He looked crooked. He looked as though he had a hunched back and a clubfoot and he could not understand how he could be like that and yet saying the right thing.

The same dream repeated itself after about two weeks and this time he thought to himself: God must be trying to speak to me. So he asked God for the meaning of the dream. God revealed to him that, that man was himself which was a shock to him. Then he realized for the first time that God was pinpointing the rebel - the old man in him. The preacher was pointed to Romans 6 and saw that the remedy was execution. But that, by the mercy of God, the execution had taken place many centuries ago when Jesus died on the cross. Our old man was crucified with him and that is a historical fact whether we believe it or not.

You can picture the hill of Golgotha with three crosses on it. The middle cross being taller than the other two crosses. The question is; for whom was that middle cross made for? That middle cross was the cross on which Jesus was crucified. It was made for Barabbas. You and I must be the Barabbas - your old self. It was there for Barabbas but Jesus took the place of Barabbas. Therefore Jesus took your place and my place.

This is a revelation to see that I am Barabbas. I am the criminal. I am the person for whom the cross was made for. I should have been on it but at the last moment an unexpected switch took place and Jesus took my place and your place. Jesus took the place of Barabbas. That is God's vivid way of demonstrating that the rebel, the old man was crucified in Jesus. What we have to do is believe.

Let us look at another picture which is from prophet Isaiah in Isaiah 1:5-6. God deals with Israel for their many sins but the root problem of Israel was rebellion and this is how he describes it:

Why should you be beaten anymore?

Why do you persist in rebellion?

Your whole head is injured, your whole heart afflicted.

*From the sole of your foot to the top of your head there is no soundness —
only wounds and welts and open sores, not cleansed or bandaged or
soothed with olive oil.* (Isaiah 1: 5-6)

In these scriptures, God is showing us how he sees and deals with rebellion. It is a very vivid picture of Jesus as he hung on the cross. He exactly fulfilled that prophecy.

Let us read the words again:

"Your whole head is injured (by countless different ways - Thorns pressed in the scalp, blows on the face, the beard plucked out,) *your whole heart afflicted* (Jesus died of a broken heart) *from the sole of your foot to the top of your head there is no soundness only wounds and welts and open sores not cleansed or bandaged.*

That is the exact picture you could give of the appearance of Jesus on the cross. What is God telling us through the Prophet? - That the rebel was punished in Jesus. Jesus bore the punishment of the rebel because of the sin in Israel. Its root problem, in the midst of all its religion, was rebellion.

Then we get in Isaiah 52 verse 13 and 14 we get this vivid prefiguring of Jesus as the sacrifice.

> *See, my servant will act wisely; he will be raised and lifted up and highly exalted.*
>
> *Just as there were many who were appalled at him — his appearance was so disfigured beyond that of any human being and his form marred beyond human likeness* (Isaiah 52:13-14)

You see, we have very many pretty pictures of Jesus on the cross with some blood trickling out of his hands and wound on his side. That does not even represent the reality. After you consider all that he had been through, to that point there was not a place on his body that was not sore. Why? It is because it had to be. It was the outworking of rebellion and that is where you and I should have been. But in the infinite mercy of God a switch took place and Jesus took the place of Barabbas and he took your place and my place.

And then if you go on in Isaiah 53:6 which is the great picture of the suffering servant. It is the key to everything and it says: *We all, like sheep, have gone astray, each of us has turned to our own way* (Rebellion); *and the Lord has laid on him the iniquity of us all.* (Isaiah 53:6)

The word iniquity in Hebrew is Awon. It means rebellion. And the punishment for rebellion and all the evil consequences of rebellion is the cross. Jesus was our substitute. The last Adam became the rebel with our rebellion and endured all the evil consequences of rebellion.

Now this is the key - **an exchange took place**. This is the door to God's treasure house. If you can grasp, what happened on the cross. Jesus became identified with our rebellion. An exchange took place. All the evil due to our rebellion came upon Jesus that all the good due to his perfect obedience might be offered to us.

Whichever way you look at it, that exchange was total:

- He was punished that we might be forgiven

- He was wounded that we might be healed
- He took our sin that we might have his righteousness
- He died our death that we might share his life
- He was made a curse that we might receive the blessing
- He endured our poverty that we might share his abundance
- He bore our shame that we might have his glory
- He endured our rejection that we might have his acceptance

You can see the picture of the rebel there on the cross. Please understand that you are the rebel but Jesus took your place. Not only did he bear your rebellion, but he also bore all the evil consequences of your rebellion that you might enter into all the blessings of his perfect obedience.

And you know what that is? It is grace. You cannot earn it, you did not deserve it. You cannot even lay a claim upon it. There is only one way to receive it, which is by faith.

It is interesting that when Isaiah presents this picture of the suffering servant in chapter 53, he begins with a warning against unbelief. Who has believed our report? The great barrier to receiving the benefits of Christ's atonement is unbelief. You need to renounce the spirit of unbelief.

In Romans chapter six we see the infinite riches opened up through the atoning death of Christ. If we do not practice baptism the way the New Testament practiced it, all this truth is concealed. It is baptism that is the vivid external acting-out of our identification with the truth, which is Christ.

Children remember 40% of what they hear, 60% of what they hear and see, and 80% of what they hear, see and do. So God being the great teacher, when it comes to this great central truth, He makes sure that we do not just hear it, but see it too and do it.

Therefore, every time a believer is baptized (through immersion in water) it is the glorious truth of our identification with Jesus in death, burial and resurrection. One of Satan's primary objectives has been to remove this practice from the church so that we might lose the glorious truth that it represents.

Looking back at Romans verse 6;

Rom 6:6 *knowing this, that our old self was crucified with Him, in order that our body of sin might be done away with, so that we would no longer be slaves to sin;*

Remember that is true whether you knew it or not, whether you believe it or not, it is true. Your knowing it and believing it, is what is going to make a difference in your life.

You can have your past sins forgiven but still continue to be a slave to sin if the old man has not been dealt with.

Rom 6:7 *for he who has died is freed from sin.*

When the law has put you to death that is the last thing it can do to you. After that the law has no more claims on you. You have passed out of the territory of the law. So when we are dead with Jesus, we are justified. There is no more claim against us. We have paid the final penalty in him. Paul says that; he that is dead is justified and acquitted from sin. He has paid the final penalty and there is nothing more that the law can demand of him.

Rom 6:8 *Now if we have died with Christ, we believe that we shall also live with Him,*

If we have been buried, we will be resurrected, but if we have not been buried, we have no right to be resurrected.

Rom 6:9 *knowing that Christ, having been raised from the dead, is never to die again; death no longer is master over Him.*

Rom 6:10 *for the death that He died, He died to sin once for all; but the life that He lives, He lives to God.*

So we die a death to sin once for all and after that the life that we live we live to God. That is the transition.

Rom 6:11 *Even so consider yourselves to be dead to sin, but alive to God in Christ Jesus.*

Reckon yourselves to be dead in sin. That is the truth. If you cannot reckon that, then you cannot believe. That is why God says my people are destroyed for lack of knowledge.

Take a moment to consider what is meant by the phrase **'dead to sin'**. Let us take a picture some terrible man who does all the things that religious people do not do. He swears, he drinks whiskey, he smokes cigars, he watches pornography on television, he is just a beast, a bad man and his wife is a believer. And he has got children who are believers too and he gives them a miserable time. He swears at them, gets angry with them and one Sunday evening they tiptoe out to the local gospel house and leave him sitting in his chair smoking his cigar, swilling his whiskey and watching something that he should not be watching on television. And they have a wonderful meeting that night and they get really high in the spirit and they come back still singing choruses. As they get in the house, suddenly they remember, he is going to curse them and they stop dead on their track but nothing happens. They tiptoe into the room. He is sitting in the chair, the smoke is coming up from his cigar but he is not smoking it. The whiskey is untouched on the table. He is not interested in the television. You know what happened to him? He had a heart attack and died. He died to sin. It means that sin has no more power over him. Sin has no more attraction for him and sin produces no more reaction from him. That is what it is to be dead to sin.

There is no disputing that he is a dead man. He does not lose his temper, does not drink whiskey, does not swear, does not do all sorts of other things, he does not gossip on them etc. HE IS DEAD TO SIN.

When we reckon ourselves dead to sin, sin has no more power over us. Sin has no more attraction for us. Sin produces no more reaction from us.

6.4 How to Apply God's Solution in our Lives

In the previous two sections, we looked at God's solution for the old man. We saw that the solution is summed up in one word: Execution.

But the mercy of God lies in this: that the execution took place when Jesus died on the cross, our old man was crucified with him and we are given the privilege through baptism of identifying ourselves with him in his death, his burial and then in everything else that follows on. God has no other program for the old man but execution.

Now we are going to move on to the second part of chapter 6 which is very practical. In the previous part of the chapter 6, Paul has given what we could call the doctrinal basis.

How do we make God's Solution work in our lives?

We will read first of all verses 12 through 14.

Rom 6:12 Therefore do not let sin reign in your mortal body so that you obey its lusts,

Rom 6:13 and do not go on presenting the members of your body to sin as instruments of unrighteousness; but present yourselves to God as those alive from the dead, and your members as instruments of righteousness to God.

Rom 6:14 For sin shall not be master over you, for you are not under law but under grace.

Now Paul gives instructions here. These instructions can only be acted on by people who have passed through the transition described in the previous part of the chapter. A person, who has not put his faith in Jesus and accepted his substitutionary sacrifice on his behalf, is not capable of carrying out these instructions. So these instructions only work on the basis of what Paul has already said in the previous part of the chapter.

Now he says you have got to take a firm stand against sin.

A preacher once said: if you ever want to get to heaven, you have got to learn to say no and that is certainly the truth. Paul says that you have got to make up your mind and say no to sin. From now on, sin, you are not going to control me. I take a stand against you. You have no more claims over me. You have no more power over me and I am not going to submit to you.

Sin and Satan are both alike: they only listen when you really mean it. They both have a way of knowing when you are just saying it and when you are saying it and meaning it. You have to say it with determination.

Applying the work of Jesus in our lives demands the exercise of our will. It is impossible if we do not exercise our will. Through faith in Jesus our wills' are liberated from the dominion of sin. After that it becomes our responsibility to use them. God is not going to do that for us. This is the point, you have got to rise up and say this is my responsibility.

For example; when you have an internal struggle against depression, what should you do? Depression can come down on you and weigh you down and give you this sense of hopelessness and failure. You will struggle against this thing in every way that you know and make no progress until you feel like giving up.

But Isaiah 61:3 (KJV) says: *'in place of the spirit of heaviness, the garment of praise '*.

But when you realize that your problem is that you are not fighting against yourself but against another person. A person without a body i.e. a spirit that is tormenting and oppressing you, you will have solved this problem over 80% of the way.

Proverbs 11:9ᵇ says: ... *But through knowledge the righteous will be delivered.*

Joel 1:32 says: *'whosoever shall call on the name of the Lord shall be delivered.'*

So go before God in prayer and pray: God you have shown me that I am oppressed by a spirit of heaviness. I am coming to you now and I am calling upon you in the name of the Lord Jesus. Deliver me from this spirit of heaviness and he will deliver you.

Therefore God has already done what you could not do for yourself. But he will show you what your responsibility is through scriptures. It is up to you to reprogram your mind, especially if you habitually think in a negative way. Are you a professional pessimist? That is a denial of you faith in Jesus. Jesus had liberated your mind from that oppressing spirit but he is not going to do for you what you should do for yourself. You have to retrain your mind. Every time a negative pessimistic thought comes to your mind, reject it and replace it by something positive based on Scripture. And with time your whole inner working changes completely.

We have a responsibility, which is to take our stand against sin. To disassociate ourselves from everything sinful and that we have to do by exercising our will.

So Paul says do not let sin reign in your mortal body that you should obey its lusts and do not go on presenting the members of your body to sin as instruments of unrighteousness, but present yourselves to God as those alive from the dead and your members as instruments of righteousness to God.

In essence what Paul is saying is; deny sin access to your members. Do not let it control your hands. Do not let it control your feet. Do not let it control your tongue. Do not let it control your mind. You have been set free and he says on the contrary yield yourself to God and your members as instruments of righteousness to God.

There is a double yielding:
1. First of all you yield your will to God. You say; "God not my will but yours be done."
2. Then having yielded our will, we have to yield our members to God as instruments of righteousness. Your tongue, your mind, your eyes etc. The translation says instruments and the Greek says weapons. These are weapons with which we fight.

First we yield our will to God, then we yield to God the one unruly member of our body which we cannot control the tongue. So we are actually fulfilling the instruction here yielding our members or physical members to God as instruments or weapons of righteousness.

When our tongue has been yielded to God and taken over by the Holy Spirit, it becomes a weapon in prayer, in testimony, in preaching etc.

When Paul finished the first 11 chapters of Romans, (all his theology) there is another therefore at the beginning of chapter 12: *I beseech you therefore brethren by the mercies of God that you present your bodies, a living sacrifice.*

So it is a question of willing and yielding. You have got to do it in that order because if you do not, you will by habit, yield to the wrong thing. You see, because you are used to yielding to sin, Paul says do not go on presenting your body and your members to sin. You have been doing so for a long while. The question really is: For how long have you been doing it, after you met the Lord? But we have to stop and say that is the end. My will has been released. I can will, one will with God and when

I have yielded my will to God, I do not have to yield my members as instruments of sin to Satan.

Then Paul comes out with a tremendously important statement in verse 14 and he says; for he says sin shall not be master over you. The old translation (KJV) says; sin shall not have dominion over you for you are not under law but under grace.

The implications of that statement are very far-reaching. Paul says you are not under law but under grace. It is either the law or the grace. It cannot be both at the same time. If you are under law, you are not under grace. If you are under grace you are not under law. You have to decide. It is a choice. Do not try and have it both ways at the same time because you cannot.

"For you are not under law but under grace": What is the implication of that? If you are under the law, sin will have dominion over you. That is a shocking statement to many people. But it happens to be what the Bible says and it says it consistently all the way through.

So we have this choice. I am not under law. I am not governed by a set of rules. I do not operate on the basis of fear. I have become a son of God. I obey Him because I love him. Love is my motivation for obedience not fear.

God does not want to make us slaves the way the law made us slaves. God makes sons and daughters, but you have to decide. It is very important that you exercise your will and exercise it right, because if you let yourself to be pushed around by Satan, he will push you around. He is a bully and he goes for the weak. You cannot afford to be weak in any area of your life.

Then in verse 15, comes the next imagined objection. Paul has a lawyers' mind and uses imagined objections.

Rom 6:15 *What then? Shall we sin because we are not under law but under grace? May it never be!*

Paul is asking. If we are not under the law, are we free to commit sinful acts when it suits us, because we are not under the law. What is his answer? Perish the thought.

Now this is Paul's answer and we read verses 15 through 22:

Rom 6:16 *Do you not know that when you present yourselves to someone as slaves for obedience, you are slaves of the one whom you obey, either of sin resulting in death, or of obedience resulting in righteousness?*

So Paul says when you yield yourself to someone to obey him, you become a slave to the one you obey. So if by a decision of your will, you decide, well I am going to commit this sinful act. Let us say an act of immorality because I am not under the law, Paul says, if you do that, you are yielding to immorality and you become a slave of immorality. You cannot yield to something without becoming the slave to it. So you have to decide who you want to yield to.

Let us turn for a moment to Joshua 24:15: Here Joshua is confronting Israel at the end of his career with a choice. Some of us do not like choices. We would rather get along without having to decide but in the spiritual life, you cannot avoid choices. He says to Israel, now therefore fear the Lord and serve Him in sincerity and truth.

"If it is disagreeable in your sight to serve the LORD, choose for yourselves today whom you will serve: whether the gods which your fathers served which were beyond the River, or the gods of the Amorites in whose land you are living; but as for me and my house, we will serve the LORD." (Joshua 24:15)

Notice: it is not 'choose whether you will serve'. It is 'choose whom you will serve'

So the only choice you have after you have been redeemed is whether to serve sin to serve righteousness. Before you were redeemed, you did not have any choice. You could not help sinning and therefore you could only serve sin. There was no other option. Those who have experienced redemption, through faith in Jesus Christ, have a choice.

Rom 6:17 *But thanks be to God that though you were slaves of sin, you became obedient from the heart to that form of teaching to which you were committed,*

That is very important. The word 'form' there is the same word that is used for putting metal in a mold to cause it to set in a certain shape.

It is amazing that when people are newly converted, they are hot and it is very important to put them in the right 'form' right at the beginning. A lot of people get wonderfully converted and they are enthusiastic. But when they go to some church or group which does not really present the truth of the Bible, they get 'set' in the wrong form and then it is hard to change them.

There are many evangelistic crusades where thousands of people go forward and are converted. But the question is: what form is that hot metal going to be poured into. How will it set? However, many times it does not come out right.

Rom 6:18 *and having been freed from sin, you became slaves of righteousness.*

So it is a choice. Something is going to control you. Is it going to be sin or righteousness? If you choose righteousness, believe me you will be tested. You will really be tested. The devil does not give up as long as he thinks he has got a chance of succeeding.

When people are tested and tempted the devil will go on until that person comes to the place where the temptation just does not mean anything. He is not even going to entertain the thought and the devil is clever enough not to waste his time on people like that. But if there is any double mindedness in you, the devil will exploit that. You have to make a firm decision.

Rom 6:19 *I am speaking in human terms because of the weakness of your flesh. For just as you presented your members as slaves to impurity and to* *lawlessness, resulting in further lawlessness, so now present your members as slaves to righteousness, resulting in sanctification.*

If you go into lawlessness, it increases and you become more and more lawless. Many of us can trace that in our own lives. You are going to go one way or the other. It is almost impossible to stand still in the spiritual life. You are either going forward or you are going backwards. Either going further into rebellion or you are going to progress in holiness but standing still in the spiritual life is almost impossible.

Rom 6:20 *for when you were slaves of sin, you were free in regard to righteousness.*

Paul goes on and again he is very explicit. Remember he was writing to a society where slavery was a very normal thing. So all these people knew what it was to be a slave. He is using a figure or reference which was very appropriate in those days.

Rom 6:21 *Therefore what benefit were you then deriving from the things of which you are now ashamed? For the outcome of those things is death.*

So Paul says think it over for a moment. When you were serving sin, when you were a slave to sin, what did you get? Well some of us got headaches and a sense of shame and many of us wondered whether life was really worth living. What was it all about? Because many times, we lived in disagreement, in contention and in disharmony with the people close to us.

So Paul says to think it over. Just bear in mind where you used to be. Do you want to go back there?

In my experience in the Christian life, I have had many temptations and many discouragements. But one thing I have never once entertained is the thought of going back to the old life because as far as I am concerned it has nothing to offer. When I shut that door, I threw away the key. By now I have gone too far to remember the way back. Thank God for that.

Rom 6:22 *But now having been freed from sin and enslaved to God, you derive your benefit, resulting in sanctification, and the outcome, eternal life.*

So Paul says stop looking back and cultivate looking ahead where are you headed. For you are headed for a life of holiness. You are headed for eternal life which does not end with this life but goes on into eternity. That is where you are going; it is difficult to walk forward if you are looking backwards.

I wonder if you realize how fortunate you are to know what to do about guilt. We know there is a solution to guilt but there are, millions of people on earth today who feel guilty and do not know where to go. They have never tasted God's goodness, his grace and his mercy. They have never heard that there is forgiveness.

Rom 6:23 *for the wages of sin is death, but the free gift of God is eternal life in Christ Jesus our Lord.*

Those are the options if you want your wages. The due reward for what you have done.

I trust that it would be appropriate at this moment to tell God once again that we yield to him our will and we yield to him our members. "Lord I yield my will to you now and I lift up my hands in token that I am yielding my physical members to you in Jesus name. Amen"

CHAPTER 7: RELEASED FROM THE LAW, BOUND TO CHRIST

(Romans 7:1 – 7:25)

Now we are moving into the final stage of this journey before we reach the conclusion which is Romans chapter 8. Romans chapter 7 is the final stage before we reach our destination which is chapter 8 and this is the hardest stage to go through.

In this stage, Paul is dealing with the law. We might think that we deal with the law before we are converted and then after that, there is nothing more about the law. But by observation and by experience that is not true.

After we have been converted, after we have experienced deliverance from the old man, we come face to face with this tremendously difficult issue: What is the place of the law? How do I relate to the law?

Let us use this little example of the man who went to see a doctor with pain in his stomach. The doctor examined him and said I think your problem is appendicitis.

Man: Well said the man. Appendicitis what is that?

Doctor: That is inflammation of the Appendix.

Man: Up till now I never knew I had an appendix that can be inflamed.

A lot of Christians are like that. They have a problem or they have a pain and when they go to the Word of God, the Word of God says your problem is that you are wrong. Your problems or pain is related to the law and the Christian says: I never knew that was a problem. This is the first time I have heard about it.

So God helping us, we are going to devote effort to the seventh chapter of Romans. Just pray for grace that you will get through it with a clear understanding. It is not easy but it is possible by God's grace.

7.1 The Relationship of the Believer to the Law

We are going to deal in this section with the first six verses, where Paul uses a metaphor from marriage to explain our release from the law and our freedom to live another way.

Rom 7:1 Or do you not know, (Paul uses that kind of phrase writing to Christian's maybe because in most places Christians do not know) *brethren (for I am speaking to those who know the law* - the Law of Moses), *that the law has jurisdiction over a person as long as he lives?* Once you are under the law there is no escape except by death. It is a lifetime commitment.

Rom 7:2 for the married woman is bound by law to her husband while he is living; but if her husband dies, she is released from the law concerning the husband.

Paul is using this analogy of marriage

Rom 7:3 So then, if while her husband is living she is joined to another man, she shall be called an adulteress; but if her husband dies, she is free from the law, so that she is not an adulteress though she is joined to another man.

Rom 7:4 Therefore, my brethren, you also were made to die to the Law through the body of Christ, so that you might be joined to another, to Him who was raised from the dead, in order that we might bear fruit for God.

Rom 7:5 For while we were in the flesh (remember the special use of the word flesh), *the sinful passions, which were aroused by the Law, were at work in the members of our body to bear fruit for death.*

Rom 7:6 *But now we have been released from the Law* (from what have we been released?), *having died to that by which we were bound, so that we serve in newness of the Spirit and not in oldness of the letter.*

Let us take the basic fact that under the law, if a man marries a woman, as long as the man remains alive, the woman is not free to marry another man. If she marries another man she would become adulterous. She would commit adultery. But if the man to whom she was married to died, then she is free to marry another man without being an adulteress.

Paul says through the law, you were married. The law was like a marriage covenant and it was for life. What were they married to? This is the difficult part. They were married to their fleshly nature (the old man).

The whole essence of the law, which is the problem with the law, is that you are required to do it in your own ability. You are relying on your fleshly nature and that is why it never works.

Coming under the law is like a marriage ceremony in which you are married to your fleshly nature. Now as long as your fleshly nature remains alive, you cannot marry somebody else because you will be an adulterer or adulteress.

But what Paul is saying is this; that your first husband died. When Jesus died on the cross, your first husband died, the old man was crucified with him.

When you grasp that you say: 'praise God! I am free'. I do not have to go on with this awful husband (called the law) who gave me an awful life. He gave me no blessings, no peace, no righteousness. I am not tied to him any longer. I can now be married to another man. The alternative is to be married to the one who rose from the dead. The risen glorified Christ. He can become your husband whether you are a man or a woman.

What we are talking about is a relationship in the spirit realm. Let us turn for a moment to 1st Corinthians 6:16-17 to see that reality.

Paul is teaching against fornication and sexual immorality and he says: *Or do you not know that the one who joins himself to a prostitute is one body with her? For He says, "the two shall become one flesh." But the one who joins himself to the Lord is one spirit with Him.* (1 Corinthians 6:16-17)

Now the picture was of sexual union between a man and a prostitute. On the basis of that picture, Paul says that there is another kind of union that you can have with the Lord. It is not sexual but it is spiritual. That is a marriage relationship with the Lord. He that is joined to the Lord is one with him. Not in soul, not in body but in spirit.

The question is; what is the act by which we are joined to the Lord in one spirit? It is WORSHIP. That is why worship is the highest activity of the human being. Worship is procreative i.e. it produces new life.

When we are joined to the Lord, in worship, that is when we begin to bring forth the things that God wants to be brought forth. That is the spiritual fruit. Worship is not a sort of appendix to the Christian life. It is not a little addition to services. It is the culmination. It is the consummation of our marriage to the Lord. We are united with him in one spirit. When we have that unity, we begin to bear spiritual fruit in our lives. You need to know which husband you are united to. Worship leaders are almost number one target for Satan.

Let us look at Galatians 5 verse 19 and following:

We are going to look at the two kinds of offspring from the two kinds of marriage Union.

19Now the deeds of the flesh are evident, which are: immorality, impurity, sensuality, 20idolatry, sorcery, enmities, strife, jealousy, outbursts of anger, disputes, dissensions, factions, 21envying, drunkenness, revelry, and things like these, of which I forewarn you, just as I have forewarned you, that those who practice such things will not inherit the kingdom of God.(Gal 5:19 – 21)

Fleshy deeds are all too evident and they will show even when you tell people that you are spiritual.

The question is; what kind of children do you want? If you are married to the law, these are the kind of children that you will bring forth. That is what the flesh brings forth. You cannot find one good thing in that entire list. The flesh cannot produce anything acceptable to God. It is corrupt - that is the key word.

Jesus said a corrupt tree cannot bring forth good fruit. Paul says in Romans 8 *"those who are in the flesh cannot please God"* it is impossible because none of the things in this list can please God.

Now what is the alternative if you are married to Christ and joined to him in this sacred spiritual union?

22But the fruit of the Spirit is love, joy, peace, patience, kindness, goodness, faithfulness, 23gentleness, self-control; against such things there is no law. 24Now those who belong to Christ Jesus have crucified the flesh with its passions and desires. (Gal 5:22 – 24)

The works of the flesh are totally bad and the fruit of the Spirit is totally good.

And then as a kind of afterthought, Paul adds about the fruit of the Spirit: *against these things there is no law i.e.* The people who bring forth that kind of fruit do not need to be ruled by the law. They are not under the law. They have escaped from their marriage to the flesh under the law and they are free to be married by the Holy Spirit to the resurrected Christ and bring forth the kind of fruit which is appropriate to that Union.

The key to successful Christian life is not effort, but it is union. Most of us are far too busy trying. Can any vine ever bring forth grapes by trying? Let us turn to the well-known parable of the vine as an example. John 15:1-5

Verse 1-5. Jesus is speaking: *"I am the true vine, and My Father is the vinedresser.* (John 15:1)

I am so glad for that statement. Incidentally there are people who try to dress and prune me but the only one who is skillful enough to prune is the father. Do not let human beings get at you with their choppers.

"Every branch in Me that does not bear fruit, He takes away (How can you be a branch in Jesus without being a believer and if you do not bear fruit, he will take you away)*; and every branch that bears fruit, He prunes it so that it may bear more fruit.* (John 15:2)

Some of you are going through pruning and you may be fighting it, wandering saying what is gone wrong. Nothing has gone wrong; this is part of the process. You are not being pruned because you are a backslider or because you are wicked or you are uncommitted. You are being pruned because you have been bringing forth fruit and you are being pruned in order that you may bring forth more fruit.

We have got to distinguish between chastisement and God's pruning.

"You are already clean because of the word which I have spoken to you. (Do you know that the word of God cleanses?) (John 15:3)

"Abide in Me, and I in you. As the branch cannot bear fruit of itself unless it abides in the vine, so neither can you unless you abide in Me. What is the key? It is abiding in Jesus. It is not effort, its union and out of that union the Holy Spirit brings forth the beautiful succulent grapes which are the fruit of the Spirit. (John 15:4)

"I am the vine, you are the branches; he who abides in Me and I in him, he bears much fruit, for apart from Me you can do nothing. (John 15:5)

That is right. When you are out of relationship with Jesus, there is nothing you can bring forth that is good. That is a beautiful parable. It contains the three persons of the Godhead: Jesus the Son is the vine, the father is the vine dresser, and the SAP that rises up through the vine into the branches and brings forth fruit is the Holy Spirit.

That is what the Christian life is about. It is not a set of rules. Rules do not have their place, but we are not made righteous by rules. If we have been made righteous by faith, we will keep the appropriate rules unconsciously, but we will never be made righteous by keeping rules.

Laws never change people's hearts. Everyone needs to take stock of himself or herself to make sure that they are bringing forth the fruit. More Laws can never change a country.

Food for thought: "which kind of country would you rather live in; a country with good laws and bad people, or a country with bad laws and good people?" The solution is not changing the laws, it is changing the people. It is only a revival that will very rapidly and thoroughly change bad people into good people and The Holy Spirit is the only one who can bring this about. Do you know that the Holy Spirit can change someone from being a bad person to a good person overnight?

7.2 The Law and Sin

Going back to Romans chapter 7, we are going to deal with the second part of this chapter which says that the law brings sin to life and out into full view.

Returning under the law, when we have been released from it, revives the old man who is still a criminal.

Let us see where this is stated and it stated several times.

First of all we will go back for a moment to Romans 3:20. Paul says: *by the works of the law no flesh will be justified in his sight.* No one will ever achieve righteousness with God by the keeping of a law and then he concludes: *for through the law comes the knowledge of sin.* The law does not enable people to become righteous but it brings out sin into the open. It makes us fully conscious of the nature and power and evil of sin. And that is one of its main purposes.

Second, Romans 7:5 just emphasizes this point: *for while we were in the flesh, the sinful passions which were aroused by the law were at work in the members of our body to bear fruit for death.* Most people do not view the law that way – that it arouses sinful passions.

Now again from Romans 7:7 – 11, we see this truth.

Rom 7:7 *What shall we say then? Is the Law sin? May it never be! On the contrary, I would not have come to know sin except through the Law; for I would not have known about coveting (lusting) if the Law had not said, "you shall not covet."*

You shall not covet, is one of the Ten Commandments. Its purpose is to bring the nature and power of lust or coveting out into the open. Paul says I would never have realized the full and true nature of lust were it not for this law. Then Paul goes on:

Rom 7:8 *But sin, taking opportunity through the commandment, produced in me coveting of every kind; for apart from the Law sin is dead.*

So far from the commandment, instead of making me able to overcome coveting, it worked in me an increase of coveting. That psychologically true. I want to say this in a way that will help you. If you are having a problem with lust or fear or hatred or resentment, you will not overcome it by rules that forbid you to do it. In fact the more you focus on the negative rules, the more power that thing will have over you. If you keep saying, I must not lust, I must not lust - your whole mind becomes full of the concept of lust. So instead of delivering you from lust, it enslaves you to it. It is the same with fear, resentment etc.

I must not resent my boss, I must not resent my boss but the next time you see your boss all you can think about is resentment. That is not the way out. Then Paul makes a very amazing statement there at the end of verse 8: *apart from the law sin is dead.* We will discuss this in more detail later.

Do you see what the commandment has done? It has caused us to take sides with the law, saying that, this is what we ought to do. Then we discover that the more we try to do it, the less we succeed. We have discovered that there is something in us which works against our own best intentions. It is the law - it forces sin out into the open.

So the law serves a God-given purpose, but it is not the purpose of making people righteous.

Rom 7:9: *I was once alive apart from the law but when the commandment came sin became alive and I died.*

Rom 7:10 *and this commandment, which was to result in life, proved to result in death for me;*

Rom 7:11 *for sin, taking an opportunity through the commandment, deceived me and through it killed me.*

Now I am going to offer you two explanations of what Paul is saying:

First of all, as a descendant of Adam, Paul was represented by Adam as we all were. Adam was alive in the Garden of Eden. He was a perfect being without corruption or flaw of any kind. We do not know how long he continued in that condition. It may have been hundreds of years but we just do not know. But when the commandment came, sin came to life. Rebellion rose up in him and he did the very thing he was told not to do. There must have been thousands of trees in that garden. But he wanted to partake of the only tree that was forbidden and when he partook of it sin came to life and he died. God had warned him. God had said to him that on the day you eat of it, you will surely die. He did not die physically because Adam lived for 900 years more. He died spiritually. He was cut off from God by his rebellion. He was no longer fit for the presence of God. When God came into the garden, he hid himself. That is one possible explanation which would apply to all of us since we are all descended from Adam. Sometimes we hide when we are confronted by God's truth. When God says to you: forgive others, you hide and try to explain your way out of forgiving others.

Secondly, Paul was an Israelite which most of us are not. We need to remember that Israel was not redeemed from Egypt and their slavery by the law. The law did not get them out of Egypt. What got them out was faith in the Passover lamb and its shed blood. But when they came to the foot of Mt. Sinai, God presented them with the law. Up to this point they were relying on God. But when they were presented with the law, what happened? They broke the first commandment – *'thou shalt have no other gods besides me'. Thou shalt make no graven images.* That is not an accident. That is the result of trusting in the flesh. The moment we trust in the flesh, we revive that rebel and all he can produce is rebellion. He is not capable of producing anything but rebellion. Paul says I know that in me, in my flesh, dwells nothing good. Please say that out aloud. Do not say it if you do not believe it. It takes most of us a long while to discover that. So that is an application to Paul as an Israelite. Israel came out of Egypt. They were redeemed by faith in the Passover lamb and they were alive to God but when the commandment came, they trusted in their own carnal ability, and sin came out alive, and they were cut off from God, and they died. That does not mean to say they were forever cut off, because God opened a way for them to return in repentance but they had to return by faith. Not by the works of the law.

Of all the difficult things in this Roman pilgrimage, this is the hardest to escape - legalism. We get born again by faith but soon after we turn back to a set of laws.

Let us look at a scripture about returning under the law.

Thus says the LORD, "Cursed is the man who trusts in mankind and makes flesh his strength, and whose heart turns away from the LORD. (Jeremiah 17:5)

That is legalism. When we have known the Lord, tasted His grace and experienced his supernatural power and his deliverance from bondage of sin and we go back to trusting in our own ability, our own rules, our own programs, our heart depart from the Lord and then we come under a curse.

In other words, this scripture says: cursed is the man who has known the Lord, experienced his power and turns back to his own strength and his own efforts.

Now you are free to make your own judgment but in my opinion that is the condition of most of the professing Christian Church today. Almost every significant movement in the church began in the power of the Holy Spirit; otherwise it would never have begun.

You cannot play around with the blessing of the Lord. He gives it freely but we are required to appreciate it. We have to recognize our total dependence upon his grace and his supernatural power. You cannot be a Christian by your own strength or efforts. It is on a level you can never attain. When you try to do it in your own strength, in your own efforts having known the supernatural grace and power of God you come under a curse.

Then the next verse reads:

For he will be like a bush in the desert
And will not see when prosperity comes,
But will live in stony wastes in the wilderness,
A land of salt without inhabitant. (Jeremiah 17:6)

What a description of somebody under a curse. The most common reason why Christians come under a curse is legalism and this is the theme of Galatians and it is summed up in Gal 3:1 *Oh foolish Galatians who has bewitched you...*

Having begun in the spirit are you now trying to be made perfect by the flesh?

Then Paul goes on, if you come back under the law, you come back under a curse. He reminds them in Gal 3:10; *"Curse is everyone who does not continue in all the works of the law to do them."*

7.3 God's Law is Holy

Now you might say well, then the Law is a bad thing. Paul says on the contrary the law is totally good. The badness is not in the law but it is in us.

Rom 7:12 So then, the Law is holy, and the commandment is holy and righteous and good.

Rom 7:13 Therefore did that which is good become a cause of death for me? May it never be! Rather it was sin, in order that it might be shown to be sin by effecting my death through that which is good, so that through the commandment sin would become utterly sinful.

Rom 7:14 For we know that the Law is spiritual, but I am of flesh, sold into bondage to sin.

So there is nothing wrong with the law. It is good it is holy. It is perfect. It is also spiritual. Do not blame the law. The problem is not in the law. The problem in us - in our flesh and there the law performs the vital function of confronting us with the real condition of our flesh.

Now we have used the word legalism. Let us define it.

Two definitions of legalism

First of all legalism is the attempt to achieve righteousness with God by keeping any set of rules.

Catholic rules, Baptist rules, Pentecostal rules etc. If you are attempting to achieve righteousness with God by those rules - you are under legalism. There is nothing wrong with rules. We need rules - what is wrong is thinking that, by keeping those rules, you will become righteous with God.

The other alternative definition of legalism is adding to what God has required for righteousness anything more of our selves. No one is authorized to add to God's requirements or righteousness. God says: all I ask is that you believe in God who delivered Jesus for our offences - that is all.

7.4 The Struggle with Sin

Being confronted with the law tends to produce in us a kind of inner spiritual conflict. A war starts within us.

Rom 7:15 For what I am doing, I do not understand; for I am not practicing what I would like to do, but I am doing the very thing I hate.

Rom 7:16 But if I do the very thing I do not want to do, I agree with the Law, confessing that the Law is good.

Rom 7:17 So now, no longer am I the one doing it, but sin which dwells in me.

Rom 7:18 For I know that nothing good dwells in me, that is, in my flesh; for the willing is present in me, but the doing of the good is not.

Rom 7:19 For the good that I want, I do not do, but I practice the very evil that I do not want.

Rom 7:20 But if I am doing the very thing I do not want, I am no longer the one doing it, but sin which dwells in me.

Rom 7:21 I find then the principle that evil is present in me, the one who wants to do good.

Rom 7:22 For I joyfully concur with the law of God in the inner man,

Rom 7:23 but I see a different law in the members of my body, waging war against the law of my mind and making me a prisoner of the law of sin which is in my members.

As a matter of fact, Paul here talks about being brought under captivity to the war of sin which is working in its members. The more the concern we have to be good and to do good, the more conscious we become of this inner conflict.

People who do not care about righteousness or goodness probably do not have much of a conflict. But the more you care, the more you have a desire to be good and to do good, the more conscious you become of this inner conflict.

The conflict between carnality and spirituality

The Bible gives us a kind of picture of this conflict in the experience of Rebekah. Rebekah was Isaac's wife and they were married for a good many years and could not have any children. It says Rebekah was barren.

Have you ever considered how many of the women of the Bible were barren, for whom God's purpose was to be, that they should become the mothers of the most significant children. Sarah, Rebecca, Hannah and many others. It is as though God brings us to the place where we have to pray through to the fulfillment of his revealed will. I think that is an experience that happens in the lives of many of God's chosen. God shows us that this is my will and He puts us in a situation where it seems impossible in order that we may learn to pray through the impossible.

So we read in Genesis 25:21 and following:

21 Isaac prayed to the Lord on behalf of his wife because she was barren and the Lord answered him and Rebecca his wife conceived.

22 but the children struggled together within her and she said; if it is so why then am I this way (God what is the meaning of this? why do I have a struggle inside me) *so she went to inquire of the Lord*

23 and the Lord said to her: two nations are in your womb and two people shall be separated from your body and one people shall be stronger than the other and the older shall serve the younger (which is contrary to natural tradition and culture especially in the Middle East)

24 When her days to be delivered were fulfilled behold there were twins in her womb. Now the first came forth red all over like a hairy garment and they named him Esau

25 and after when his brother came forth with his hand holding on to Esau's heel so his name was called Jacob (the word Jacob is derived from the word for a heel the Hebrew) and Isaac was 60 years old when she gave birth to them.

Rebecca felt this struggle going on inside her and she could not understand what was going on. So she went and asked the Lord and the Lord said you have got two kinds of men inside you. He did not give much detail but He said contrary to normal culture and custom when they come out the older one will be the servant of the younger.

Now Esau is portrayed all through the Bible as a type of what we would call the carnal nature or the carnal man and Jacob is a type of the spiritually disposed man. That does not mean that Jacob was always good.

You might wonder why God said *Esau I have hated Jacob I have loved* (Malachi 1:2). Today in our culture, Esau would be the good guy and

Jacob would be the one that people would be displeased with. That is a remarkable fact, but it is true.

Now Esau did not do anything very wrong, but the thing about him that God hated was that he was not concerned about his spiritual birthright. He was prepared to sell it for a bowl of soup. God hates that indifference and lack of concerned about the grace. The spiritual blessings of God are something that provokes God's wrath.

Jacob's one redeeming feature was that he esteemed birthright and the blessing. He was very crooked in the way that he went to get it. He did a lot of things he should not have done and he paid for them. But all through he still had this one redeeming feature. He was determined to get the birthright and the blessing. That really is about the best that can be said of any of us.

So here are two kinds of nature:

- **The carnal nature** is unconcerned about the things of God and the blessings of God. It just wants a good time and plenty to eat and plenty of money and a nice house etc.

- **The spiritual man** is not good. There is a lot of crookedness in him, but he has this one redeeming feature that he really is determined to get the blessings of God. You remember it ended up in a wrestling match where Jacob wrestled all night against an angel.

Now they are not many of us that would wrestle all night against an angel. He was a man of strength and determination and he walked away from that wrestling match with his thigh out of joint and from then on he limped. There are lots of men and women who have to have a meeting with God that leaves them limping, so that, for the rest of their days they do not walk in their own strength. At last Jacob had a learned he could not do it by his own efforts. The last thing he said to that angel who was his Redeemer, who was to be his Messiah - unless you bless me, I will not let you go. One thing I must have is your blessing. That is how a spiritual man thinks.

What I am trying to say is this; do not be disturbed if there is a conflict in you. Not every one of us has a Jacob in him. If there is a Jacob as well as an Esau there is going to be conflict. These two natures cannot agree.

7.5 The Way Out of This Conflict

In Romans 7:17 to 23, we saw that a confrontation with the law provokes an internal conflict within the one who wants to do the will of God. Romans 7 verse 24 and following and gives us the way out of this conflict. It is very obvious that Paul had this conflict in a very marked degree himself and he says:

Rom 7:24 Wretched man that I am who will set me free from the body of this death?

Or from this dead carnal nature that always fights against the things of God. Which resists my best intentions to do good and to keep God's law. Who will deliver me? It is a cry of anguish.

Rom 7:25 thanks be to God - through Jesus Christ our Lord!

What he is really saying is this; thanks be to God, there is a way out through Jesus Christ. The way out is through the cross. It is through the substitutionary sacrifice and death of Jesus.

Romans 6:6 says: our old man (our fleshly nature) was crucified with him. It was put to death and because of that we can be delivered from the fleshly nature and come into the fullness of the freedom and the life in the spirit. But it is through the substitutionary sacrifice of Jesus on the cross.

If there is one thing you should always remember in Roman 6, it is that our old man was crucified with him. Reckoning that the old man is dead and as long as we continue reckoning that in faith we will experience it.

7.6 The Two Options

We are therefore confronted with the fact that we only have two possibilities:

- We are either under the law dominated by sin or
- Under grace, led by the Holy Spirit and free from the law and from sin.

These possibilities are mutually exclusive alternatives you cannot be in both. Romans 6:14 says: *for sin shall not be master over you for you are not under law but under grace.*

That clearly implies that if you are under the law, sin will be master over you. If you are under grace, you cannot be under law and therefore sin will not master you. You cannot be under the law and under grace at the same time. You have to make up your mind.

Being under grace and being led by the Holy Spirit is extremely important. A lot of people say; well if I am not under the law, then I can do whatever I please. That is totally incorrect. The alternative to being under the law is not doing what you please but it is to be led by the Holy Spirit. One thing for sure is that the Holy Spirit will never lead you to do anything evil or displeasing to God. You can trust him better than you can trust your own efforts to keep the law.

Let us look at this statement made in Roman's 8:14 (we will get there later): *for all who are being led by the Spirit of God these are sons of God.*

The word means mature sons. In order to become a child of God, you have to be born of the Holy Spirit but in order to become mature in Christ you have to be led by the Holy Spirit. The only path to maturity is being led by the Holy Spirit. There are countless children of God who have been born of the Spirit but never learned to be led by the Holy Spirit. They remain spiritual babies all their lives because the only path to maturity is being led by the Holy Spirit.

For as many as are regularly led by the Holy Spirit (it is a continuous present tense) these and these only are the sons of God. Therefore, the alternative to being under the law is to be under grace and if you are under grace you are being led by the Holy Spirit.

Galatians 5:18 says: *but if you are led by the spirit you are not under the law*

This is very clear. If you are under the law you are not being led by the Holy Spirit. The only way to maturity is to be led by the Holy Spirit. You cannot come to maturity by being under the law.

1st Timothy 1: 8 – 11 says:

8 We know the law is good if one uses it lawfully,

9 realizing the fact that the law is not made for a righteous man (have you been made righteous by faith in Jesus Christ? yes or no. If yes, then the law is not made for you. Then Paul lists the kind of people that the law is made for. Then ask yourself if you I want to be among that list.)

The law is made for those who are lawless and rebellious, for the ungodly and sinners, for the unholy and profane, for those who kill their fathers and mothers, for murderers,

10 and immoral men and homosexuals and kidnappers and liars and perjurers and whatever else is contrary to sound teaching or doctrine.

Do you want to be in that list? Well those are the people that the law is made for.

Then Paul sums it up:

11 according to the glorious gospel of the Blessed God with which I have been entrusted

This is the message of the gospel. You cannot be made righteous by keeping the law. The only way you can achieve righteousness is through faith in the atoning death and resurrection of Jesus Christ.

7.7 The Product of Faith vs. the Product of Flesh

Now in Galatians 4, Paul uses an analogy from again the experience of the patriarchs - the two sons that were born to Abraham - first Ishmael and then Isaac. (Gal 4:21 – 31)

21Tell me, you who want to be under law, do you not listen to the law?

22For it is written that Abraham had two sons, one by the bondwoman and one by the free woman.

23But the son by the bondwoman was born according to the flesh and the son by the free woman through the promise.

24 This is allegorically speaking, for these women are two covenants: one proceeding from Mount Sinai bearing children who are to be slaves; she is Hagar.

25 Now this Hagar is Mount Sinai in Arabia and corresponds to the present Jerusalem, for she is in slavery with her children.

26 But the Jerusalem above is free; she is our mother.

27 For it is written, "Rejoice, barren woman who does not bear; break forth and shout, you who are not in labor; for more numerous are the children of the desolate than of the one who has a husband"

28 And you brethren, like Isaac, are children of promise.

29 But as at that time he who was born according to the flesh persecuted him who was born according to the Spirit, so it is now also.

30But what does the Scripture say? "Cast out the bondwoman and her son, for the son of the bondwoman shall not be an heir with the son of the free woman."

31 So then, brethren, we are not children of a bondwoman, but of the free woman.

So Ishmael is the product of the law. He is the work of the flesh. He is the result of Abraham doing his best to achieve God's purpose by his own efforts. He lost patience and got tired of waiting for the son that was promised and he listened to his wife and said well let us have a child by my maid Hagar which was not immoral in those days. It was perfectly legitimate within the culture of that day. Nonetheless it was out of faith. It was not in faith and the Bible says whatsoever is not based on faith is sin.

But he who doubts is condemned if he eats, because his eating is not from faith; and whatever is not from faith is sin. (Rom 14:23)

God forgave Abraham but he paid a heavy price for that act which is still being paid today - four thousand years later. It is the descendants of Ishmael who are the main source of problems to the descendants of Isaac.

Could that be interpreted as a warning? It does not pay to get things in the flesh because we will have to live with them. One interesting fact about Abraham is that his only errors did not come from failing to do what God told him to do. They came from doing more than God told him to do.

I suppose that is true for most committed Christians. Our problems will not be in disobeying and failing to do what God says. They come from going beyond what God says and doing our own thing and taking our own initiative and the result will always be an issue.

The hardest thing to do sometimes is to wait. We usually jump in and beget an Ishmael because we get tired of waiting.

Genesis 21:9-10 says...*But Sarah saw that the son whom Hagar the Egyptian had borne to Abraham was mocking her son, and she said to Abraham, "Expel the slave woman and her son, for the slave woman's son will never share in the inheritance with my son Isaac!*

Paul says here in Galatians that when Isaac came, Ishmael immediately started to make fun of Isaac (the flesh always ridicules or strives with the spirit) and Sarah got angry and she counteracted her own advice.

Abraham took her advice the first time which was wrong and the second time it was right. Now, this is the message when the child of faith and grace comes, there is no room for the slave woman and her child. Cast out the law and the products of the flesh, when the faith child comes.

Notice Isaac was not the product of Abraham's ability. He was the product of a supernatural impartation from God. What we can do in our own ability is never sufficient to please God. We have to operate on a supernatural level. You cannot live the Christian life on the level of your own ability.

When you read through the Sermon on the Mount (Mathew 5: 1-11), ask yourself how much of that you can do on your own ability and own will.

Therefore Christianity is not a set of rules. You cannot be saved by grace and live under the law.

Galatians 5:3-4 says: *For I testify again to every man that is circumcised, that he is a debtor to do the whole law.* (You cannot just keep one point of the law you either keep it all or you are not under it at all.) *Christ is become of no effect unto you, whosoever of you are justified by the law; ye are fallen from grace.*

What it means is they were no longer living in the grace of God. That is a very solemn statement "you have been severed from Christ". Like many churches today, what was the problem of the Galatian Church? They had known God's supernatural grace and power in a wonderful way and then because of false teachers, they had felt that they had to go back and keep the Law of Moses. This applies to millions of Christians across the world today.

So Paul was more upset with the Galatians than any other church. It is the only church he wrote to that he did not thank God for. He could thank God for the Corinthian church even though there was adultery and incest and drunkenness. But when he started to write to the

Galatians, he got so upset and instead of saying I thank God for you, he said I marvel that you are so soon turned away from the grace of Christ. (Galatians 1:6)

7.8 The Response We Have To Make

We saw that a confrontation with the law provokes an internal conflict within the one who wants to do the will of God.

We pictured it like the situation of Rebecca when she was pregnant with twins Esau and Jacob. Esau the type of the carnal man and Jacob a type of the spiritual man and we said that that Paul himself obviously went through the same kind of spiritual conflict and at the end of Romans chapter 7 he cried out in agony in verse 24: *Wretched man that I am! Who will set me free from the body of this death?* And then he came out with a triumphant response in verse 25: *Thanks be to God through Jesus Christ our Lord!*

That is the way out. It is through the cross. It is through the substitutionary sacrifice of Jesus. Because on the cross, and in Jesus, our old man, this body of sin, was put to death and through that execution on the cross we can be delivered from the Dominion of the old carnal nature. We can be released to serve God in the spirit. (Romans 6:6).

That is a historical fact - whether you know it or you do not - It is true. Knowing it, and believing it, will change you. It was done in order that our body of sin might be done away i.e. rendered ineffective or put out of action, that we should no longer be slaves to sin.

The implication is that, as long as the old man is still allowed to have his way, we will be slaves to sin. In Romans 6:6 this is presented as something that was done for us. Our old man i.e. our fleshy nature, was crucified with him but there is another side to that truth which we are going to deal with.

Now, there is something we have to do. It does not all happen because Jesus did it. There is a certain response of faith that we have to make. Let us turn to Galatians 5:24, which is the response that we have to make.

Now those who belong to Christ Jesus have crucified the flesh with its passions and desires. (Gal 5:24)

This is the distinguishing mark of those who truly belong to Jesus. It is not a doctrine, it is not a denomination. It is something that has taken place in them. By an act of their own will and faith they have crucified the flesh.

Romans 6:6 is God's side that our old man was crucified which then lays the basis that Galatians 5:24 is the response required from us i.e. those who belong to Christ have crucified the flesh on the basis of what Jesus did for us. We apply the cross to our own fleshly nature.

Now the cross is not an easy way to die. It is painful and there is a certain amount of pain, which is inevitable, in entering into this life of freedom and victory. We can only do it as we crucify our flesh. In a certain sense, we have to take the nails and drive them through our own hands and our feet and take our place willingly on the cross and be identified with Jesus in his death.

The emphasis here is that this is not free from pain.

Forasmuch then as Christ hath suffered for us in the flesh, arm yourselves likewise with the same mind: for he that hath suffered in the flesh hath ceased from sin; That he no longer should live the rest of his time in the flesh to the lusts of men, but to the will of God. (1Peter 4:1-2)

Now that is an astonishing statement. Many Christians would say: I thought Jesus did all the suffering? All was done on the cross. Why do we have to suffer in the flesh?

The statement that should attract us should be: *he suffered in the flesh and has ceased from sin.* Is not wonderful to have ceased from sin? Then the next verse says: no longer to the lusts of men but for the will of God. Many Christians will be attracted to the possibility of living the rest of their life, no longer for the lusts of our fleshly nature, but to do the will of God.

Our hearts could be sincere with the desire to do the will of God, but according to this scripture, it seems that the way is going to be painful. In a sense, you have got two options. You can suffer God's way or you can suffer your own way, but suffer you will. Anybody who tells you there is no suffering in the Christian life is deceiving you and he is going contrary to Scripture.

To understand this, Let us take the following narrative as an example:

There is this beautiful young Christian lady and she is about 20 years old. She had a wonderful encounter with the Lord and has been filled with the Holy Spirit. She really desires to serve God. She is also a member of a good church and has a loving gracious mature pastor. Then a young man comes into her life and he is not a committed Christian. But he gets very interested in her and he says well, I will go to church with you, I will do whatever you want and I want to marry you. Anything I have to do to marry you I will do. Sounds familiar?

So he comes to church and sings the hymns and listens to the sermons and the young lady goes to her pastor and says this is the man that has come into my life. He wants to marry me. What should I do? And the pastor says do not marry him because he has never made his own personal commitment to the Lord. He is only coming to church because he wants you. When he has got you and you are married to him, there is no guarantee that he will go on coming to church.

So now, the young lady has got two options:
The right thing is to apply the cross to her fleshly nature. Her fleshly nature longs for this man. She has all sorts of beautiful pictures of a home and children and happiness. She continually pictures the man she wanted and the way she wants him to be. Have you noticed how

easy it is for us to do that with people? We do not see them as they really are. We see them the way we would like them to be and then in due course we are horribly disillusioned when we discover who they really are.

So option number one is: I will obey the Word of God through the mouth of my pastor. I realize he has my best interests at heart and so I am going to put the nails in my own fleshly nature. I am going to take my place on the cross and say I am crucified with Christ. Those desires in me that are not godly, that are out of the will of God, I am putting them to death. Today I am taking my place on the cross. I am driving those nails through my own urges and desires and passions. Now that is painful but the pain does not last long. The pain leads to something that is beautiful and wonderful - a life that is truly lived for God.

The other option is the bad solution. She does not listen to her pastor and goes ahead and marries this man. 15 years later, he leaves her with three children for another woman and she has had a miserable life for 15 years. Do not say that that is not painful. That is a lot more painful than taking God's solution. At the end of 15 years she has got the message, it does not pay to marry the wrong man. But it has been a very long painful way to get the message.

Therefore, whichever way she comes in to the purpose of God and the understanding of God's will, it is going to cause pain. You can have pain God's way by applying the cross in your own life or you can have pain the world's way and that is very unpleasant. It is a long way back when you have stepped out of the will of God and followed your own desires. It is painful but you have to deny yourself. You have to take up your cross.

Jesus said in Matthew 11:29 - 30: *Take My yoke upon you and learn from Me; for I am gentle and humble in heart, and you will find rest for your souls. For My yoke is easy and My burden is light."*

Someone defined the cross this way - two ways

1. First of all it is the place where your will and God's will cross. A place when we say "no to my will but thy will be done."
2. Secondly, the cross is the place where you die. It is the place of your execution. God will not impose the cross on you. Jesus said: if anyone will come after me, let him take up his cross and follow me. You cannot follow Jesus until you have denied yourself and taken up your cross. The cross is the instrument of execution but it is the way of deliverance. It is the only way out.

Let us close this section by describing the difference between obeying God, under the law and obeying God under grace. In each case, the ultimate purpose is to obey God, but it is done in different ways.

To illustrate this, Let us take a simple commandment which is given both in the: Old Testament (under the Law of Moses), and in the New Testament (under the law of grace). Exactly the same words and which apply whether we are under the law or whether we are under grace.

The commandment is – **"Be holy for I am holy"**

In Leviticus 11 verse 45, God speaks through Moses to Israel and he says: *For I am the LORD that bringeth you up out of the land of Egypt, to be your God: ye shall therefore be holy, for I am holy.* (Leviticus 11:45)

Now in this context, it means that you have got to keep an immensely complicated set of rules, which were given in the preceding verses of Leviticus 11. In this type of holiness, you have the do's and the do not's. That is the response of legalism.

From the beginning of the 11th Chapter, God gives to Moses commandments regarding clean and unclean Animals.

E.g. In Leviticus 11:26, The Lord says: *"concerning all the animals which divide the hoof but do not make a split hoof, or which do not chew cud, they are unclean to you: whoever touches them becomes unclean.*

So if you touch one of those animals like a camel, which divides the hoof but does not chew the cud, you become unclean. You are shut out from the fellowship of God's people until sunset and you have to go through a lot of cleansing rituals.

Read through the whole chapter and you will see the list. It is very elaborate and it gives a lot of tremendously complicated details and at the end of this list, the Lord says you shall be holy for I am holy.

In this context, it means that to be holy means to keep every one of those rules. That is the holiness of the law. It is perfectly valid if you can do it. Paul said that the law is perfect; however it is pretty hard to keep it.

Then Peter addresses Christians who have accepted the redemption of Jesus on their behalf as obedient children.

As obedient children, do not be conformed to the former lusts which were yours in your ignorance, but like the Holy One who called you, be holy yourselves also in all your behavior; because it is written, "YOU SHALL BE HOLY, FOR I AM HOLY." (1st Peter 1:14 – 16)

Is Peter telling us that we have to observe all these rules about lizards, cats and dogs? It is obviously not so. He must be expecting something different. In this context, Peter is talking about a response which is faith in Jesus. Jesus in me is my holiness. I do not rely on myself, I do not follow a set of rules, and I let Jesus be holy in me and through me. The holiness of the law says; I have got to keep all these rules. I have got to do this; I must not do that etc.

There was a certain lady who was asked what makes her to be so victorious in life and she said: every time Satan knocks at the door, I just let Jesus answer. That is the simplest description of the holiness of faith. I do not meet Satan in my own strength; I do not face these challenges in my own strength. I know I will be defeated. You just turn to Jesus and you and ask him to take care of the situation.

Let us just read just a few verses about this:

But by His doing you are in Christ Jesus, who became to us wisdom from God, and righteousness and sanctification (That is Holiness), *and redemption,* (1st Corinthians 1:30)

So if I am faced with the situation in which I need wisdom, what do I do? Will I come up with my own clever way? NO. I say Jesus you are my wisdom. I release you to be my wisdom.

If I am faced in a situation where I am tempted and my righteousness is challenged, what do I do? Am I going to try hard? No, I am going to say; "Jesus, you are my righteousness. Take care of this situation." If I am faced with this challenge of holiness I will say; "Jesus in me is my holiness." I do not have to strive. I do not have to struggle. All I have to do is to let Jesus take control of me and the situation.

Another beautiful scripture on this is Philippians 4:13. It says...*I can do all things through him who strengthens.* How much can I do? I can only do all things that express obedience to God through him who strengthens me. That does not mean I can do anything I want.

Then Hebrew 12:10 which deals specifically with this theme of holiness, it says; *For they disciplined us for a short time as seemed best to them, but He disciplines us for our good, so that we may share His holiness.*

Speaking about earthly human fathers, the writer says for they disciplined us for a short time as seemed best to them but He God disciplines us for our good that we may share his holiness. Notice that it is not our own holiness. We become partakers of God's holiness through Jesus - the holy one dwelling in us. The key here is not to flex our faith muscles and say I can handle this situation. It is to say God, I cannot handle this situation, and I am weak. I know my own weaknesses. I am just going to yield to you Jesus. I am going to let you take over.

Now that is by no means easy, and depends so much on our individual backgrounds. People who are wired to rely on their own abilities will not find it so easy. It takes strength, but it takes a different kind of strength - saying I will not trust myself but I will yield to Jesus. I will let him take control.

This is not something we can do immediately. It is something we have to learn stage by stage. We say to God; "I cannot handle this problem. I am not equal to this, I do not have the wisdom, I do not have the strength, but Jesus you are in me and I can do everything that God tells me to do through the one who is in me - the one who empowers me from within."

We have to learn to bring all the issues and problems in our life to God.

One weakness with many people is that we only turn to God with the big problems, but when we are faced with little problems, we try to handle it on our own. But when the little problems become big, we run back to God. We have to take all our problems to God.

CHAPTER 8: DELIVERANCE FROM BONDAGE

(Romans 8:1 – 8:4)

We have now completed all the stages of the Roman pilgrimage and we stand now at the entrance to our destination which is Romans chapter 8. It is a beautiful unfolding of the nature of the Spirit controlled or spirit filled life of the Christian who meets God's conditions.

Now we come to the entrance to this destination which is extremely important:

8.1 There Is No Condemnation

Rom 8:1 Therefore there is now no condemnation for those who are in Christ Jesus.

The critical phrase here is 'no condemnation'. As long as there is any kind of condemnation in your life, you cannot live and function in Romans chapter 8 and the purpose of God.

In the previous seven chapters, we were supposed to eliminate every possible cause of condemnation in our lives. And if we have faithfully followed through, understood it and believed it, we should be able to say now that - there is therefore no condemnation in my life. Condemnation is the devil's favorite and strongest weapon. There are countless numbers of Christians who are not free from condemnation. The reason is that they have not taken the pilgrimage. They have not worked through the percolator (Coffeemaker). A lot of people as we said earlier are like instant coffee. Romans chapter 8 does not work in them.

You have to deal with every possible cause of condemnation. We cannot enumerate them all now but bear in mind that in chapter 3, we dealt with the fact that all our past sins could be forgiven (Justification by Faith) and then in chapter 6 we went through the execution of the rebel - the old man. Then we went through the hardest stages of all, which was chapter 7 where we see believers united to Christ and the conflict of two natures. Now, we have come to the place where there is no condemnation from the law.

In Colossians 2:13-16: Paul describes what God accomplished for us through the death of Jesus on the cross and he says he spoiled or stripped principalities and powers - that is the principalities and powers of Satan.

When you were dead in your transgressions and the uncircumcision of your flesh, He made you alive together with Him, having forgiven us all our transgressions, having canceled out the certificate of debt consisting of decrees against us, which was hostile to us; and He has taken it out of the way, having nailed it to the cross. (Colossians 2:13-14)

Beyond the cross, the law has no claims on you. Through the cross, you have been justified and you have paid the last penalty. The law has no more claims on you.

When He had disarmed the rulers and authorities, He made a public display of them, having triumphed over them through Him. (Colossians 2:15)

Those are Satan's evil hosts in the heavenly places that seek to dominate us and destroy us.

Therefore no one is to act as your judge in regard to food or drink or in respect to a festival or a new moon or a Sabbath day. (Colossians 2:16)

Paul does not say that we are not to observe the Sabbath – that is a matter of personal decision. Nobody should condemn us in respect to them. Instead being free from condemnation, demands a certain amount of backbone, because there are a lot of religious people, whose favorite occupation is to bring you under condemnation. You have got to learn where you stand in Christ.

You have to say that: I am not going to let anybody condemn me in respect of any of the requirements of the law including the Sabbath, which as you know is the fourth of the Ten Commandments.

Let us now go back to Romans chapter 8.

Rom 8:2 *For the law of the Spirit of life in Christ Jesus has set you free from the law of sin and of death.*

There are two laws at work. One is the law of sin and death which pulls you down and the other is the law of the spirit of life only operating in Christ Jesus. It does not operate outside of Christ Jesus.

A very simple example of this is the law of gravity. For example; take a booklet in your hand. If you let go of the booklet, the law of gravity operates and it will fall down.

If however, you take the booklet with your left hand and put it into my right hand, the law of your will overrules the law of gravity and your right hand can lift that book up, which would otherwise have fallen. That is what it means to be in Christ. You are delivered from the law of sin and death (the left hand) to the law of the spirit of life in Christ Jesus (the right hand).

Rom 8:3 *for what the Law could not do, weak as it was through the flesh,* (Paul points out that there was nothing wrong with the law. It was our fleshly nature that was the problem) *God did: sending His own Son in the likeness of sinful flesh and as an offering for sin, He condemned sin in the flesh,* (in the flesh of Jesus)

On the cross, God finally condemned and disposed of sin. There are two scriptures in Hebrews that we need to look at for a moment - Hebrews 9:26b and Hebrews 10:3.

But now once at the consummation of the ages He has been manifested to put away sin by the sacrifice of Himself. (Hebrews 9:26b)

What did Jesus do by the sacrifice of himself? He put away sin. He disposed of sin. He put it right out of the way. He terminated its power and its claims.

Side by side with that, we need to look at Hebrews 10:3 talking about the sacrifices of the law it says: *But in those sacrifices there is a reminder of sins year by year.* The sacrifices of the Law never put away sin. All they did was remind people of their sins and cover their sins until the next sacrifice was due. So, instead of disposing of sin, the sacrifices of the Law constantly and continually brought it up again.

This is what this means: If I am under the law of sin and death and sacrifice, then I will have to do the sacrifice again and again for the same sin. But when Jesus offered the sacrifice of himself, he put away sin and therefore there now remains no further sacrifice for sins. Nothing more will ever be needed. It has all been done by the death of Jesus on the cross.

8.2 Love - The Righteous Requirement of The Law

Now we come on to the important practical issue which comes out in Romans 8 verse 4: God did this through the sacrifice of Jesus in order:

Rom 8:4 *that the requirement of the law might be fulfilled in us who do not walk according to the flesh but according to the spirit*

Now notice that, it is not the law that needs to be fulfilled, but the requirement of the law. Let us look at two other places where this word is found: In Romans 5:18 (the second half of the verse) speaking about what Jesus did.

So then as through ones transgression, there resulted condemnation to all men, even so through one act of righteousness there resulted justification of life to all men. (Rom 5:18)

That is the same word 'an act of righteousness'

Then in Revelation 19:8 we have a picture of the bride ready for the marriage supper. This is a glorious picture: *It was given to her to clothe herself in fine linen, bright and clean; for the fine linen, is the righteous acts of the saints (Revelation 19:8)*

Remember Isaiah 64:6. It says; *all of us have become like one who is unclean and all our righteous acts are like a polluted garment; we all wither like a leaf, and our iniquities carry us away like the wind.*

What is a righteous act? If the law says, I should not commit adultery and I say to myself, I will not commit adultery. What I have really done is committing a righteous act. But if I still harbor lustful thoughts in my heart, this righteous act is only outward and cannot make me righteous before God. It is like buying a beautiful new dress to attend an important event, but when the day of the event comes, I put on the suit or dress without taking a bath. Outward, I will look clean to men, but inside I will be filthy and when someone comes too close, I become nervous because I know that I might not smell too pleasing.

So it is the righteous acts of the law or the righteous requirement of the law that is to be fulfilled in us. We are not going to keep that law, but we are going to fulfill the righteous requirement of the law.

Therefore, the million dollar question is: what is the righteous requirement of the law?

If you do not know that, you are groping in the dark and you have no real idea of what is expected of you. The answer to that that question is LOVE. There is a whole list of scriptures which state this.

First,

In Matthew 22 there is a conversation between Jesus and a teacher of the law and one of them, a lawyer asked him a question testing him:

"Teacher which is the Great Commandment in the law" Jesus said to him you shall love the Lord your God with all your heart and all your soul and with all your mind. This is the great and foremost commandment and the second is like it. You shall love your neighbor as yourself on these two Commandments, depend or hang the whole law and the prophets. (Mat 22:36-40)

So Jesus gave a very clear specific answer. The keyword in both Commandments is love. Jesus said on these two commandments all the law and the prophets hang. If you wanted to hang your jacket up on a wall, there must be a peg there. So you take your jacket off and go and hang it on the peg. Very simply, the peg has to be there before you can hang your jacket on it. Love is the peg for all the commandments. Love for God (by keeping his commandments) and love for your neighbor - that is the righteous requirement of the law

Second,

Owe nothing to anyone except to love one another; for he who loves his neighbor has fulfilled the law. For this, "You shall not commit adultery, you shall not murder, you shall not steal, you shall not covet," and if there is any other commandment, it is summed up in this saying, "You shall love your neighbor as yourself." Love does no wrong to a neighbor; therefore love is the fulfillment of the law. (Rom 13:8-10)

That is very clear. God does not leave us any reason to doubt that Love is the fulfillment of the law.

Third,

For the whole Law is fulfilled in one word, in the statement, "You shall love your neighbor as yourself." (Gal 5:14).

Notice that, that is the whole law.

Fourth,

But the goal of our instruction is love from a pure heart and a good conscience and a sincere faith. For some men, straying from these things, have turned aside to fruitless discussion, wanting to be teachers of the Law, even though they do not understand either what they are saying or the matters about which they make confident assertions. (1 Tim 1:5-7)

The one thing we are aiming at when we preach and teach is love. There are three requirements for love: a pure heart, a good conscience and sincere faith. In other words, any kind of talk about the law that does not direct people to love is fruitless discussion.

How much fruitless discussion do we have in our churches today? A story is told about a mother and her son who were arguing. The mother wanted the son to go to church and the son did not want to go to church. So the son said:

Son: I do not want to go to church. I do not like those people and they do not like me. Why should I go to church? Give me two reasons.

Mother: First of all, you are 40 years old and second you are the pastor of the church.

What volumes does that story tell us? He is the pastor of the church and he does not like those people and they do not like him. Are there many churches like that today? A lot of time is wasted on religious activity that does not produce the one thing that really matters which is Love.

Therefore we have to constantly take stock of what we are doing. If we are not producing love then we are wasting our words, our time and our strength and the time of all the people listening to us.

Brethren, how much time is wasted in the church today? The results show, we do not love one another the way Jesus said to his disciples. Jesus said: *By this shall all men know that ye are my disciples, if ye have love one to another.* (John 13:35). There are many brethren today who complain that the world is judging the church. The truth is that Jesus had given the world the right to judge the church by these words. In other words, through this scripture, Jesus said that: If the world does not see you loving one another, they have got every right to say you are not my disciples.

Now that you know the righteous requirement of the law, you are answerable for what you know.

8.3 The Nature of This Love

First of all, this love is supernatural. It can only come from God. There is no way you can work it up. Religion will not give it to you. It comes only through the new birth. Peter says;

Since you have in obedience to the truth purified your souls for a sincere love of the brethren, fervently love one another from the heart, for you have been born again not of seed which is perishable but imperishable, that is, through the living and enduring word of God. (1 Peter 1:22-23)

Notice what Peter is saying. Your ability to love one another only comes from the fact that you have been born again. If you have not been born again, of the seed of God's word, this kind of love would be impossible.

Romans 5:5 says; *and hope does not disappoint, because the love of God has been poured out within our hearts through the Holy Spirit who was given to us.*

First of all, it is brought forth out of the seed of the word of God as a nature within you. Then the whole of the fullness of God's love is poured out into your heart through the Holy Spirit. It is totally supernatural. No human effort can ever produce anything, even a counterfeit of the love of God.

The next thing we need to see is that love is inseparable from obedience. Love is not some sentimentality or sweet words. It is manifested in obeying Jesus in everything. In John 14:21 Jesus says: *he who has my Commandments and keeps them he it is who loves me.*

Who is the person who really loves the Lord? Is it the one who prays the loudest and the longest? Not necessarily. It is the one who has his Commandments and keeps them. That is the proof of love. Furthermore love is the motive for our obedience. In John 14:15 Jesus said... *if you love me you will keep my Commandments.*

So if we do not keep his Commandments, the problem is that we do not love him. We can say we love him. If we are disobedient we do not love him. Love is the motive for obedience.

And in John 14:23 Jesus comes back to them with this same truth: *Jesus answered and said to him, "If anyone loves Me, he will keep My word; and My Father will love him, and We will come to him and make Our abode with him.*

Obedience is the test of our love and it is the motive of our love. Our love is not motivated by fear. Paul says in Romans 8:15 ...*you have not received the spirit of slavery again to fear.* You have not come back under the law where you are threatened with penalties every time you do something. We are motivated by a totally different motivation and it is love.

If you love your children, they will love you even when they are grownups. If however, their love for you is motivated by fear, they will become rebels when they become teenagers. Love is a much more powerful motive than fear and God is wise enough not to base his relationship with us on fear but on love.

The moment you were born again and even baptized in the spirit, you are not perfect in love. You have only just started. Love is progressive. Paul says in Philippians 1:9; *and this I pray that your love may abound still more and more in real knowledge and all discernment so that you may prove things that are excellent.*

So we have love, but it needs to abound more and more. We need to increase in love. The more we have of love the more sensitive we will be about the things that please God. A child that really loves you is sensitive to your smallest requirements. You do not even have to say it. That is the relationship that we should have with God. It is an ever increasing love which expresses itself, in an ever increasing sensitivity to what pleases God, our father.

The good news is that, even if we fail, our faith is still reckoned to us as righteousness. So we do not have to be perfect the first five minutes or the first five years as long as we are in the faith. God will deal with our imperfections just as he dealt with Abraham's. Even when Abraham was doing the wrong thing, his faith was still counted him as righteousness.

Even when we are doing wrong, as long as we are in the faith, our faith is still reckoned to us for righteousness and God says I will take care of the consequences. I will straighten them out. I have got my own way of doing it. But meanwhile their faith is reckoned to them as righteousness.

Then 1st John 2:5 tells us how love is made perfect: *but whoever keeps His word, in him the love of God has truly been perfected. By this we know that we are in Him:*

How do we affect the love of God? It is by keeping his word. Please, do not trying to feel loving, because that is not the way to get love.

Suppose you said to your wife *"I am really trying to love you"* do you think that would please her? You will definitely have a problem. We do not have to try to love. Do not focus on your feelings, focus on obedience. Just obey his word. That is all you need to do.

8.5: Your Legal Inheritance

From verse 5 of Romans 8, Paul now focuses on fact that there is a total opposition between the flesh and the Spirit of God. You understand by now that the flesh in this context does not mean our physical body but it means the nature we have received by inheritance from Adam – the rebel.

Remember God dealt with the rebel on his side in Romans 6. As far as God is concerned the rebel has been executed.

Now what I am seeking to unfold to you is what I would call your legal inheritance. You have heard the people who say I got it all. In a certain sense what they say is true. Legally they have got it all. They were entitled to everything but there is a vast difference between having it legally and having it experientially. That is really the nature of the Christian life; moving from the legal to the experiential.

We can illustrate this by the children of Israel moving into the Promised Land. In Joshua 1:2, God said to Joshua; *"I am giving them the land"*. In verse 3 God said: *"I have given them the land"*. From then on, legally the whole land of Canaan belonged to them. But experientially they did not have one inch of it. They could have lined up on the east bank of the River Jordan and folded their arms looked westward and said we have got it all. But the truth will be that the Canaanites would still be dwelling in the land.

God brought them into the Promised Land by two major miracles; by the crossing of the river Jordan and by the destruction of Jericho. From that time onward they, had to fight for everything. If they did not fight, they did not get it.

That is true in the Christian life. Paul here indicates very clearly that, it is one thing to have the legal inheritance, but it takes a lot of determination, faith and patience to move from the legal to the experiential.

8.6 The Opposition Between The Flesh and The Spirit

Rom 8:5 For those who are according to the flesh set their minds on the things of the flesh, but those who are according to the Spirit, the things of the Spirit.

Those who set their minds on the flesh, think like the flesh. Those who set their minds on spiritual things, think like the spirit. The difference is not just external. It is in the way they think. When God changes us, he does not start from the outside. He starts from the inside. Religion starts from the outside i.e. you have got to change your clothes, stop smoking, straighten out your hair, and take off your makeup or whatever else it might be. God does not start that way and sometimes religious people get frustrated with him because he starts in the heart. When God has changed your heart and your mind, ultimately He will change your external appearance. So the people who are operating in the realm of the Spirit think spiritually and the people operating in the realm of the flesh think carnally.

Rom 8:6 For the mind set on the flesh is death, but the mind set on the Spirit is life and peace,

The King James Version says: to be carnally minded is death, but to be spiritually minded is life and peace. You will know whether you are spiritually minded or not, because if you have life and peace that comes from being spiritually minded. If you are still anxious, troubled and tormented and uncertain you have not yet moved into your inheritance. You are entitled to it but you have not come into it.

Rom 8:7 because the mind set on the flesh is hostile toward God; for it does not subject itself to the law of God, for it is not even able to do so,

King James Version says; the carnal mind is enmity with God. That is very important to note. You have inside you an enemy of God. Your natural mind is enemies with God.

I hope it is not offence to say that the majority of Christian seminaries or bible colleges today are educating the carnal mind. They are educating the enemy of God and what they are producing are educated enemies of God. That might not be true of all seminaries or bible colleges, but is true of the majority of them today.

There was a certain minister of God who years ago went to a seminary and on the first lecture; the first thing the lecturer said was "First, I want to tell you all that I am an atheist". That is not surprising though, when there is that kind of infiltration in Christian seminaries and colleges. So inside a carnal mind is an enemy of God. That is the important thing for us to realize.

Also, a carnal mind does not subject itself to the law of God. For it is not even able to do so. The rebel cannot change. Not even God can change that rebel. What he does is to him put him to death.

Rom 8:8 *and those who are in the flesh cannot please God.*

As long as you are operating in your own natural ability and your unconverted condition, you may be very religious and very zealous. You may go to church every day of the week, but you cannot please God. That is the bottom line.

Now, what we need to note is that this enmity is in the mind. Consequently, to get right with God there has to be a change in our minds. Let us look at two statements to this effect:

The first statement is in Ephesians 2:3. It is talking about all the people in the world. *Among them we too all formerly lived in the lusts of our flesh, indulging the desires of the flesh and of the mind, and were by nature children of wrath, even as the rest.*

So it is not just the flesh, but the mind also that is at enmity with God.

Then in Colossians 1:21, Paul says speaking about those who had not been reconciled with God: *And although you were formerly alienated and hostile in mind, engaged in evil deeds,*

So true conversion absolutely demands a total change of mind and the proper scriptural word for that is REPENTANCE. The Greek word for repentance is METANOIA which means change your mind. It is not an emotional experience. It is primarily a change of the will and of the mind.

Repentance is probably the most neglected foremost doctrine of the Christian faith. It is described very clearly in Isaiah 55:7;

Let the wicked forsake his way And the unrighteous man his thoughts; (Notice: It not just your way but also your thoughts). *And let him **return** to the LORD, And He will have compassion on him, And to our God, For He will abundantly pardon.*

Thank God, he is waiting to have compassion and to pardon. But it is not enough to just turn from our outward ways. We have to turn from our inward thoughts. They are all in hostility toward God. This could be said of religion. It turns us from our outward ways but not our inward thoughts.

In Romans 12:2 Paul says; *and do not be conformed to this world, but be transformed by the renewing of your mind, so that you may prove what the will of God is, that which is good and acceptable and perfect.*

Therefore, when our minds change, our renewal or transformation is complete. Religion is just about getting people to change externally and it does not work. But when your mind has changed, your external behavior will change automatically. Therefore, not being conformed to the world is not primarily a dress code change. It is a change of the way we think. Some of the people, who have got the strictest dress code, have never had their minds change.

Now we come back to Romans 8 and the transition from the flesh to the spirit in verse 9:

Rom 8:9 *However, you are not in the flesh but in the Spirit, if indeed the Spirit of God dwells in you* (Really occupies all of you). *But if anyone does not have the Spirit of Christ, he does not belong to Him.*

I have always had some difficulty with that because I know of people who say that they walk in the spirit (and I believe them) yet they act in the most carnal way. When Spirit baptized people are carnal, they are the most carnal of all and the hardest to deal with.

People ask, how can a person who is baptized in the spirit have demons if he is filled with the spirit?

Well, a lot of people baptized in the spirit are not filled with the spirit. There are lots of areas in their lives that the spirit has not taken over yet.

Example: when you pour water into a bottle, the water may begin to run over but there may be a lot of bubbles inside the bottle. A lot of spirit-filled people still have got bubbles inside them. How do we know? A tree is known by its fruit. If it gives forth bitterness, unkindness, unfaithfulness and criticism, that is not the fruit of the Spirit. The potential is there, if you let the Holy Spirit indwelling control you.

And then it says *if anyone has not got the Spirit of Christ he does not belong to him.* He may belong to any church but he does not belong to Christ.

What is the spirit of Christ? What are its marks? It is: meekness, humility, purity, honesty, does not boast etc.

Rom 8:10 *If Christ is in you, though the body is dead because of sin, yet the spirit is alive because of righteousness.*

King James Version says: *And if Christ be in you, the body is dead because of sin; but the Spirit is life because of righteousness.*

The body is dead. What body? It is the fleshly nature and not your physical body. But the Spirit is alive. The Spirit is life. The Holy Spirit provides a totally new life. The old life has come to the end and a new life has started initiated by the Holy Spirit.

Listen, this is really where we are at the legal. It is not always the experiential. So there is the potential. When Christ comes into you, all that fleshly life dies as far as God is concerned i.e. at least on his side it is dead. You may say - well how do I go on to living a new life? It is born into you by the Holy Spirit - a totally new life. Not an improved life, nor a reformed life but a new life.

We said this earlier; just to emphasize again, corruption is irreversible. The key word that describes our carnal nature is corruption. Paul says; 'the old man is corrupt according to the deceitful lusts.'

Just like a fruit. You can put it on the kitchen table and leave it for 5 days. When you come back, you find it has spoilt. That is corruption. You can put it in the refrigerator but that will only give it a couple of more days before it spoils. The only solution is a new creation. God is not going to patch the rebel up. He is going to put him to death and start anew and that is what we have in Christ.

Therefore if anyone is in Christ, he is a new creature; the old things passed away; behold, new things have come. (2 Corinthians 5:17)

The new creation is totally of God. It has got nothing of the old creation. It is a totally new beginning. If we really realize what we had in the new birth, we would get excited about it. But a lot of people think that this is just another religious phrase. They do not really have any conception of what it is.

Rom 8:11 But if the Spirit of Him who raised Jesus from the dead dwells in you, He who raised Christ Jesus from the dead will also give life to your mortal bodies through His Spirit who dwells in you.

To me, that is the basic principle of divine healing. The same power that raised the body of Jesus from the tomb and sat him on God's right hand is now working in our physical bodies. If you can really believe that, it will be the basis of faith for any kind of physical healing or miracle that you need.

8.7 Put To Death The Body of Sin

Rom 8:12 so then, brethren, we are under obligation, not to the flesh, to live according to the flesh—

Rom 8:13 for if you are living according to the flesh (he is writing to spiritual Christians), *you must die; but if by the Spirit you are putting to death the deeds of the body, you will live*

When you visit our hospitals there are an awful lot of sick Christians. Here we are, believing in divine healing, we have got all the scriptures, then - why so many sick Christians?

The answer is in this scripture: *if you live after the flesh you will die*. This scripture is to the saints. They are not lost souls, but Christians living more in the flesh than in the spirit. They spend much more of their time in front of the television set than they do reading their Bible. Most of their conversation, has very little to do with God. They are living according to the flesh and Paul says this to spirit-filled Christians: if you live according to the flesh, you are nurturing that thing in you which is corrupt and all you get out of it is corruption.

So we have to put to death this body of sin. We have to refuse the demands of the flesh. We have to refuse our members to sin and yield our members to God and to righteousness - That is an exercise of the will. Then Paul comes to this beautiful scripture:

Rom 8:14 For all who are being led by the Spirit of God, these are sons of God.

We have dealt with that already, but just to emphasize, The Holy Spirit is a person. He is not a theological concept. He is not a little sentence at the end of the Apostles doctrine. He is a person and if you want to be led by him, you have got to develop a personal relationship with the Holy Spirit. You have got to let him take you by the hand. You have got to listen to his quiet whispers. You have got to sense his gentle nudges. He is a very sensitive person. He is pictured as a dove - a dove is timid (shy) bird and it is easily scared away.

The only person who never scared the Holy Spirit away was Jesus because he had the lamb nature in John chapter 1. If you want a real intimate personal relationship with the Holy Spirit, you have got to cultivate the lamb nature – meekness, purity and a life laid down in sacrifice.

John 1:12 says: *But as many as received Him, to them He gave the right to become children of God, even to those who believe in His name,*

It is very important to see that, when you are born again, what you get is authority and you do not become fearful anymore. Authority is useless if it is not exercised. Therefore, the new birth is just a potential. It is an opportunity to develop into something wonderful if you will use the authority. But if all you do is keep telling everybody you are born again and never take any intelligent attempts to exercise authority in a scriptural way, over the problems that confront you and the sins that still beset you, you will make no progress at all.

So Paul says that we have to move out of our way of thinking and living in the flesh, into a totally different one and we need the help of the Holy Spirit. And he, the Holy Spirit is willing to help us.

8.8 No Longer Slaves But Sons

Then Paul then says:

Rom 8:15 For you have not received a spirit of slavery leading to fear again, but you have received a spirit of adoption as sons by which we cry out, "Abba! Father!"

Rom 8:16 The Spirit Himself testifies with our spirit that we are children of God,

You are no longer slaves but sons. You are not motivated by fear but you are motivated by love and guided by the Holy Spirit.

We have not come under a spirit of slavery. Legalism brings people under the spirit of slavery. He is contrasting Sinai with Golgotha. In Sinai, the children of Israel were frightened and they backed off from the mountain. They said we do not want to hear that voice again. But God does not want to make slaves. He wants to make sons who are motivated by love and respect and who cry out Abba Father. In this, the Spirit helps us, because he bears witness that we are the children of God. Every one that is born of God has the witness in himself.

It is quite powerful to have the supernatural testimony of the Holy Spirit - that you are a child of God. If the Holy Spirit tells you that you are a child of God, it really does not matter much what other people say. He is the one that matters.

8.9 Our Inheritance Depends On Our Willingness To Suffer With Christ

Now Paul goes on in verse 17:

Rom 8:17 and if children, heirs also, heirs of God and fellow heirs (joint heirs) *with Christ, if indeed we suffer with Him so that we may also be glorified with Him*

According to the laws of inheritance, it does not mean that every one of us gets a little part of that inheritance. It means that we all share the total inheritance together.

That is a tremendous statement. We are heirs to all that Jesus's has inherited because we are his younger brothers. But there is a condition at the end of verse 17 - *if indeed we suffer with him in order that we may be also glorified together.*

So our inheritance depends on our willingness to suffer with him. You cannot become an heir of God without being willing to suffer with Jesus. If you reject the suffering, I do not believe that you can claim your inheritance. There is a certain tendency in the church today to dismiss suffering as something that does not belong to the Christian life.

Let us go on and consider the nature and the purpose of suffering which is something that every one of us will partake to some degree. Paul says in the next verse:

Rom 8:18 For I consider that the sufferings of this present time are not worthy to be compared with the glory that is to be revealed to us.

Coming from Paul that is rather an impressive statement considering what he suffered. Let us read the list of Paul's sufferings for a moment in the following scripture.

Are they servants of Christ?—I speak as if insane—I more so; in far more labors, in far more imprisonments, beaten times without number, often in danger of death. Five times I received from the Jews thirty-nine lashes. (195 lashes altogether). *Three times I was beaten with rods, once I was stoned, three times I was shipwrecked, a night and a day I have spent in the deep. I have been on frequent journeys, in dangers from rivers, dangers from robbers, dangers from my countrymen, dangers from the Gentiles, dangers in the city, dangers in the wilderness, dangers on the sea, dangers among false brethren; I have been in labor and hardship, through many sleepless nights, in hunger and thirst, often without food, in cold and exposure.* (2 Corinthians 11:23-27)

The remarkable thing is that in the same epistle a little earlier on, in 2nd Corinthians 4:17, he says *our light affliction which is but for a moment worketh for us a far more eternal and exceeding way to glory*

So what are you complaining about brother? How heavy is your affliction compared with Paul's? Paul said his affliction was a light affliction. Here in Romans he says: *the sufferings of this present time are not worthy to be compared with the glory that shall be revealed in us.* What made the difference with Paul was that he had a vision of the glory. If we lose the vision of the glory, we will not benefit from our sufferings.

Paul said; *while we look not at the things which are seen, but at the things which are not seen; for the things which are seen are temporal, but the things which are not seen are eternal.* (2 Corinthians 11:18)

So suffering will work God's purposes in your life, while you are looking at the things which are not seen. Paul had a vision of the unseen glory and nothing he suffered was worthy to be compared with the glory that he saw in the future. Whether we lose the vision of the eternal or not we will still suffer but we will get no benefit from it.

8.10 The Redemption of all Creation

Now Paul comes to one of the most profound revelations.

Rom 8:19 *for the anxious longing of the creation waits eagerly for the revealing of the sons of God.*

What Paul is saying is this: we are not the only ones that are suffering. The whole creation is suffering because of our sin. Because it was man's sin that plunged al creation into chaos and futility and that creation will not be redeemed until we are redeemed. So the whole creation is waiting for us. That is a tremendous statement.

All creation is waiting for us to be revealed in our resurrection glory. You see, creation is lot more alive to the promises of God than many Christians.

Let us turn briefly to Psalms 96.

Let the heavens be glad, and let the earth rejoice; Let the sea roar, and all it contains; Let the field exult, and all that is in it. Then all the trees of the forest will sing for joy, Before the LORD, for He is coming, For He is coming to judge the earth. He will judge the world in righteousness and the peoples in His faithfulness. (Psalms 96: 11-13)

All nature is anticipating the coming of the Lord except the church. The church is asleep but the trees are awake, the mountains are awake, the seas are awake, the animals are awake and the church is still sleeping. We are out of harmony with God.

Listen to this scripture again.
Let the sea roar and all it contains, the world and those who dwell in it.
Let the rivers clap their hands, Let the mountains sing together for joy
Before the LORD, for He is coming to judge the earth; He will judge the world with righteousness and the peoples with equity. (Psalm 98:7-9)

That is exciting because Jesus said right at the end of this age; men's hearts will fail them for fear and for the things that are coming upon the earth. So as the Lord's coming is imminent, the sea is going to get so excited. The rivers will clap their hands and the mountains will sing. Have you ever pictured rivers with hands or mountains with voices?

All creation is longing for the Lord to come and put things right. Man was made the steward of the earth, but after his fall, man raped the earth. He has left the earth in many areas desolate, stripped, bare, and exploited and the earth is crying out to God - how long are you going to let these people trample over us and tear us up, defile us and fill our atmosphere with that horrible pollution. Can you picture that?

The trouble with most of us is that we are so self-centered. Somebody said that the typical prayer of the average church member is - God bless me and my wife, my son John and his wife - Amen. That is sad.

Rom 8:20 for the creation was subjected to futility (vanity, emptiness, frustration), *not willingly, but because of Him who subjected it, in hope*

Rom 8:21 that the creation itself also will be set free from its slavery to corruption into the freedom of the glory of the children of God

Notice that, it is only when the children of God come, that creation will be set free. Creation also suffered a curse after man sinned. Let us look for a moment in Genesis 3.

Then to Adam He said, "Because you have listened to the voice of your wife, and have eaten from the tree about which I commanded you, saying, 'You shall not eat from it'; Cursed is the ground because of you; In toil you will eat of it all the days of your life. (Genesis 3:17)

See, God's pronouncement of a curse for the ground because of the sin of man. Man was the steward of the whole earth. He was answerable to God and his fall brought disaster on all that he was responsible for. This principle of responsibility is one we run away from today. The fact is we are responsible before God for certain things. As parents, we are responsible for our children.

Proverbs 22:6 says: *Train up a child in the way he should go, even when he is old he will not depart from it.*

This is a command we will have to answer to on the Day of Judgment. If parents fail, children suffer. They do not deserve it, but it comes because of the failure of the steward who was over them. The same principle applies to the whole earth.

God set Adam over the whole earth. He said to him; subdue the earth and rule over it, it is under your stewardship, but when Adam fell, he brought a disastrous consequence upon the whole earth. It is a frightening thought.

"Both thorns and thistles it shall grow for you; and you will eat the plants of the field; (Genesis 3:18)

What was the mark of the curse upon the ground? It was two things; 'thorns' and 'thistles'. Who provided redemption from the curse? Jesus. Have you ever noticed that they gave him a crown of thorns and they gave him a purple robe which is the color of the thistle? That was God's attestation that Jesus was redeeming both man and the earth from its curse. But the redemption will not come until man's Redemption is complete.

Rom 8:22 *For we know that the whole creation groans and suffers the pains of childbirth together until now.* (Did you know that?)

Rom 8:23 And not only this, but also we ourselves, having the first fruits of the Spirit, even we ourselves groan within ourselves, waiting eagerly for our adoption as sons, the redemption of our body.

Rom 8:24 *For in hope we have been saved, but hope that is seen is not hope; for who hopes for what he already sees?*

Rom 8:25 *But if we hope for what we do not see, with perseverance we wait eagerly for it.*

Now let me ask you frankly. Do you ever have this experience of the Holy Spirit groaning within you? Not for some problem in your life but for the redemption of creation. Do you ever empathize with this creation on which we men brought such terrible consequences by our sin and continue those consequences?

We have not acted as stewards of the earth; we have acted as exploiters of the earth. Our selfishness and our greed are rapidly ruining this earth but we who have the first fruits of the Spirit should have a totally different attitude. We should have empathy with the earth with its groaning sharing in its groaning and it is longing for redemption.

When will Redemption come? - When Jesus comes back. What will happen to us? Our bodies will be changed. That will be the redemption of our body. Paul says very clearly at the end of verse 23; *waiting eagerly for our adoption as sons, the redemption of our body.*

Remember, the end of the Christian life is not to get to heaven. That is just a stage in the journey. The end of the Christian life or the goal of the Christian life is the resurrection and only then will our redemption be complete.

That I may know Him and the power of His resurrection and the fellowship of His sufferings, being conformed to His death; in order that I may attain to the resurrection from the dead (Philippians 3:10-12)

So the whole creation is groaning in childbirth pain. Let us talk about this regeneration which is not just our personal regeneration but the regeneration of creation.

Jesus said in Matthew 19:28 to his disciples: *And Jesus said to them, "Truly I say to you, that you who have followed Me, in the regeneration* (that means the rebirth) *when the Son of Man will sit on His glorious throne, you also shall sit upon twelve thrones, judging the twelve tribes of Israel.*

From this scripture, there is a rebirth coming which is the rebirth of creation. Then Jesus said in Matthew 24:8 about the signs that mark the close of this age: *"But all these things are merely the beginning of birth pangs."*

The birth pangs of a new age.

Then Jesus said in Luke 21:28: *But when these things* (what he was describing in Matthew 24) *begin to take place, straighten up and lift up your heads, because your redemption is drawing near."*

You see, the climax it is not just our personal Redemption, it is the redemption of all creation and all creation is groaning in birth pangs or longing for that and we who have the first fruits of the Spirit.

God's purpose is that we should be groaning together. We should not be wrapped up in all our little personal problems and church squabbles. We should see the glorious vision of what God has in mind and we would give ourselves in prayer to bring it about.

8.11: Our Victory in Christ

In the previous section we looked at verses 19 through 25 which is an amazing revelation of God's total purpose for creation. We find that, as believers in Jesus, who received the Holy Spirit we are not to be exclusively preoccupied with our own little concerns or with the affairs of this age or even with the total destiny of the church.

God wants us to have an enlarged understanding so that we can identify with God's total program for creation. One reason for this is that we the human race are responsible for all the trouble that has come upon creation. God made Adam steward over the creation and Adam was unfaithful and failed in his stewardship. This brought disaster not only upon Adam and his descendants but upon the whole creation. So God in his limitless wisdom has ordained that the redemption of creation will be closely tied in with the redemption of the Adamic race and that creation will not be redeemed until our redemption is complete. Because our sin brought corruption and disaster upon all creation, it will be our redemption that will bring back redemption to creation.

So Paul speaks about praying not just for our own concerns, but being concerned with creation too and for the return of righteousness to the earth.

Now as we contemplate this, our minds and our hearts can hardly comprehend what Paul is saying to us and this could be the reason for what Paul says next in verses 26 and 27. He talks about the part of the Holy Spirit in our prayer. A casual eye, cannot comprehend, why the complete change of context.

However, what Paul is saying is that: do not try to attain this in your own limited understanding or your own limited emotional capacity. Let the Holy Spirit come in and do it for you. In a certain sense, what Paul is saying in these verses is this – 'just release yourself to the Holy Spirit and let him set up a prayer meeting inside you'. Just let the Holy Spirit pray.

8.12 The Holy Spirit Helps In Our Weaknesses

Let us look at these verses:

Rom 8:26 In the same way the Spirit also helps our weakness; for we do not know how to pray as we should, but the Spirit Himself intercedes for us with groanings too deep for words;

We are not enlarged enough in our understanding and our feelings to respond to this challenge that has been unfolded to us. When we consider what Paul has been saying about groaning for the whole creation. It is perfectly true that we just do not know how to pray right. Therefore, the Holy Spirit, when he comes in (if you know how to relate to him) you can release him to pray in you and through you.

Rom 8:27 and He who searches the hearts knows what the mind of the Spirit is, because He intercedes for the saints according to the will of God.

God the Father knows what the mind of the Spirit is. We do not know how to pray. Many times we do not know what to pray for. Sometimes when we know what to pray for, we do not know how to pray for it. That is the truth and we do not need to remain helpless and incapacitated because, the Holy Spirit as a person, comes in and takes control.

Rom 8:28 And we know that God causes all things to work together for good to those who love God, to those who are called according to His purpose.

That is a wonderful scripture. We notice that it does set certain parameters. You cannot say that everything that happens to you is God working something for your good. It only applies to those who love God and those who are called and who are walking in God's purposes. In such a case, everything that happens to you is the out working of God's plan no matter what may appear to be the case.

Alternatively, if you love God and you are called and you are not walking in his purposes, God will intervene and he will do something to stop you. That is also working for your good even if it does not appear so. God said about Israel *'I will hedge up her ways and she will not be able to find her ways.'* (Hosea 2:6).

Many times when God's children begin to go astray, God builds a hedge in front of them and there is just no way through. That is God working everything for your good as long as you are sincere and in faith walking in the purposes for which God called you.

Sometimes you may feel that God is not answering your prayers. If God would answer all our prayers, we would find ourselves in a lot of problems. Therefore even when our prayers do not get answered, it can be part of God's provision and care for us.

8.13 God's Total Plan For Us

Now the next statement in verses 29 and 30 is tremendous because this explains why we know everything is working together for our good and it tells us God's total plan for us from eternity to eternity. We will spend some time to outline that plan because; I believe that if we really grasp that plan, believe it and align ourselves with it, we will have total security.

Many of God's people are insecure today. They are troubled and they are like a drowning man grasping for air because they do not know what to hold on to. God keeps them afloat but they are not secure. The real basis for security is to understand God's eternal plan. The first thing we need to understand is that, it did not start with us, but it started with God and whenever God started on anything, he would take it to completion. Once we know that God initiated this then we will have confidence that He will complete it.

Therefore let us read what Paul says here in these verses and then we will supplement it from some other scriptures elsewhere to get a full picture of God's plan from eternity to eternity.

Rom 8:29 For those whom He foreknew, He also predestined to become conformed to the image of His Son, so that He would be the firstborn among many brethren;

Now, predestination can be presented as a very twisted doctrine. We are not predestined to be saved. We are predestined to be conformed to the image of Jesus. If you see somebody really being conformed to the image of Jesus, the only explanation is that God predestined him.

Rom 8:30 and these whom He predestined, He also called; and these whom He called, He also justified; and these whom He justified, He also glorified.

Now here is a kind of outline, but you have to look at a number of different passages in the scripture to get the total plan, complete and in the right order.

This is the outline of this program of God,

The first stage is that **God foreknew us**.

He knew us in advance. This is stated by Paul in Romans 8:29 (for whom he foreknew). It is also stated in 1st Peter 1: 1, 2. He addresses his epistle to the aliens scattered throughout various places and then he says who are chosen according to the foreknowledge of God the Father.

So that first the origin of everything is God's fore knowledge. He did not act in ignorance. He did not experiment. He knew in advance what kind of people we would be. How he would deal with us. How he could work out his plan for us. So we begin with God's foreknowledge which was before creation ever took place. That is a staggering thought. Before anything was ever created God foreknew each one of us. You are not an accident looking for a place to happen. Everything has been foreknown and fore planned by God from eternity.

The second stage is **God chose us**.

In 1st Peter we are chosen according to the foreknowledge of God. It is important to see that God's choice of us is based on his knowledge of us. He chooses us because he knows us in advance. He knows what we will be like and he knows what he can make of us. This is also stated in this scripture:

Blessed be the God and Father of our Lord Jesus Christ, who has blessed us with every spiritual blessing in the heavenly places in Christ, just as He chose us in Him before the foundation of the world, that we would be holy and blameless before Him. (Ephesians 1: 3-4)

So God foreknew us and on the basis of his foreknowledge, he chose us. You are not where you are because you made the choice. You are where you are because God made the choice. That makes a lot of difference to your attitude toward yourself and to your situation. It was started with God. And then

The third stage is **he predestined us**.

The word predestined merely means that God arranged in advance the course that our life would follow. This is stated in Romans 8:29 and 30. For whom he foreknew he also predestined. And in verse 30 whom he predestined these he also called. So the next stage is, God worked out in advance, the course that our life was to follow. He predestined us. This is also stated here; *In love, He predestined us to adoption as sons through Jesus Christ to Himself, according to the kind intention of His will,* (Ephesians 1:5)

He worked it all out in advance. Then also in Ephesians 1:11; *we have obtained an inheritance, having been predestined according to His purpose who works all things after the counsel of His will,*

So that should give you security. You have been predestined. The course of your life has been arranged in advance by the one who works everything, the way he wants it. He works all things according to the counsel of his own will.

Then in Ephesians 2:10: *for we are God's workmanship created in Christ Jesus for good works which God prepared beforehand that we should walk in them*

You understand we do not have to make our own decisions as to what to do. We have to find out the works that God has planned beforehand for us to do them. We are not required to make those decisions for ourselves. We are only required to find out the plan, the pattern, which God has for us. That relieves us of a whole lot of anxiety. If we can only see that God created us to do things which he created us to do. So we can do the things that he has ordained for us to do because he created us for that purpose.

If you are continually frustrated and feel unable to do what you are trying to do, you are probably trying to do the wrong thing. You are probably trying to do your own thing and not God's thing. So you need to change.

The fourth stage is **he called us**.

Back to Romans 8:30. *and these whom He predestined, He also called…* the word call also means invite.

Now this is the point at which God's plan comes out of eternity and into time. This is the point in our lives when we are confronted with eternity when God calls us. It is a very solemn and sacred moment. Looking on in Romans 11:29 a short but very powerful verse… *for the gifts and the calling of God are irrevocable.* God never changes his mind. He never withdraws his gifts. He never changes his calling. You are set on something that is totally secure and the creator of the universe is the author of it. His offer is behind it all.

Then we look in 2nd Thessalonians 2:14 for a moment - speaking about sanctification and faith, Paul says… *It was for this He called you through our gospel, that you may gain the glory of our Lord Jesus Christ.* The presentation of the gospel to you is God's invitation to share the fellowship of the father and the son. You will find that in 1st John 1:3, 4 …*what we have seen and heard we proclaim to you also, so that you too may have fellowship with us; and indeed our fellowship is with the Father, and with His Son Jesus Christ. These things we write, so that our joy may be made complete.*

Therefore, you are called by an invitation to share the fellowship of the Godhead in heaven. That is a pretty invitation. If you had an invitation from the president, you will get excited about it. Think of what this is. It is an invitation from the almighty eternal God to share fellowship with him in heaven forever!

The Fifth Stage is **he saves us**.

Then having called us, when we respond, he saves us. Let us look at 2nd Timothy 1:9… *who has saved us and called us with a holy calling, not according to our works, but according to His own purpose and grace which was granted us in Christ Jesus from all eternity,*

So when you are saved you are also called. Every person who is saved is called. You may not know it but you are called - called to a certain task.

Then in Titus 3:5: *He saved us, not on the basis of deeds which we have done in righteousness, but according to His mercy, by the washing of regeneration and renewing by the Holy Spirit.* There is a definite moment in time when you respond to the call God and he saves you. You pass out of death into life and out of condemnation into the righteousness of God. It is the greatest single transition that can take place in the life of any person. It is our response to God's call that plugs us in to God's eternal plan. That is why the calling of God is tremendously important and it is sacred.

Paul said eternity has called us with a holy calling brothers and sisters. Your calling is holy it should be the first priority in your life to fulfill your calling. A lot of Christians do not sufficiently appreciate their calling. Everyone's calling is sacred no matter what you are called to be, whether it is a housewife or a physician or a missionary, God planned it all in advance. You do not have to work it all out. You just have to walk in the good works which God has prepared for you to walk in.

The sixth Stage is he **justifies us**

After calling comes justification. You are acquitted. You are declared not guilty. You are reckoned righteous and made righteous. You are just as if you had never sinned.

Romans 8:30: *and these whom He called, He also justified;*

When you respond to the call, when you accept Jesus and his sacrifice on your behalf, you are not only saved but you are justified. You are reckoned righteous. Your clothed not merely with a garment of salvation but you are covered with a robe of God's righteousness (Isaiah 61:10).

The Seventh stage is **Glorification**

Romans 8:30 - *whom he justified these he also glorified.* Notice that it is in the past tense. It is not something that is going to happen after we die. It is done now through our faith in Jesus Christ. This is so exciting and so few Christians seem to realize it. Let us look for a moment in 1st Corinthians 2:7 - *but we speak God's wisdom in a mystery, the hidden wisdom which God predestined before the ages to our glory;*

We speak a secret hidden wisdom of God. We have been let into the secret hidden wisdom of God. And the end of this scripture says that - he had ordained it for our glory. Just think about that. The whole wisdom of God from eternity is directed towards getting us into his glory.

But God, being rich in mercy, because of His great love with which He loved us, even when we were dead in our transgressions, made us alive together with Christ (by grace you have been saved), and raised us up with Him, and seated us with Him in the heavenly places in Christ Jesus, (Ephesians 2: 4-6)

So we are made alive, then we were resurrected and then we are enthroned. That is God's plan.

Let us recapitulate those seven stages.

1. God foreknew us
2. He chose us
3. He predestined us

All that happened in eternity, then in time

4. He called us
5. He saved us
6. He justified us and
7. He glorified us (he invited us to share the throne of glory with him right now in this present age)

If you really can grasp God's plan, there can be no further room in your life for insecurity. Everything has been taken care of.

8.14 More Than Conquerors

Let us now go through the closing verses of Romans chapter 8. You will notice as we turn to it, that Paul returns again to this theme of no condemnation with which he began this chapter. Remember the first verse: *there is therefore now no condemnation*

Our greatest enemy and the greatest tool of Satan against us is condemnation i.e. being made to feel guilty. There is a great difference between being made to feel guilty and being convicted of sin. The Holy Spirit convicts us of sin. He is specific and practical. He says you did this and you should not have done it. This is what you have got to do and the moment you put it right, it is all over.

But guilt is something you can never fully define. Did I say the right thing? Maybe I did not say? Maybe I have not done enough, maybe I did not treat her right, and maybe what she said about me was right, maybe I am not really true or sincere. There is no end to guilt. The further you go into it, the deeper you sink. Guilt comes from the enemy and conviction comes from our friend the Holy Spirit.

Be very cautious about anybody who makes you feel guilty. Because more often, what they say is not from God. God is not in the business of making people feel guilty.

Let us look now verse 31:

Rom 8:31 *what then shall we say to these things? If God is for us, who is against us?*

He does not say nobody is against us but what he says is - what does it matter who is against us. There is simple saying: one plus God is a majority. In any circumstance one plus God is a majority.

Rom 8:32 *He who did not spare His own Son, but delivered Him over for us all, how will He not also with Him freely give us all things?*

This is a tremendous verse. If you want to know how committed God is to you, look at the cross. God gave His only Son to die in agony and shame on your behalf. Paul says very logically that if God did that, there is nothing good that he will withhold. When you are in times of darkness and temptation and doubt, do not try and reason it out. Just turn to the cross and say - that is the measure of God's love and commitment to me. I may not understand what is going on but I know that God is totally committed to me.

Once God has accepted you as his child, he is totally committed to you. It is a lifetime commitment. God said I will never leave you nor forsake you. Do not get involved in arguments with the devil about minor details. Focus on the cross and he cannot defeat you. At the foot of the cross, you are on undefeatable ground.

Rom 8:33 *who will bring a charge against God's elect? God is the one who justifies;*

The question is, if God has justified you, who can make you feel guilty?

Rom 8:34 who is the one who condemns? Christ Jesus is He who died, yes, rather who was raised, who is at the right hand of God, who also intercedes for us.

Though there will be people who will try to condemn us, God has done everything conceivably possible to keep us from coming under condemnation. If people accuse us, he says I have justified you. If people condemn us he says, the price has already been paid by the death of my son. He paid the full penalty by his death and he rose from the dead that he might be our intercessor forever.

Christians actually wound one another with words spoken out of the Spirit and become each other's accusers. What kind of arrogance is that? We accuse others before God; somebody that God has undertaken to justify. We accuse someone for whom Christ died for?

It our duty is to pray for them. It is a tremendous responsibility upon us when we pray for our fellow Christians so that God can turn them. If you cannot thank God for a person, do not pray for them. You find that almost every time Paul prayed for people, he began by thanking God for them.

You cannot know how dangerous and subtle the power of condemnation and guilt is. So many times, it does not come from our enemies. It comes from our friends. Somebody once said – "with friends like that who needs enemies".

But I am emphasizing this point - God will not tolerate condemnation of his chosen. He has pledged himself to maintain our cause and we have an expert advocate. In Hebrews 3:1 it says *Jesus is the high priest of our confession* and in Hebrews 7:25 speaking about this high priest: he is able to save forever or he is also able to save to the uttermost.

It is interesting to think of the life periods of Jesus ministry. 30 years of perfect family life earning his living, three and a half years of public ministry and nearly 2,000 years of intercession. What does that tell us about our priorities? We have an intercessor 1st John 2:1...*my little children I am writing these things to you that you may not sin* (thank God he did not end there) *and if anyone sins, we have an advocate with the father Jesus Christ the righteous*. We have got the most expert advocate in the universe pleading our case. There is no reason ever to be condemned. God is on our side and Jesus is at the right hand of God and he is our advocate. God has undertaken to justify us. He will not tolerate condemnation of us.

The Christian life is like a soldier's life. You cannot go to the battle field alone. You need your colleagues to cover you. However, if one of your colleagues is slackening, the whole troop suffers. Worse still, if one of your colleagues begins to collaborate with the enemy giving away your position, the whole troop is in danger.

I hope you can see how serious this matter of guilt and condemnation is. Let's look at a beautiful scripture from Isaiah 54:17: this is spoken to God's people... *no weapon that is formed against you shall prosper and every tongue that accuses you in judgment you will condemn*.

Notice that God does not say I will do it. He says I have given you the basis for you to do it did. Realize that every tongue that will rise against you, you will condemn. This is the heritage of the servants of the Lord and their vindication is from me declares the Lord. Amen

Now, having once again dealt with this matter of condemnation and guilt, we come to the beautiful and glorious climax but you cannot get there under condemnation.

The climax in a simple phrase; It is eternal unity in spirit with Messiah and that is where we are headed. Jesus is the goal – he is the beginning and he is the end. He is the first and he is the last. He is the alpha he is the omega. And you have not arrived until you have this union with Jesus in the spirit.

Rom 8:35 *who will separate us from the love of Christ? Will tribulation, or distress, or persecution, or famine, or nakedness, or peril, or sword?*

Do you think Paul would have listed those things if they had never happened to us? It would have been a waste of words. Paul says we may encounter any or all of those things, but one thing they can never do is separate us from the love of God. Then he quotes from Psalm 44, a very somber song just as it is:

Rom 8:36 *Just as it is written, "For your sake we are being put to death all day long; we were considered as sheep to be slaughtered."*

That was God's people under the Old Covenant. Those words are going to be true of the church before this millennium ends. God has not promised to keep us from persecution. In fact he has warned us to anticipate. But he said persecution can never separate you from the love of God.

All around this earth our brothers and sisters are laying own their lives. They are being imprisoned they are being beaten. They are being persecuted. But thank God because they are not being separated from the love of God.

Rom 8: 37 *But in all these things we overwhelmingly conquer through Him who loved us*

In all these things (tribulation, distress, persecution, famine, nakedness, peril and sword) we overwhelmingly conquer. KJV says that in all these things, we are more than conquerors.

It means that you will go into tests, you will go into battles but when you come out, you will have more than when you went in. You have not only won but you have gained spoils. That is what it means to be more than a conqueror. That is what Paul promises us. In all these things we overwhelmingly conquer.

Then we come to this glorious conclusion:

Rom 8:38 *For I am convinced that neither death, nor life, nor angels, nor principalities, nor things present, nor things to come, nor powers,*

Rom 8:39 *nor height, nor depth, nor any other created thing, will be able to separate us from the love of God, which is in Christ Jesus our Lord.*

It is something when a person says I am convinced. It carries conviction with it. What is Paul talking about is an eternal and inseparable union with Jesus our Savior and Messiah through the spirit which nothing can ever break. And this is the goal of the Christian life.

Let us close with this scripture: *For you have died and your life is hidden with Christ in God. When Christ, who is our life, is revealed, then you also will be revealed with Him in glory.* (Colossians 3: 3-4)

When did we die? We died when Jesus died on the cross. We have a hidden life which the world cannot see. Christ is our life. That is all you need to know. It is a hidden life.

Then in verses 10 and 11: *and have put on the new self who is being renewed to a true knowledge according to the image of the One who created him — a renewal in which there is no distinction between Greek and Jew, circumcised and uncircumcised, barbarian, Scythian, slave and freeman, but Christ is all, and in all. (Colossians 3: 10-11)*

And you know that is it. Christ is all. When we have him we have everything. He is all we need.

PART 2 - THE DESTINY OF ISRAEL AND THE CHURCH

Romans Chapter 9 - 11

This is the first of four teaching sections in which we will be working through Romans chapters 9, 10 and 11. We will work through them systematically. These chapters focus on the destiny of Israel.

Without an understanding of these chapters, the Gospel is incomplete. For too long, God's people have been denied the precious truths which they contain. Yet without them, the church cannot truly understand her destiny.

Some theologians and preachers think that these chapters (9, 10 and 11) are a digression. That dealing with Israel is a sort of side issue that really is not of importance. To classify those chapters as a digression or an afterthought is an expression of Gentile bias. In these chapters, God's dealings with Israel, which is the main theme, but by no means the exclusive theme, provides a historical demonstration of many vital spiritual principles which apply equally to Christians. They have been out worked in the history of Israel, but they are there for our benefit because God has not changed his principles. These same principles are working in our lives and we need to know them.

The title of this section is: THE DESTINY OF ISRAEL AND THE CHURCH and the central theme is: God's sovereignty and grace operating through his choice.

Now these are great central truths of the New Testament and very few modern day Christians have laid hold upon them because there is a wide gap in the understanding of Christians today.

If we could draw a little comparison, much of the church today is like what astronomy was before. When people believed that the Sun revolved around the earth. It was an intellectual and a religious revolution before the truth could be established that the Earth actually revolves around the Sun. Before that, man's view of the universe, was earth cantered. Because of that, there were many areas that man could not accurately measure or understand.

To draw a comparison, many Christians have a view of God which is man cantered. They view Jesus Christ as someone revolving around us and that he is there to meet our needs and answer our prayers and do what we want. That is a totally distorted picture of God. Thank God that Jesus is there. He answers our prayer. He takes care of us. He loves us and provides for us but we are not the centre.

Jesus Christ is like the Sun and our little Earth revolves around him. When you comprehend that Jesus is the centre, then other things begin to fall into place which you cannot accurately understand, if you are viewing everything from a self-cantered perspective.

CHAPTER 9: THE SOVEREIGNTY OF GOD

(Romans 9:1 - 9:33)

9.1 Introduction to God's Sovereignty

What is the meaning of the word sovereignty? This is a word that is rarely used amongst modern Christians. Sovereignty means this: 'God does what he wants, when he wants, in the way he wants and he asks no one's permission.'

There are a lot of Christians who think that God needs their permission to do things in their lives. That is not so. Sovereignty means that God will have everything in your life the way he wants and without your permission. That is sovereignty. Your reaction is to try to see how you can adjust to it.

God does what he wants, when he wants, the way he wants and he does not ask my permission and he does not ask your permission.

Now, there is a contrary philosophy, which is also a kind of religion which is very prevalent in our modern society. It is called HUMANISM. Humanism says man is at the center. If God does anything he has to get our approval and if we do not approve, God will not do it.

These are two opposing views of the world and of life. The biblical view is God centered: everything begins with God and ends with God. The humanistic view which has infiltrated the church to a remarkable extent says that God needs our permission before he does anything. If we do not like what he does we will withhold our permission. That is the attitude.

We can look at a number of key verses from these chapters: chapters 9 10 and 11, which pick out the main themes.

The first Key Scripture is Romans 9:11: '*...that God's purpose according to his choice might stand not because of works that because of him who calls.*'

That is God's sovereignty. It happens because God chose and God did not choose because we earned it or deserved it. He just chose because he chose.

There is a very important question you need to ask yourself. Do you trust God to choose? It is a very important question in your life. Many people especially those who have lost loved ones really struggle with this question.

Job said: *...the Lord gave and the Lord took away.* (Job 1:21)

If you trust God to give, do you also trust him to take away? It is completely illogical to only trust God to give and not to take away. Many of us need to ask ourselves: do I trust God? Do I trust his choice? Do I trust his timing? When you can come to the point of trusting Him, you will be a much more peaceful person.

The second key scripture is Romans 9:16: '*So then it does not depend on the man who wills or the man who runs, but on God who has mercy.*'

Ultimately it is not our effort. It is not our cleverness. It is God's mercy. There is this kind of silence inside when you try to absorb this. Maybe some of you scarcely ever really face that. It is the results that really matter in your life. Nothing comes because of all your efforts or of your cleverness. They come because God is merciful. It is good because we can trust God's mercy much more, than we can trust our own cleverness.

The third Key scripture is Romans 10:4: '*For Christ is the end of the law for righteousness to everyone who believes.*'

Many of us are familiar with that Scripture but many of us have not really applied it in our religious lives. We are still somehow trusting in keeping a set of rules to achieve righteousness with God and it does not work.

Christianity is not a set of rules. What is it? That is another question Romans 10:9 says... *if you confess with your mouth Jesus as Lord, and believe in your heart that God raised Him from the dead, you will be saved;*

That is the most important single piece of information you need in your whole life. How can I be saved? And that is the answer.

The fourth Key Scripture is Romans 11:5 - says... *'In the same way then, there has also come to be at the present time a remnant according to God's gracious choice.'*

We are back again. It all depends on God's grace and his choice.

Then the fifth Key Scripture is Romans 11:22 words that are desperately needed in the contemporary church: *'Behold then the kindness and severity of God; to those who fell, severity, but to you, God's kindness, if you continue in His kindness; otherwise you also will be cut off.'*

A lot of preaching only deals with God's kindness but there is another side to God - Its severity. It is the way we relate to God that will determine which side of God we see.

Then the sixth Key Scripture is Romans 11:29 *'for the gifts and calling of God are irrevocable'*

Once God has given something he never withdraws it. Once God has called someone, he never withdraws his calling.

Then the seventh Key Scripture is Romans 11:36 *'for from him (God) and through him and to him are all things.'*

Everything starts with God, is maintained by God and ends with God.

9.2 Paul's Agony Over Israel

Now we will go into a more detailed review of these chapters starting with chapter 9. We need to bear in mind that the chapter divisions were not in the original letter. They were put in by a translator.

It is important for modern readers to have those breaks, but you have to bear in mind that they are subjective. They are not necessarily correct. They are just the best that the translator could do and so we should not make too big a gap between chapter 8 and chapter 9.

Chapter 8 ends with this glorious conclusion: that nothing can separate us from the love of God in Christ and then Paul goes on with what is a remarkable contrast. He actually says I wish I could be separated from the love of God for the sake of my fellow Israelites, but of course God does not agree with that. You need to understand that Paul has always been viewed with real hostility by the Jewish people. A lot of Jewish people say Jesus we can accept but Paul no. One reason is that they consider him to be a source of anti-Semitism and even in his own life he was bitterly persecuted by the Jewish people because he was taking the gospel to the Gentiles. His own Jewish people felt that he was taking something that belonged exclusively to them and giving it to people whom they considered to be very inferior and unworthy. If you study the life of Paul as revealed in the New Testament, you will find that that was the main reason why he was persecuted by his own people.

So you have to bear in mind that Paul who deeply loved his own Jewish people had this tremendous burden all through his ministry, that they regarded him as a traitor.

So here he begins this chapter by declaring his complete commitment to the well-being of his own people and you have to understand it from that background.

Rom 9:1 I am telling the truth in Christ, I am not lying, my conscience testifies with me in the Holy Spirit,

Something he takes very serious

Rom 9:2 that I have great sorrow and unceasing grief in my heart

What is the cause of his sorrow and his grief?

Rom 9:3 *for I could wish that I myself were accursed, separated from Christ for the sake of my brethren, my kinsmen according to the flesh,*

He was so deeply concerned about the condition of his fellow Jewish people that he said that; I wish that I would become lost if God could accept them in my place. That is an amazing statement.

I think when someone is called to the ministry; one of the conditions for doing what God wants done is to bear a real burden for the well-being of God's people.

In Exodus 32, which is the scene after Israel had made the golden calf and Moses had to come up and intercede with God on their behalf and following:

Then Moses returned to the LORD, and said, "Alas, this people has committed a great sin, and they have made a god of gold for themselves. "But now, if You will, forgive their sin—and if not, please blot me out from Your book which You have written!" (Exodus 32:31, 32)

God's answer is worth listening to.

The LORD said to Moses, "Whoever has sinned against Me, I will blot him out of My book. (Exodus 32:33)

Do you think that still applies? I think God only has one book. I think it is very rushed to assume automatically that because of some event in your past your name still remains permanently in the book of the Lord.

Moses and Paul, were the only two men who had that intense devotion to God's people that they were willing to become lost if that could bring salvation to them. Of course it could not and there was only one person who could do that – Jesus.

Then he describes what makes them a special people, which was God's dealing with them for over a period of say 2000 years. And he speaks about eight specific distinctive privileges which Israel enjoyed.

Rom 9:4 who are Israelites, to whom belongs the adoption as sons, and the glory and the covenants and the giving of the Law and the temple service and the promises,

Rom 9:5 whose are the fathers, and from whom is the Christ according to the flesh, who is over all, God blessed forever. Amen.

1. The adoption as sons: When the Lord was telling Pharaoh to release Israel in Exodus 4:22, he said; Israel is my son, my firstborn. Let him go that he may serve me. Then he said to Pharaoh if you do not let him go I will demand your firstborn and that is what happened. So there is God's declaration - Israel is my son, my firstborn amongst the nations.

2. The glory: The visible manifest of God's presence in various forms - as a cloud, as a fire and so on.

3. The covenants: All the covenants of the Bible from Noah onwards and were revealed to Israel.

4. The giving of the law: On Mount Sinai.

5. The temple service

6. The promises: The promises of God were all given to the Jewish people.

7. The fathers: The patriarchs

8. From whom The Messiah according to the flesh i.e. according to his human nature.

Then it says of Jesus: who is over all God blessed forever amen. This is one of the various places in which Paul specifically gives the title of God to the Lord Jesus Christ.

9.3 God's Sovereign Choice Determines Who His People Are

Here, we are now dealing with the sovereignty of God and the calling of God. This is where it is brought out more clearly than in any other passage in the Bible. Two examples are given from the early history of Israel to emphasize that; it is not our decision that really matters, but God's decision.

Let us consider this. You are not a Christian because you decided to be a Christian. Primarily you are a Christian because Jesus chose you. If Jesus had never chosen, you could never have made the choice. So the initiative does not come from you but from the Lord. You have the privilege of responding, but you do not take the initiative and this is what Paul is emphasizing here.

Let us look at what Paul says. He takes two examples where God made a choice in the descendants of Abraham. In each case and in a certain sense it was seemed unnatural choice. But it was God's choice that determined history. So he says in Romans 9:6

Rom 9:6 But it is not as though the word of God has failed.

That is the Word of God that came to Israel. You might say well Israel failed in a certain sense. That is true although not entirely true. But God's Word did not fail. It accomplished his purpose.

For they are not all Israel who are descended from Israel;

That is very important to understand. What Paul is saying is that, not all people who are Israelites by natural birth are accepted as Israel by God. Paul says God did not include all who might have been included, but he separated out some to whom he gave the title.

Rom 9:7 nor are they all children because they are Abraham's descendants, (Then he quotes the words that God spoke to Abraham about the son whom he promised) *but: "Through Isaac your descendants will be named."*

So what he is saying is that Abraham had two sons - Ishmael and Isaac. Ishmael by Hagar and Isaac by Sarah but the only one that is counted as descendants of Abraham in this sense are the ones descended from Isaac. So out of the two God excluded the older and chose the younger.

There is no suggestion here that God gives the name Israel to us as Christians. That is not even near what God is saying. What God is saying is he reduces the number of people to whom the word Israel applies, who are recognized as Abraham's descendants. The descendants of Ishmael in that sense are excluded and only the descendants of Isaac are included.

But that is not the end because when we go to the next generation and we go to Isaac's wife Rebecca, Rebecca became pregnant with twins who were struggling in the womb. When she went to inquire of the Lord in prayer, the Lord told her that you have got two different kinds of Nations in your womb. He said one will be stronger than the other and the older will serve the younger. That is contrary to the normal tradition of the Middle East. Twice God excluded the older and chose the younger.

Here is where Paul does everything he can to emphasize that it did not depend on anything that Esau or Jacob had done because before they were born, God said I reject Esau and I choose Jacob. What Paul is emphasizing here is that it really depends on God's choice.

Do you trust God to make the right choice? Do you or do you not? A lot of people do not. It is a personal decision and each one of us has to make that decision.

Rom 9:8 That is, it is not the children of the flesh who are children of God, but the children of the promise are regarded as descendants.

It is not merely fleshly descent by natural inheritance that makes Israel. Let us turn for a moment to 1st Peter 1:23. Speaking to born-again Christians, Peter says… *for you have been born again not of seed which is perishable but imperishable, that is, through the living and enduring word of God.* (1Peter 1:23)

So what is the generative seed that makes us God's people? It is God's Word. This principle goes back right into the history of the patriarchs because it was not a natural descent that determined the ones that I were to be accepted by God as his people but the embracing of the promise of God's Word. The seed was the Word of God. So to be a true Israelite, you had to first of all be descended from Abraham, Isaac and Jacob and you also had to have the seed of God's Word received by faith in your heart to make you really part of God's chosen people.

Let's read Romans 9:8 again. *That is it is not the children of the flesh who are children of God not by natural descent only but the children of the promise are regarded as descendants.*

The promise is the Word of God. And then he gives this word of promise. That is, the word which the Lord God spoke to Abraham.

Rom 9:9 *For this is the word of promise: "At this time I will come, and Sarah shall have a son."*

So that is the first example of the promise. So within all those that descended from Abraham, only those who have received the promise of God by FAITH in their hearts are considered the people of God. That is what makes them truly God's people.

Then we take this second example which is even more remarkable.

Rom 9:10 *And not only this, but there was Rebekah also, when she had conceived twins by one man, our father Isaac;*

Rom 9:11 *for though the twins were not yet born and had not done anything good or bad, so that God's purpose according to His choice would stand, not because of works but because of Him who calls,*

Rom 9:12 *it was said to her, "The older will serve the younger."*

Paul here emphasizes that it was God's choice that was decisive. This is a very difficult truth for people to accept in our modern civilization. Everything in our civilization has been permeated by the influence of humanism - even the church.

So we really have an attitude which says: God if you are going to do that, you better give an account to me why? The Bible says 'God does not give an account of anything'.

Remember what sovereignty means: God does what he wants, when he wants, the way he wants and he does not ask our permission.

So to demonstrate this, with the utmost clarity, God took the case of twins in a woman's womb, both from the same father even before they were born. Before they had any opportunity to do anything good or bad and He said:

Rom 9:13 Just as it is written, "Jacob I loved, but Esau I hated."

God said; I am rejecting the older i.e. Esau. If you follow the life of the two of them, by modern day standards – Esau would pass as the good guy and Jacob as the bad guy. Esau did nobody any harm whereas Jacob cheated him. The things that Jacob did would be frowned upon today. I am not saying that God endorsed the things Jacob did, but that God does not choose the people we might choose. That is why some of us got chosen.

I mean if I had been God, I would have never chosen myself.

When I first told my former friends that I had given my life to Christ, most of them said – of all the people you! They could not believe it had happened to me. Some of them still do not believe up to date. I am glad that the choice was not left to them. I am glad the choice was not left to me either. If I had been God, I do not think I would ever have taken the risk he took when he chose me.

The question is: Do you really trust God to make the right choice. Sometimes we tend to think that God made the right choice with me, but not some of the people. If it would have been up to you, you would not have chosen them.

Verse 13; *just as it is written, Jacob I loved but Esau I hated* is quoted from the last prophet of the Old Testament – Malachi.

The book of Malachi begins by God telling Israel, "I have loved you" and he says Esau I hate. That is something to ponder about God. Is God a hater as well as a lover? - In a way yes. You cannot love if you are not also prepared to hate. The Bible says: he that loves the Lord hates evil. Your capacity to love is probably determined by your capacity to hate. You have got to be sure that you love the right thing and hate the wrong thing.

9.3.1 Who is an Israelite?

Now, we are going to clear the air regarding: who in the New Testament is called Israel. This is important for us to be able to understand these chapters because there is a wrong teaching today that Israel is no longer Israel and that the church is now Israel. Whom does the New Testament give the title Israel? Has the New Testament withdrawn the title from historical Israel - the Jewish people? And has the New Testament now given the title to the church?

We are going to look at some objective statements from the Bible and principally from the New Testament. The word Israel or Israelite (they are interchangeable) are used 74 times in the New Testament.

There is no possibility that they could be applied to the church. In fact in many passages they are applied in a sense that distinguishes Israel from the church.

Israel is never used in the New Testament as a title for the church. In Galatians 6:15 and 16 we have a phrase which has confused many:

For in Christ Jesus neither circumcision availeth anything, nor uncircumcision, but a new creature. And as many as walk according to this rule, peace be on them, and mercy, and upon the Israel of God. (Galatians 6:15-16)

Now there we have the phrase 'The Israel of God'. Most people today especially in the west interpret the Israel of God as the church. However Romans 9:6-8...*For they are not all Israel who are descended from Israel; or are they all children because they are Abraham's descendants but: "Through Isaac your descendants will be named. "That is, it is not the children of the flesh who are children of God...but the children of the promise are regarded as descendants."*

This gives us two kinds of Israel:

1. The Israel of God who are the children of promise and,
2. The children of the flesh who still go by the name - Israel

Therefore in reference to the Phrase: 'Israel of God', Paul is talking about those Israelites who have been completed by their relationship to the Messiah and have thus become the Israel of God in this sense. Paul is applying the word Israel only to those Israelites or Jews who are not merely Israelites by birth but who have also received the seed of the promise of God's Word and experience new birth in Christ.

Now the difference is this, the Gentiles are an un-ploughed field. God had never dealt with them in this way. So they are a new creation. They simply stepped out from the old into the new. Whereas Israel of the Jewish people was a people with whom God had been dealing for 14 or 15 centuries and they already had some kind of a relationship with God which only had to be completed by the acknowledgment of the Messiah.

In Isaiah 43:21 speaking about Israel as heirs, the Lord says: *This people have I formed for myself; they shall shew forth my praise.*

The word form is the word that is used of a potter molding a vessel. God had been molding Israel for 15 centuries. It was a people that he had already formed for himself. They needed to be completed by the acknowledgment of Messiah.

On the other hand, if they fail to acknowledge the Messiah as Paul says in Romans 11, they were broken off. Then in Romans 15 verse 8 Paul says: *For I say that Christ has become a servant to the circumcision* (that is the Jewish people) *on behalf of the truth of God to confirm the promises given to the fathers,*

It was not something new. They had the promises for many centuries. To them Jesus was a servant to confirm the promises they already knew and were expecting to see fulfilled. Then Paul goes on in the next verse: *and for the Gentiles to glorify God for His mercy; as it is written, "Therefore I will give praise to you among the gentiles, and I will sing to your name." (Romans 15:9)*

You can see the difference: that the Jewish people had many promises already given to them which had to be fulfilled and the Gentiles had no promises. They did not depend on God's faithfulness to fulfill a promise but they only depended on God's mercy.

That is why there is a difference between those who have merely come into the new creation out of nothing, spiritually, and those that have been completed because they already had received the promises.

Now there is another passage that we need to look at in Romans chapter 2 verses 28 and 29. These verses speak about the one who is a true Jew. Again this is extremely controversial.

For he is not a Jew who is one outwardly, nor is circumcision that which is outward in the flesh. But he is a Jew who is one inwardly; and circumcision is that which is of the heart, by the Spirit, not by the letter; and his praise is not from men, but from God. (Romans 2:28-29)

Again this scripture is not extending the use of the term Jew. It is restricting the term. What Paul is saying is that, it is not sufficient merely to be Jew outwardly, merely to have natural descent or to have physical circumcision. It has to be the circumcision of the heart. It has to be something inside you which receives God's praise. So again it is restricted.

In John 1:47 Jesus saw Nathanael coming to him and said of him *behold a true Israelite in whom is no deceit.*

Nathanael was a true Israelite because he was not merely was an Israelite by natural descent, but he had the inner attitude of heart which God requires.

So the Israel of God or the true Israelite is not somebody who is a Gentile and has come to Christ. It is a Jew or an Israelite who has been completed, out of all his background, in the promises of God extending over many centuries.

One other example is in 1st Corinthians 10:18. Paul says *Behold Israel after the flesh: are not they which eat of the sacrifices partakers of the altar?*

What is Paul saying when he says look at Israel according to the flesh is - look at those who are only Israelites by natural descent but do not fulfill the inner conditions of heart. The reason is claimed because they have gone into idolatry. So they were still Israelites by natural descent, but they certainly were not accepted by God because of their inner condition of heart.

Therefore, Israel in the New Testament means precisely the same as Israel in the Old Testament. But there are a few passages maybe two or three where Paul uses Israel in a restrictive sense - meaning people who fulfill two qualifications.

1. They are Israelites by natural descent

2. They fulfill the inner requirements in the heart which God looks for to make them truly his people.

9.3.2 Proof That Israel is Israel & The Church is The Church

In the previous section, we considered the use of the word Israel in the New Testament and we saw that in the New Testament, Israel is never a synonym for the church. Israel is one thing and the church is another. However Israel is many times a type of the church. Many of the things that happened to Israel, as Paul says in 1st Corinthians 10, are written to warn us so that we may not make the same mistakes that Israel made. Therefore, Israel in the New Testament is never used as a name for the church.

On the other hand, Israel all through the Bible is a type of the church. The things that happened to Israel contain very important lessons for us as Christians today.

There has been in the church, for probably at least 16 centuries, a theory or a theology that because Israel were so rebellious and disobedient, and also because to a certain extent, they were responsible for the crucifixion of the Lord Jesus. They were not solely responsible. Because of that, this theory evolved that God has set aside Israel and that he has replaced Israel by the church.

This is a very popular theory today and a lot of people are propagating it. It cannot be accepted and I want to give you three reasons why we should not accept it.

The theory says that: God has finally and forever rejected Israel as a people and that in their place he has chosen and put up the church and that all God's commitments and covenants and promises to Israel are no longer valid.

9.3.2.1 First Reason why we cannot accept this theory of replacement

First of all this theology discredits the reliability of Scripture because the Bible contains many very clear specific statements of what God says he will do which will never be fulfilled if God has finally and forever set aside Israel. In other words, the proponents of this theory imply that the Bible is no longer a reliable book. This is a tremendously serious objection.

Let us look through a number of scriptures which clearly state God's purpose and plan for Israel and what he's going to do. Then consider for yourself whether these could possibly be fulfilled if God had permanently set aside Israel.

Isaiah 11: About the 'Restored Remnant', says:

Then it will happen on that day that the Lord Will again recover the second time with His hand The remnant of His people, who will remain, From Assyria, Egypt, Pathros, Cush, Elam, Shinar, Hamath, And from the islands of the sea. And He will lift up a standard for the nations and assemble the banished ones of Israel, and will gather the dispersed of Judah from the four corners of the earth. (Isaiah 11: 11, 12)

Those words were written before the Babylonian captivity of Israel. But even before that took place, Isaiah predicted there would be a second re-gathering not from Babylon, but a secondary re-gathering. Of the many places mentioned, Jews have not fully returned to Israel.

On the other hand, every statement in these scriptures is being fulfilled in this century i.e. the re-gathering of the Jews. This means that God is still dealing with Israel as a nation.

Then in **Jeremiah 30:** Jeremiah was not overindulgent to the sins of Israel. A few prophets have taken so much time to tell Israel all the evil things that they have done. Jeremiah is certainly not biased but he says in Jeremiah 30 verse 3: *'For behold, days are coming,' declares the LORD, 'when I will restore the fortunes of My people Israel and Judah.' The LORD says, 'I will also bring them back to the land that I gave to their forefathers and they shall possess it.'"* (Jeremiah 30:3)

Now, there is only one land that agrees to that description. The land that God gave the forefathers of Israel and Judah and God says I will bring them back and they will possess it. They never possessed it after the Babylonian captivity. They were always as if they were tenants in a land at the discretion of a Gentile empire. And eventually, they were uprooted and driven out of the land by the Roman Empire in 70 AD. So nothing in that period answers to these words. But again everything that is written there has been fulfilled and is being fulfilled in our days. This is very real but that is not the primary reason. The primary reason is, because God says it in his word.

Then in **Jeremiah 31:10:** *Hear the word of the LORD, O nations,* (that is the Gentiles) *and declare in the coastlands afar off,* (All parts of the earth that border on the oceans) *and say, "He who scattered Israel will gather him and keep him as a shepherd keeps his flock."*

Again, this scripture is being fulfilled in our day.

Then in **Jeremiah 31:35-37:** *Thus says the LORD, Who gives the sun for light by day and the fixed order of the moon and the stars for light by night, Who stirs up the sea so that its waves roar; The LORD of hosts is His name: "If this fixed order departs from before Me," declares the LORD, "Then the offspring of Israel also will cease from being a nation before Me forever. "Thus says the LORD, "If the heavens above can be measured and the foundations of the earth searched out below, Then I will also cast off all the offspring of Israel for all that they have done," declares the LORD.*

Very simply stated, that means that as long as you can go outside, and look up in the sky and see that the Sun and the Stars are still there in their divinely appointed order. As long as you can stand on the border of the sea and look at the waves roaring, by that alone you will know that Israel is still a nation before the Lord.

Then in **Jeremiah 32: 37-42** (This is specifically referring to Israel)

37 "Behold, I will gather them out of all the lands to which I have driven them in My anger, in My wrath and in great indignation; and I will bring them back to this place and make them dwell in safety. 38 "They shall be My people, and I will be their God; 39and I will give them one heart and one way, that they may fear Me always, for their own good and for the good of their children after them. 40"I will make an everlasting covenant with them that I will not turn away from them, to do them good; and I will put the fear of Me in their hearts so that they will not turn away from Me. 41"I will rejoice over them to do them good and will faithfully plant them in this land with all My heart and with all My soul. 42"For thus says the LORD, 'Just as I brought all this great disaster on this people, so I am going to bring on them all the good that I am promising them.

When God says that he will do something with all his heart and all his soul, there is not really much choice for anybody else. Notice this final verse 42: *for thus says the Lord just as I brought all this calamity on this people so I am going to bring on them all the good that I am promising them.*

The calamity that God has brought on Israel is a historical fact. History records all that has happened to Israel. It was not literal or spiritual. It has happened and God says: in just the same way as I brought the calamity upon them, I am going to bring all the good upon him. It is going to be real in the records of history. Again we live in an exciting time when we can see God doing the very thing he said he would do.

Then in **Ezekiel 20:40-44**

40"For on My holy mountain, on the high mountain of Israel," declares the Lord GOD, "there the whole house of Israel, all of them, will serve Me in the land; there I will accept them and there I will seek your contributions and the choicest of your gifts, with all your holy things. (Again, there is only one place of answers to that description – the whole house of Israel.) *41"As a soothing aroma I will accept you when I bring you out from the peoples and gather you from the lands where you are scattered; and I will prove Myself holy among you in the sight of the nations.* (God says my name will be glorified. Holiness will be demonstrated in what I do in you) *42"And you will know that I am the LORD, when I bring you into the land of Israel, into the land which I swore to give to your forefathers. 43"There you will remember your ways and all your deeds with which you have defiled yourselves; and you will loathe yourselves in your own sight for all the evil things that you have done.* (God does not diminish the evil. In fact he emphasizes it.) 44*"Then you will know that I am the LORD when I have dealt with you for My name's sake, not according to your evil ways or according to your corrupt deeds, O house of Israel," declares the Lord GOD.'"*

The Lord is very clear. He said, you do not deserve it but I am doing it that my name may be glorified and to prove my faithfulness.

Then in **Ezekiel 36:22-28**: This is like a recapitulation of the history of Israel over the last 60 years or so.

22*"Therefore say to the house of Israel, 'Thus says the Lord GOD, "It is not for your sake, O house of Israel, that I am about to act, but for My holy name, which you have profaned among the nations where you went.*

Again God emphasizes that you have not deserved it. You have got no claim on it, but I am doing it because I have committed myself to do it. I am demonstrating who I am in the eyes of the nations because of my faithfulness to you.

I think we should all be glad that God does not remember our corrupt deeds. How many of us would feel confident before the Lord if he would not say I will not remember all the bad things you have done? These are very important principles because we need them just as much as Israel does.

23*"I will vindicate the holiness of My great name which has been profaned among the nations, which you have profaned in their midst. Then the nations will know that I am the LORD,"* declares the Lord GOD, *"when I prove Myself holy among you in their sight.* (This is God's testament to all nations) 24*"For I will take you from the nations, gather you from all the lands and bring you into your own land.* (Why is it their land? because God gave it to them and that settles it.) 25*"Then I will sprinkle clean water on you, and you will be clean; I will cleanse you from all your filthiness and from all your idols.*

I will re-gather you still in your filthiness. Many people think that if Israel is to be re-gathered, first of all they must repent and then God will take them back. God says: that is not the way I am going to do it. I am going to take them back and then I am going to deal with them so that they will repent.

26"*Moreover, I will give you a new heart and put a new spirit within you; and I will remove the heart of stone from your flesh and give you a heart of flesh.*

God has never said to any other nation that they have a heart of stone. But he says to Israel, you have a heart of stone. What is a heart of stone? It is a heart that cannot respond to the Spirit of God. It is incapable of doing it and that was a judgment of God upon them.

27"*I will put My Spirit within you and cause you to walk in My statutes, and you will be careful to observe My ordinances.*

What Israel is going to discover is that, the only way you can ever walk in God statues, is when God puts his spirit within you. The same principles apply to you and me.

28"*You will live in the land that I gave to your forefathers; so you will be My people, and I will be your God.*

Again there is only one land that answers to that description. Notice the end purpose of all God's dealings with Israel. You will be my people and I will be your God. In a certain sense God has taken special responsibility for dealing with the Jewish people.

Then in **Amos 9:14-15:** Amos is another prophet that did not have much good to say to Israel. That is about nine chapters of condemnation and judgment and when you think, that the situation is hopeless, in the last two verses suddenly came out with what is like dawn after a long dark stormy night. God says in in these scripture: 14"*Also I will restore the captivity of My people Israel, and they will rebuild the ruined cities and live in them; They will also plant vineyards and drink* *their wine, and make gardens and eat their fruit. 15"I will also plant them on their land, and they will not again be rooted out from their land which I have given them," Says the LORD your God. (Amos 9:14-15)*

Every one of those things is happening now. They have rebuilt at least nine biblical sites in the last 50 years. They have also made gardens. If ever, there have been an agricultural people, it is Israel. They have also restored vines cultivation, which failed completely under the Muslims, because they do not believe in alcohol.

So, in this present restoration of Israel, that they will never lose the land again. In the midst of innumerable forces arrayed against them, which have always been since the day, the state of Israel was born. Every day that Israel exists, is a miracle. But that miracle is going to continue until God has fulfilled his word.

Then in **Zechariah 14** in verse 2 and following: *2For I will gather all the nations against Jerusalem to battle, and the city will be captured, the houses plundered, the women ravished and half of the city exiled, but the rest of the people will not be cut off from the city.* (This is going to be a serious situation) *3Then the LORD will go forth and fight against those nations, as when He fights on a day of battle. 4In that day His feet will stand on the Mount of Olives, which is in front of Jerusalem on the east; and the Mount of Olives will be split in its middle from east to west by a very large valley, so that half of the mountain will move toward the north and the other half toward the south.* (It is going to happen here the way God says it) *5You will flee by the valley of My mountains, for the valley of the mountains will reach to Azel; yes, you will flee just as you fled before the earthquake in the days of Uzziah king of Judah. Then the LORD, my God, will come, and all the holy ones with Him! (Zechariah 14:2-5)*

At the end of verse five, we get to the climax then the Lord my God will come and all the Holy Ones with him.

Here is the clearest single prediction. This is the place to which the Lord Jesus will return. This is where he ascended to heaven – the

Mount of Olives. And the angels that came and spoke to the disciples said this same Jesus who is taken up from you, will come in like manner as you have seen him go into heaven. He went up in clouds and he will come in clouds.

God is literally going to do all these things.

9.3.2.1 Second reason why we cannot accept this theory of replacement

Now the second reason why we cannot accept this theory of the replacement of Israel is that it discredits the faithfulness of God. Let us read one passage from the Living Bible because it is so vivid. Jeremiah 33 beginning at verse 24:

People say that the Lord chose Judah and Israel and then abandoned them. They are sneering and saying that Israel is not worth to be counted as a nation. But this is the Lord's reply:

24"Have you not observed what this people have spoken, saying, 'The two families which the LORD chose, He has rejected them'? Thus they despise My people, no longer are they as a nation in their sight. 25"Thus says the LORD, 'If My covenant for day and night stand not, and the fixed patterns of heaven and earth I have not established, 26then I would reject the descendants of Jacob and David My servant, not taking from his descendants rulers over the descendants of Abraham, Isaac and Jacob. But I will restore their fortunes and will have mercy on them.'" (Jeremiah 33:24-26)

How exactly is that applicable to our day? People are sneering at Israel asking whether they should be considered a nation because they crucified the Lord. The Bible is so perceptive and it looks ahead with divine telescopic sight and sees how things will be thousands of years after the words were actually written.

9.3.2.1 Third reason why we cannot accept this theory of replacement

Then the third reason why we cannot accept this theory is that it undermines the security of the church. If God can replace Israel in the light of all the statements that he has made, all the covenants and commitments, then why can he not replace the church? What guarantee is there that the church will not be replaced? If I believe that God was replacing Israel, then I would be looking over my shoulder all the time to see who is going to replace us. If you had to consider which group had been less faithful, Israel or the church, it would be very hard to pick. Let us read a few words that Jesus said to two churches, in Revelation chapter 3 the first three verses:

1"To the angel of the church in Sardis write: He who has the seven Spirits of God and the seven stars, says this: 'I know your deeds, that you have a name that you are alive, but you are dead. 2'Wake up, and strengthen the things that remain, which were about to die; for I have not found your deeds completed in the sight of My God.3 'So remember what you have received and heard; and keep it, and repent. Therefore if you do not wake up, I will come like a thief, and you will not know at what hour I will come to you. (Rev 3:1-3)

That does not seem to be better in any way, from what the Lord said to Israel. It seems that they are just about the same. Again in the last message to the church the Church of Laodicea in chapter 3 of Revelation verses 14-16:

14"To the angel of the church in Laodicea write: The Amen, the faithful and true Witness, the Beginning of the creation of God, says this: 15 'I know your deeds, that you are neither cold nor hot; I wish that you were cold or hot. 16 'So because you are lukewarm, and neither hot nor cold, I will spit you out of My mouth. (Rev 3:14-16)

That is very plain speaking. Could that be applied to sections of the church? Are there sections of the church that are neither cold nor hot? How many are there that are not like that?

Now, I want to point out to you that, everything that people have reservations about concerning Israel applies to the church also. God is dealing with the church in precisely the same way as he has dealt with Israel. The origin of all this, is not because we are good or because we merit it, but it is God's sovereign choice. You are not a Christian because you chose Christ. You are a Christian primarily because Christ chose you. If Christ had never chosen you, you would never have been able to choose him. The origin of everything is God's will, God's sovereignty and God's choice. This is just as true of the church as it is of Israel.

In fact in studying God's dealings with Israel, we get a very wonderful lesson of how God deals with us. Let us just take a few scriptures from the New Testament and try and bring this home.

Let us look at 1st Peter 1: 1 & 2:

1Peter, an apostle of Jesus Christ, to those who reside as aliens, scattered throughout Pontus, Galatia, Cappadocia, Asia, and Bithynia, who are chosen,2 according to the foreknowledge of God the Father, by the sanctifying work of the Spirit, to obey Jesus Christ and be sprinkled with His blood: May grace and peace be yours in the fullest measure. (1Peter 1: 1-2)

Although this letter was primarily addressed to Jewish believers, it says of these people at the end of verse one… *who are chosen according to the foreknowledge of God the Father.* So why are we believers? It is because God choose us. God knew what he could make out of each one of us.

Once you grasp this fact, your insecurity begins to dissolve. You do not have to try so hard. You have to accept the fact God chose you. I might not have chosen myself, but God chose me. Why did he choose me? It was according to his foreknowledge. In other words God knew from eternity what he could do with me. God knows from eternity what he can do with each one of you. What a relief. It is not all your effort. Paul says - It is not him who wills or of him who runs but its God who shows mercy.

Most Christians today have completely lost sight of this fact. You are a Christian because God chose you, knowing what he could do with you. So do not complain about your inadequacies because God knew all about them but he still chose you, in a certain sense, because of them. God has chosen the weak things to demonstrate his power.

Verse 2 says: *according to the foreknowledge of God the Father, by the sanctifying work of the Spirit* (So when God has chosen you, his spirit begins to work on you and most of us when it started we were not aware what was happening.), *to obey Jesus Christ and be sprinkled with His blood:* (You see the Holy Spirit brings you to the place where you encounter Jesus Christ and obey) *May grace and peace be yours in the fullest measure.* Peter is actually writing to believing Jews.

The Spirit of God begins working on us long before he brings us to Jesus to be sprinkled with His blood. The blood is not sprinkled on the disobedient. You have to come to the place of obedience before you come under the sprinkling of the blood. When you get out of the place of obedience, you are getting out of the direction of the blood. The blood is not sprinkled on the disobedient.

This is a very important message. If we walk in the light, as he is in the light, the blood of Jesus continually cleanses us from all sin.

Let's look at another scripture. In Romans 8:29 and 30 which is speaking about you and me, it says:

29For those whom He foreknew, He also predestined to become conformed to the image of His Son, so that He would be the firstborn among many brethren; 30 and these whom He predestined, He also called; and these whom He called, He also justified; and these whom He justified, He also glorified. (Rom 8:29 - 30)

Where does it all begin? It begins as Peter said with God's foreknowledge and after God foreknew us he chose us. He made this choice before creation and before the world's came into being. God chose you and me and having chosen us he predestined us i.e. he planned the course that our life would follow. This happened in eternity long before there were a people called Israel. Long before there was anything called the church. God foreknew us and he chose us, he predestined us.

Do not be so worried and concerned. God has got the situation under control. He has made his choice and he is not going to change his mind. Everything in history is working out for the purpose of God. You are not an accident looking for somewhere to happen but you are part of God's eternal plan.

All this is true of the church but it is equally true in Israel. If we discard these truths in regard to Israel we will not retain them in regard to the church.

Having done those three things foreknown, chosen and predestined, then he called us. That is the vital moment in every life i.e. when God calls you. When you hear the call, you better respond. God may never speak to you again.

This is the moment that your destiny is being decided. Once God has called us and we have responded then he justifies us. He acquits us of all sin. Justify means not guilty. When God gives us the garments of salvation, he adds something. He clothes us with a robe of righteousness. That is being justified.

You did not earn that. I did not earn that. None of all our struggles and our religiosity will ever do anything toward that. It happens because God decided it would happen. All you ought to do is trust him. Take a deep breath and relax knowing that God is in control in your life and you can trust him.

The problem is that the church has lost the message partly because of its wrong attitude to Israel. God said the one that touches Israel touches the apple of my eye.

Then once you are justified, you are glorified. To glorify means that you are on the throne with Jesus. He has not only made us alive (Ephesians 2:4-6), he not only resurrected us, he also enthroned us. Spiritually you are seated on the throne with Jesus.

It is ridiculous to think we could ever earn that or deserve it or be good enough. We only get it because God decided to give it to us. The best you can do is to say thank you.

One other beautiful scripture 2ⁿᵈ Timothy 1:9: *who has saved us and called us with a holy calling, not according to our works, but according to His own purpose and grace which was granted us in Christ Jesus from all eternity,*

This is a breathtaking scripture. Another translation says *which was granted us before time.* Again God's purpose and grace was settled for us before time began. Your scenario was written in eternity. All you have got to do is to play your part.

Then in 1ˢᵗ Thessalonians 5:23-24

23Now may the God of peace Himself sanctify you entirely; and may your spirit and soul and body be preserved complete, without blame at the coming of our Lord Jesus Christ. 24Faithful is He who calls you, and He also will bring it to pass. (1 Thessalonians 5:23-24)

You think you can achieve that by your own efforts? What do we depend on? It is His faithfulness. Not our efforts, not our righteousness nor our religiosity. What a breathtaking revelation. You could spend time contemplating these truths and not even begin to touch the reality that they represent. You see, if the church ignores Romans 9, 10 and 11, the church is the poorer one and not Israel.

9.4 God's Will Have Mercy On Whom He Chooses

Having seen God's sovereignty, Paul now goes on to emphasize that we cannot charge God, based on His sovereignty, to choose, in the following verses.

Rom 9:14 *What shall we say then? There is no injustice with God, is there? May it never be!*

Rom 9:15 *For He says to Moses, "I will have mercy on whom I have mercy, and I will have compassion on whom I have compassion."*

You see God's justice is settled. It is un-wavering and you cannot change one jot or one tittle of it.

Romans 6: 23 say: *For the wages of sin is death, but the free gift of God is eternal life in Christ Jesus our Lord.*

What we all deserve is death. But God has chosen you and me to give a gift of eternal life. It is a Gift. The wages of sin is death but the alternative is the free gift of God which is eternal life.

Rom 9:16 *So then it does not depend on the man who wills or the man who runs, but on God who has mercy.*

Rom 9:17 *For the Scripture says to Pharaoh, "For this very purpose I raised you up, to demonstrate my power in you, and that my name might be proclaimed throughout the whole earth."*

Rom 9:18 *So then He has mercy on whom He desires, and He hardens whom He desires.*

You may say, well that is not fair. God will give you justice if you want it. But if you want mercy then do not ask for what is fair because it is not. It goes beyond anything you can earn.

Consider this scripture in Proverbs 16:4: *The LORD has made everything for its own purpose, Even the wicked for the day of evil.*

That is a profound statement. Even the wicked have got their place in God's plan. Pharaoh is perhaps the outstanding example. God says I have raised you up because I wanted to show everybody my power in your wickedness.

Everybody knows that God is fair, and how he hardened Pharaoh's heart, but most people never bother to study the whole record. If you study the whole account of Moses encountering pharaoh, very carefully, you will find that Pharaoh hardened his own heart seven times before God did anything. Then the Lord hardened Pharaoh's heart once. Then Pharaoh hardened his own heart twice more. Finally the Lord hardened Pharaoh's heart six more times. God did not harden Pharaoh's heart until he had hardened it himself seven times. God said in effect, if you are going to be stubborn and determined, then I will see just how stubborn and determined I can make you because I want to demonstrate my power in you.

The two words that are used for the heart of Pharaoh are hard and heavy. We can say Hard is stubborn and heavy is insensitive. So God often let's wickedness run its course to fulfill his purpose. This is very important to understand. Why does God allow those wicked people to go on? It is because He is using them. They are part of his plan. Therefore, even the wicked serve God.

That should set our minds to rest. When we look at the injustice and the wickedness in the world and we confront God, God's answer is "I know all about it and I am in control because the wicked are also serving my purpose".

In Genesis 15, God had promised Abraham that he will give him the land of Canaan but he says until after four generations later.

"Then in the fourth generation they will return here, for the iniquity of the Amorite is not yet complete." (Genesis 15:16)

The Amorites were already a wicked, idolatrous, perverted people. But God said their wickedness has not yet come fully. When it is fully ripe, I will cast in my sickle and reap them and your descendants will take this land.

So when you look at things that are happening in the world today, just think of it as wickedness that is not fully ripe in God's eyes. When eventually, It is fully ripe, God will cast in the sickle reap.

9.5 The Calling of the Gentiles

Rom 9:19 You will say to me then, "Why does He still find fault? For who resists His will?"

In other words everything is working out according to God's purpose. So nobody in a sense is doing other than what God has planned. Then Paul answers:

Rom 9:20 On the contrary, who are you, O man, who answers back to God? The thing molded will not say to the molder, "Why did you make me like this," will it?

What Paul is saying is that: God knows his business. Do not try and instruct him and Paul compares a human life to what a sculpture does. The one who molds the vessel is the one who decides what it will be like.

Then he says in verse 21:

Rom 9:21 Or does not the potter have a right over the clay, to make from the same lump one vessel for honorable use and another for common use?

Rom 9:22 What if God, although willing to demonstrate His wrath and to make His power known, endured with much patience vessels of wrath prepared for destruction?

When you see the wicked flourishing, think of it as God's patience, God is enduring that because his purposes are being worked out.

Peter said: *Consider also that our Lord's patience brings salvation, just as our beloved brother Paul also wrote you with the wisdom God gave him.* (2 Peter 3:15)

One of the most amazing things for all of us is God's patience. How long he endures wickedness. But he does it for the sake of his elect i.e. the chosen ones.

God knows his business and when his purposes are worked out in his chosen ones, he will deal with the wicked. Then we get this beautiful statement in verse 23:

Rom 9:23 *And He did so to make known the riches of His glory upon vessels of mercy, which He prepared beforehand for glory,*

Rom 9:24 *even us, whom He also called, not from among Jews only, but also from among Gentiles.* The Living Bible says *'vessels that God prepared to pour his glory into'* that is you and me.

Therefore when you ask why God permits that in my life, the answer is that he is making you the kind of vessel that will take his glory.

Rom 9:25 *As He says also in Hosea, "I will call those who were not my people, 'my people,' and her who was not beloved, 'beloved.'"*

Rom 9:26 *"and it shall be that in the place where it was said to them, 'you are not my people,' there they shall be called sons of the living God."*

God extends mercy both to the Jews and to Gentiles. Not to Jews only nor to Gentiles only but to both.

And Paul quotes two passages from Hosea in which it is clear that God is going to reject Israel for a time, but then he says in the same place: where it was said to them you are not my people, there it will be said to them you are my people. That is very important for us to remember because God is gathering Israel to the place where it was said "you are not my people that he might declare to them that that they are his people.

Rom 9:27 Isaiah cries out concerning Israel, "Though the number of the sons of Israel be like the sand of the sea, it is the remnant that will be saved;

God has a remnant, whom he has foreknown and chosen. Whom he is going to bring through.

Rom 9:28 For the lord will execute his word on the earth, thoroughly and quickly."

Rom 9:29 And just as Isaiah foretold, "unless the Lord of Sabaoth had left to us a posterity, we would have become like Sodom, and would have resembled Gomorrah."

Then goes on to point out that if God had not left Israel a remnant they would have been totally destroyed and wiped out. So those prophecies of Isaiah indicate very clearly that it is only a chosen remnant of Israel that will ultimately come into the fulfillment of God's purposes.

Then Paul tries to explain why Israel missed it and it is important for all of us because it could happen to you and me. You need to understand that in Paul's perspective 19 centuries ago, it was still an amazing thing that the Jewish people rejected their Messiah. We have got so used to the fact that, 19 centuries later, that it does not surprise us. It takes Paul a great deal of explanation and a great deal of quotation from the Old Testament to convince those who read that this was the way it was going to be.

You see, when we look back 2000 years ago when, in a certain sense, the Jews have been displaced from their position and we are so used to it that we do not really expect an explanation. But if you go back to Paul's time, you will realize that for him and for many others like him, it was a baffling mystery that he had to go to the scriptures to find an answer.

This is his answer: though Israel be multiplied and become exceedingly numerous, it is only the remnant that ultimately will be saved. When we come to the end of chapter 11 it says...all Israel will be saved. All Israel by then will be the chosen remnant.

9.6 Israel's Unbelief

Then Paul goes on:

Rom 9:30 What shall we say then? That Gentiles, who did not pursue righteousness, attained righteousness, even the righteousness which is by faith;

Rom 9:31 but Israel, pursuing a law of righteousness, did not arrive at that law.

Rom 9:32 Why? Because they did not pursue it by faith, but as though it were by works. They stumbled over the stumbling stone,

And he concludes the chapter by saying the Jews who sought to achieve righteousness by keeping a law failed. The Gentiles who did not know anything about a law achieved righteousness.

They tried to earn God's righteousness. But God's righteousness on the standard in which he offers it can only be received by faith. They did not receive it by faith.

The same applies to many church-going Christians today. They still think they have got to earn God's righteousness. If you think you have got to earn it, you will not receive it because, faith and works are mutually exclusive. This is the pattern for the church.

Majority of professing Christians think that they have got to do something to earn God's righteousness. The truth is that it cannot be earned.

Then he comes to the closing in verse 33 (again it is a quotation from Isaiah)

Rom 9:33 just as it is written, "Behold, I lay in Zion a stone of stumbling and a rock of offense, and he who believes in him will not be disappointed."

Another translation says *"and he who believes in him will not be put to shame."*

This is the puzzle. The Jews failed because they rejected Jesus, the Messiah. They rejected the stone that God had laid, on which to build his church.

So the stumbling block over which the Jews fell was the Messiah. In Isaiah 8:14, speaking about the Lord, the Messiah who was also predicted.

"Then He shall become a sanctuary; But to both the houses of Israel, a stone to strike and a rock to stumble over, and a snare and a trap for the inhabitants of Jerusalem. (Isaiah 8:14)

So Jesus is either a sanctuary if you believe and receive him by faith or he's a stone that you stumble over and fall. That is still true today. He is always that way. Either you enter by faith into the sanctuary or you stumble over the stumbling stone. The real essence of the stumbling stone is that you cannot achieve God's righteousness by your own effort. That never suits religious people. Religious people never want to hear that because somehow they think that we can do something to earn it.

There are two other scriptures which we can look at: 1st Corinthians 1:23: Paul speaking about his message: *but we preach Christ crucified, to the Jews a stumbling block and to Gentiles foolishness,*

So again you see the crucified Messiah is the stumbling block. Then Galatians 5:11: *But I, brethren, if I still preach circumcision, why am I still persecuted? Then the stumbling block of the cross has been abolished.*

Always bear in mind that the cross is always a stumbling block because it abolishes all human pride and self-righteousness and leaves us with no claim of our own but only to trust and receive the undeserved mercy of God. It is not sufficient to make that decision once when you get saved. We need to make the decision afresh every day.

CHAPTER 10: THE WORD OF FAITH BRINGS SALVATION

(Romans 10:1 - 21)

10.1 Righteousness based on Faith

Paul begins by a plea for Israel's salvation. We need to bear this in mind. Although it is very exciting about what is going on in the land of Israel today and the many prophecies that are being fulfilled, the one thing that can meet the need of Israel is salvation. Without that, the land and all the other exciting things are ultimately valueless.

So Paul says:

Rom 10:1 Brethren, my heart's desire and my prayer to God for them is for their salvation.

Rom 10:2 For I testify about them that they have a zeal for God, but not in accordance with knowledge.

That is a very unpopular statement with the Jewish people. If there is one thing they do not want to hear it is that they do not know. You can understand why Paul was always persona grata with them.

Rom 10:3 For not knowing about God's righteousness and seeking to establish their own, they did not subject themselves to the righteousness of God.

Notice the phrase – *'they did not subject themselves'*. What was their problem? That phrase indicates pride. That is true for Christians today too. It was not only for the Jews but for every one of us. It is a very humbling thing to have to acknowledge – "I have no claim on God except his undeserved mercy" and the fact that "Jesus took my place and died on the cross for me."

Then we come to this very significant statement:

Rom 10:4 *For Christ is the end of the law for righteousness to everyone who believes.*

This statement applies to all believers. Whether Jew or Gentile, Catholic or Protestant, Baptist or Methodist, it makes no difference. This statement primarily speaks about the Law of Moses. Notice that the Law of Moses is simply a pattern of any law.

That is a very far-reaching statement. If you believe in Jesus, then the death of Christ on the cross has terminated the law as a means of achieving righteousness with God. Again everything religious in us will revolt against that statement. It means I cannot do anything. I can do absolutely nothing but believe and trust God and rely upon his mercy.

Now Christ sacrificial death was both goal and end of the law, as a means of achieving righteousness with God. The whole law looked forward to Jesus. He is the only one who kept the law perfectly in him. The law was perfectly fulfilled in him. In him, the claims of the law were settled so that we can be free from those claims through his substitutionary sacrificial death on our behalf.

Therefore on this particular issue of achieving righteousness with God, Christ is the end of the law. However it is very important to understand and remember that the other purposes of the law, which still apply for you and me, and which we enumerated in chapter 3 of this study, still stand. To recapitulate the purpose for which the law was given, we saw that the law (Torah in Hebrew):

1. Uniquely reveals God's righteousness, holiness, wisdom and justice.

2. Shows men the reality and power of sin. There is nothing else in human experience that can diagnose sin but the law.

3. Shows men they are unable to achieve righteousness by their own efforts.

4. Foreshadows the Savior, the Messiah and foretelling him in prophecy.

5. Kept Israel as a separate nation to which the Messiah could come. Paul used the words: to keep Israel in custody or shut up a nation.

6. Provided humanity with a pattern of a nation that is governed by just laws.

7. Provided inexhaustible material for spiritual meditation.

Paul goes on and says:

Rom 10:5 *For Moses writes that the man who practices the righteousness which is based on law shall live by that righteousness.*

What Paul is saying is this, if you keep the whole law all the time, you do not need any other righteousness. But the fact of the matter is no one ever has. So we cannot depend on that. And James says if you break one commandment you are guilty of the whole law. Therefore you cannot split the Law up into little sections and say well I will keep this part but not that part. It is one single system. You either observe it all, all the time or you do not achieve righteousness by it.

And then he goes on

Rom 10:6 *But the righteousness based on faith speaks as follows:* (Paul is quoting from Deuteronomy) *"Do not say in your heart, 'who will ascend into heaven?' (that is, to bring Christ down),*

Rom 10:7 *or 'Who will descend into the abyss?' (that is, to bring Christ up from the dead)."*

What Paul is saying is that, the righteousness of faith does not depend on something that has got to be done but on something that has already been done. You do not have to go up to heaven or you do not have to descend into the abyss. Christ came from heaven and he went down into hell and he has finished the atonement. It is settled you do not have to do it.

10.2 How Do We Receive Righteousness on The Basis Of Faith?

Then Paul goes on, and these are some of the most important verses we encounter in the New Testament.

Rom 10:8 But what does it say? "The word is near you, in your mouth and in your heart" — that is, the word of faith which we are preaching,

So this righteousness comes through a word - that is the word of the gospel. The message of the gospel is the only key that opens to you the door to the righteousness of faith.

That is how important is the preaching of the Gospel. Until this message is proclaimed, people even though they long for righteousness, they cannot attain it. What an obligation Christians have to proclaim it to the whole of the human race! Not just sit in church on Sunday morning and sing a few hymns. That does not discharge our debt to humanity.

What does it say? *The word is near you in your mouth and in your heart that is the Word of Faith which we are preaching.*

Notice that to achieve righteousness by faith; there are two parts of the human personality must be involved i.e. the mouth and the heart. In these three verses (8, 9, and 10); Paul uses each of them three times. The first two times, it is the mouth and then the heart and the last time it is the heart and then the mouth. That is very significant. It is not easy to know what is in our heart. The only person who really knows the heart is the Lord.

So if you want something in your heart, how do you get it there? By saying it with your mouth and then repeating it. It may seem as though nothing is happening but after a while it happens. It is very interesting because when we say in English 'to learn by heart', the Hebrew say 'to learn by mouth'. How do you learn by heart? It is by repeating with your mouth the same phrase again and again until it is got into your heart.

That is why, it is very important to memorize scripture. When you have memorized it, there is no more effort. It comes from your heart because you have repeated them so often and they are in our heart.

Therefore, if you believe the Bible or you receive the message, then the only way to get it into your heart is by way of your mouth. This is a real important key.

Let us just read verse 9

Rom 10:9 that if you confess with your mouth Jesus as Lord, and believe in your heart that God raised Him from the dead, you will be saved;

That is the clearest single statement on how to be saved. You confess with your mouth Jesus is Lord you believe in your heart that God raised him from the dead. Notice, if you do not believe in his resurrection you cannot be saved.

Then the third time Paul changes the order:

Rom 10:10 for with the heart a person believes, resulting in righteousness, and with the mouth he confesses, resulting in salvation.

We need to know the meaning of the word confess. The English word is derived from a Latin word which means 'to say the same as'. So confession for us, as Bible believing Christians means, we say the same thing with our mouths as God has said in his word. You are not free to add to the word and you should not take away from it.

You may not immediately believe it or feel like it. But if you continuously repeat it, your heart picks it and begins to work in you. E.g. for a sick man he may say: *Jesus himself took our infirmities and bore our sicknesses, by his wounds we are healed.* You may say, "But I am sick"? Well that is perfectly correct. You are sick, but it is not what the word says. So you have to make a decision, whether you are going to side with the word or side with the symptom. This is not a quick and easy decision. It is something that you have to work out.

Here, I am just talking about healing of sickness because the word salvation is the all-inclusive biblical word for everything that was accomplished by the death of Jesus on the cross.

This is not a system you can just make it to work. It has to come from the heart. You see you have got to believe in the heart. It is one thing to believe in the mind and another thing to believe in the heart. How do you get it to the heart, by way of the mouth?

Therefore to receive salvation, you have got to do two things. Confess Jesus with your mouth as Lord and believe in your heart that God raised him from the dead. That is the basic requirement for salvation. And if you are not sure whether you believe it, but you are sincere and you believe the Bible is God's Word, just keep saying with your mouth. That is God's Way.

Going on with Romans 10 verse 11;

Rom 10:11 *For the Scripture says, "Whoever believes in him will not be disappointed."*

Paul goes on to point out in verses 11 and following that this plan of salvation is open to everybody. It is not restricted to Jews only, but it is for whoever believes in Him will not be disappointed. That is Isaiah 28:16.

Rom 10:12 *for there is no distinction between Jew and Greek* (In this respect that we are all sinners); *for the same Lord is Lord of all, abounding in riches for all who call on Him;*

Rom 10:13 *for "Whoever will call on the name of the lord will be saved"*

So you believe in your heart, you confess with your mouth and call upon the name of the Lord. It works for whoever it is.

It is easy when you have the privilege of dealing with people who have no religious or Christian background. You simply explain it to them and they do it and it works and that is wonderful.

Rom 10:14 *how then will they call on Him in whom they have not believed? How will they believe in Him whom they have not heard? And how will they hear without a preacher?*

Rom 10:15 *how will they preach unless they are sent? Just as it is written, "How beautiful are the feet of those who bring good news of good things!"*

This message must be proclaimed by messengers who are sent.

1Now there were at Antioch, in the church that was there, prophets and teachers: Barnabas, and Simeon who was called Niger, and Lucius of Cyrene, and Manaen who had been brought up with Herod the tetrarch, and Saul. 2While they were ministering to the Lord and fasting, the Holy Spirit said, "Set apart for Me Barnabas and Saul for the work to which I have called them." 3Then, when they had fasted and prayed and laid their hands on them, they sent them away. 4So, being sent out by the Holy Spirit, they went down to Seleucia and from there they sailed to Cyprus. (Acts 13:1-4)

Now let's jump to verse 17 before we return to verse 16.

Rom 10:17 so *faith comes from hearing, and hearing by the word of Christ.* Or the Word of God

If you do not have faith, you can get it. It comes. You do not have to sit there in despair and say I have no faith. There is a way to get faith. It is important to understand how faith comes. This scripture tells us that faith comes by hearing and by hearing the Rhema or the proclaimed Word of God. The first step is hearing then out of hearing faith comes.

One problem with many of us as Christians is that we do not take time to hear. We open our Bible read a chapter and close the Bible and go off to work. You must cultivate time to read and listen to the word of God. Today, we can listen to the word of God anywhere because of Technology. Through Podcasts we can download and listen to numerous teachings on the word of God in public transport, in the restaurant, in our car etc. But you need to make time for the word God if you need faith. Out of that faith, you can fulfill the requirements for salvation. You can call upon the name of the Lord and you will be saved.

Now Paul comes back to a thing which was a great problem for him. You can see him struggling with it. Why did my Jewish people not believe? So we are going to look at that for a moment going back to Romans 10 verse 15 and 16.

Rom 10:15 how will they preach unless they are sent? Just as it is written, "How beautiful are the feet of those who bring good news of good things!"

Paul here is quoting Isaiah. He is saying that this is a picture of the people carrying the message of the gospel. Then he says

Rom 10:16 However, they did not all heed the good news; for Isaiah says, "Lord, who has believed our report?"

That quotation is taken from the first verse of Isaiah chapter 53. Isaiah chapter 53 is the most complete prophetic unveiling of the atonement of Jesus Christ, but there is a warning that not everybody is going to believe. The problem is not that God has not provided the solution. The problem is we do not accept it with faith. So Paul is wrestling with this issue and going to verse 18.

Rom 10:18 But I say, surely they have never heard, have they? Indeed they have; (then he quotes Psalm 19 about the testimony of the Sun, the Moon and the Stars but he applies it to the message of the gospel) *"Their voice has gone out into all the earth, and their words to the ends of the world."*

So he said, it is been proclaimed. When Jesus said to his disciples in Mark 16:15 *"go into all the world and proclaim the Gospel to every creature".* From that time, Jesus had released the word into all the world. Until Jesus spoke those words, there was no authority for anybody to go and do it.

So Paul says now the word has been released and then he says verse 19:

Rom 10:19 But I say, surely Israel did not know, did they?

Then he answers his own question. On the contrary Moses the great Authority, warned us and he quotes from Deuteronomy 32:21. Here Moses says to Israel:

"I will make you jealous by that which is not a nation; by a nation without understanding will I anger you."

What is this foolish nation? It is the Gentiles. You and I, the Gentiles, are a foolish nation by comparison with Israel. Israel had 15 centuries of God's instruction. They were set apart, but God is going to anger the Jews by accepting other people whom they despised.

So God took in the silly Gentiles to provoke the religious and clever Jews. He warned them that he was going to do it. In Deuteronomy 32:21 Moses said: *They made me jealous by what is no god and angered me with their worthless idols. I will make them envious by those who are not a people; I will make them angry by a nation that has no understanding.*

Now we also are a people that have a covenant relation with God. That is, the Church of Jesus Christ. That was designed by God to provoke the Jews to jealousy. One thing that is tragic is that over the centuries, the church has done so little to make the Jews jealous.

A story is told of one enthusiastic believer who was working for a very intelligent and influential Jew. The believer with enthusiasm was witnessing to this man with wisdom. The Jewish man did not reject his witness, but he said "when I find something in Christianity that is better than what I have as a Jew, I will accept it". That is the attitude of many Jewish people. Honestly, if you were a Jew and you looked at the church from the outside as presented in the media, and in the lives of some people why would you want to change? The Jewish people take much better care of their own than the church does. You know, when the Jewish people see something that works, they want it.

Still in this theme of - how come that Israel did not believe? And Paul always goes for an answer in the Bible. He goes to the prophets and so he quotes in verse 20 something that is found in Isaiah 65:1

Rom 10:20 *And Isaiah is very bold and says, "I was found by those who did not seek me, I became manifest to those who did not ask for me."*

Who were those who did not seek? Those who did not ask? It is the Gentiles.

Rom 10:21 *But as for Israel He says; "All the day long I have stretched out my hands to a disobedient and obstinate people."*

So Paul says (with his Jewish brothers in mind) we were warned. We could not say that it would never happen to us because our own prophets told us. Our own Moses said God's going to make us jealous for people that really are not the people. By people that are on a different level from us spiritually and even intellectually.

Then through Isaiah, the Lord said I have stretched out my hands to you all day long and you have not reached for me but I have been found by people that are not even looking for me.

So, to sum it up, the difference between the righteousness of faith and the righteousness of law is that: The righteousness of law says, I do this and I do that, I keep this law and I keep that law, therefore I am righteous. Paul said earlier that boasting is excluded by the law of faith.

What does that imply? That if you are righteous by keeping a law, you have got something to boast about. And what is the motive that makes you want to do that? It is Pride. The root problem is Pride. In the history of the universe what was the first sin? It was pride. When the devil comes to tempt you and me he cannot do anything more than what brought about his own disaster. That is where he always aims at.

And what is the greatest single factor that creates pride in human beings? It is religion.

In fact today, the many wars and strife in the world are not caused by the fight between communism and democracy. They are caused by religion. This is a much more dangerous alternative - the rise of religious systems which will be much more enslaving.

If you ever fall into deception or erroneous teaching, your root problem will be pride. The only thing that opens the way to deception in a believer is pride.

Catchy phrases like:

"If you join this group you will be more spiritual"

"This is the group of overcomers"

"We are the ones who have got the answers - join us" etc.

If you join them you can be sure of one thing. You are wrong. This is the motive behind almost every cult. We are the right people, we are better than others, we have more knowledge than others, and we have a higher revelation than others etc.

The only solution is humility. We have to humble ourselves. Humility and faith go together. Pride and unbelief go together. You see, God's method of salvation through faith undercuts all human pride. It leaves us nothing to boast about except as Paul said the cross.

CHAPTER 11: THE ELECTION BY GRACE

(Romans 11:1 - 36)

In this chapter 11, Paul is pointing out that there is amongst the Jewish people, a remnant of believers according to the election by grace. There has always been a remnant. There has never been a time when there have not been Jewish people who believed in Jesus as their Messiah from the first century until this time. Sometimes it is been a small remnant but at this time it is increasing rapidly.

11.1 The Remnant of Israel

Paul raises this crucial question which keeps coming up and which is also one of the primary questions in the church today.

Rom 11:1 I say then, God has not rejected His people, has He? May it never be! (How can we entertain such a thought?) for I too am an Israelite, a descendant of Abraham, of the tribe of Benjamin.

So Paul says I am proof that God has not rejected the entire Jewish people. God has not rejected his people whom he foreknew. We come back again and again to that decisive fact. Those whom God has chosen and foreknown are his people. I do not think there is going to be any surprises for God in eternity. There may be a lot of surprises for us in eternity like…

"Well brother, I never expected to see you, yet you did not have the right doctrine".

"Hey, you did not belong to the right group; I do not know how you made it."

The most shocking surprise of all would be, if we did not get there.

Rom 11:2 God has not rejected His people whom He foreknew. Or do you not know what the Scripture says in the passage about Elijah, how he pleads with God against Israel?

King James says he makes intercession against Israel. Here is a prophet of God interceding against God's people. I do not think we should ever make intercession against the people of God. We might feel that they have strayed but the only intercession we can make is to ask for God's will to be done. We should never yield to interceding against God's people. When I say God's people, I mean the elect… whether Israelites or Christians.

And Elijah said:

Rom 11:3 "Lord, they have killed your prophets, they have torn down your altars, and I alone am left, and they are seeking my life."

And he had to go all the way to Mount Sinai and get back to where the law was given and have this personal interview with the Lord. Remember it was a dramatic interview. He was there on the mountain and a wind passed by and the Lord was not in the wind. Then there was an earthquake but the Lord was not in the earthquake. Then there was a fire but the Lord was not in the fire. Then there was what a still small voice. A sound of gentle blowing that was more impressive and more authoritative than the wind, the earthquake and the fire.

And so the Lord corrected Elijah and said you have got your figures wrong.

Rom 11:4 But what is the divine response to him? "I have kept for myself seven thousand men who have not bowed the knee to Baal."

Notice again the emphasis on God's grace. I have kept for myself. They did not keep themselves. I have kept them they are my reserved remnant. Then Paul goes on to say:

***Rom 11:5** In the same way then, there has also come to be at the present time a remnant according to God's gracious choice.*

The literal translation is, according to the choice of grace. And so we come back to this theme. It is grace that makes God's sovereign choice. God's choice is what settles who his people are to be. God has a remnant both in Israel and in the church. You have to accept that. The same principles apply to us Christians too and it is important that we study the facts about Israel because they apply in principle to us too.

11.2 The Remnant by Grace

Speaking about this remnant that is there by grace, Paul says in verse 6:

***Rom 11:6** But if it is by grace, it is no longer on the basis of works, otherwise grace is no longer grace.*

That is extremely important. If you can earn it, it is not grace. If you deserve it, it is not grace. Grace is not earned and it is not deserved. It is received only by faith. That is why Paul said in Ephesians 2:8: *"by grace you have been saved through faith".* Then he said *"and that not of yourselves, it is the gift of God".* You cannot even boast about the fact that you have faith because God gave you the faith by which you receive His grace. So grace begins where human ability ends. God is continually thrusting us out beyond the level of our own ability so that we may move into his grace.

We will spend a moment to look at the word grace. More often than not, many people who talk about grace know very little about it. This is also so even for the so called evangelicals and Pentecostals. They say, we are not under the law, but they are under their own little laws. Each group has its own set of rules which they keep to achieve a certain end. However, grace is very different from that.

One of the hardest things that humanity faces is to be dependent on God because the very essence of the fall at the Garden of Eden was the desire to be independent of God. Being descendants of Adam, it is the hardest thing for us to overcome and it is the hardest thing for God to deal with, in us.

One of the main tasks of The Holy Spirits' work in you and me is to bring us to the place where we are willing to be dependent on God and on His grace.

Consider these three questions.

- Are you willing not to be in control?
- Are you willing not to be esteemed? and
- Are you willing not to be secure?

That is not easy, but that is the essence of being dependent. You are not in control; your security does not depend on you. You have to depend on the grace of God every moment. That is grace and it is supernatural grace. It does not operate on the natural realm. If you can do it on the natural realm by your natural ability, you do not need grace.

So the question is: Are you willing to accept God's grace on God's condition? Are you willing to move on beyond the level of: what you can handle? Or what you know?

You will notice that all the people that were truly called of God in the Bible immediately said I cannot do it. Moses, Jeremiah etc. This is for a fact. If you ever meet someone who says: "I was called by God and I knew I could do it", Most certainly, they were not called by God because God only calls people who do not know how to do it and who know they do not know. That is how he gets them depending on his grace.

This applies to the church and many men of God. They start off depending on the grace of God and then they become so clever and so efficient that they can do without his grace. If you can do it without

God's grace, you will do it without His grace. He does not force his grace upon anybody. It is received freely by faith.

Hebrews 4:16 says: *Therefore let us draw near with confidence to the throne of grace, so that we may receive mercy and find grace to help in time of need.*

Bear in mind when you are seeking God in your need, you are coming to a throne - the throne of the one who rules the universe and it is a throne of grace. It is a throne that makes God's grace available to you.

The writer says let us come boldly that we may obtain two things: mercy and grace to help us in time of need. Everybody who comes to obtain mercy and grace receives it. The only reason people do not receive mercy and grace is because they do not come to ask for it. Either, they have their little plans and only come to the throne for God to endorse them. It does not work like that.

God has made mercy and grace available to every one of us. The first thing we need is mercy to cover up all our failures and transgressions. Then we need grace to enable us to move into the will of God, beyond the level of our own ability. God does not ever force us to do things, but he knows what we are going to do, because he knows us from inside out.

Let us direct our attention to one passage in Genesis 18:19. In regard to Abraham, this is what God says: *"For I have chosen him, so that he may command his children and his household after him to keep the way of the LORD by doing righteousness and justice, so that the LORD may bring upon Abraham what He has spoken about him."*

The Hebrew says literally I have known him instead of I have chosen him. God never forced Abraham to do anything but he chose him because he knew he could trust Abraham to do what he told him to do.

God knew that Abraham would teach his children and his household to keep the ways of the Lord that God might bring upon Abraham the promise that he had made. So God made the promise freely. He did not compel Abraham, but he knew Abraham and He knew that he would do the things that would entitle him to the promise.

So when God makes a commitment to you, he never compels you to do anything. But he knows you and he knows that he can trust you to do the very thing that he has called you to do. God's trust in humanity is astonishing.

God can never trust you with something that he does not think you can do by his grace. That is what he said about Abraham. "I have known him he will do it". What does God say about each one of us who are called? I have known him or I have known her. He or she will do it.

That should motivate each one of us much more than a set of rules, the fact that God has something for you to do and that he trusts you to do it. You could easily be tempted to break rules but, when you think about the trust God has put in you, you would not want to fail God's trust. If you think about the trust of God in you, it can be overwhelming. That is all part of this wonderful teaching about God's grace.

2nd Timothy 2:19 says: *Nevertheless, the firm foundation of God stands, having this seal, "The Lord knows those who are His," and, "Everyone who names the name of the Lord is to abstain from wickedness."*

The second one is easy to understand. If you claim to belong to Jesus Christ, you have got to abstain from ungodly evil behavior. But the first one is a secret seal. The Lord knows those who are his and we do not know. I do not know everybody who is God's chosen but God knows.

11.3 Why did Israel not believe in their Messiah?

In verses 7 and 8 Paul is still dealing with this problem of why Israel did not believe. If you have followed, you will see that Paul was continually wrestling with this issue. 'Why did my Jewish brothers and sisters not believe in their own Messiah?' And so he says in verse 7:

Rom 11:7 What then? What Israel is seeking, it has not obtained, but those who were chosen obtained it, and the rest were hardened;

Those who were chosen are the elect. Those whom God foreknew and chose have obtained it and the rest he says were hardened. And then he quotes first of all from Jeremiah 5:21:

Romans 11:8 just as it is written, "God gave them a spirit of stupor, eyes to see not and ears to hear not, down to this very day."

And then he quotes from the psalm of David. Psalm 69

Rom 11:9 And David says "Let their table become a snare and a trap, and a stumbling block and retribution to them.

Rom 11: 10 "Let their eyes be darkened to see not, and bend their backs forever."

That is because they rejected the truth of God. This is one of the most frightening facts in the spiritual life. If we persistently and stubbornly reject the truth of God, God will withdraw from us the ability to understand the truth and open up to us some kind of spirit, a spirit of stupor, a spirit of error and deception.

That is one of the most terrible judgments that can come upon those who deliberately reject God's revealed truth. There are two examples we can look at here: In 1st Samuel 16, this is the story of king of Saul who rejected God's revealed purpose and turned against it. It says about him: *14Now the Spirit of the LORD departed from Saul, and an evil spirit from the LORD terrorized him. 15Saul's servants then said to him, "Behold now, an evil spirit from God is terrorizing you. (1st Samuel 16:14-15)*

Can you absorb that? God permitted an evil spirit to have access to Saul because he had rejected the truth. That is frightening. We have to continually ask ourselves "am I hardening myself against the truth". I do not want God to take his spirit from me and release an evil spirit in its place. David knew this truth and in his prayer in psalms 51, pleading for God's mercy after killing Uriah and taking Uriah wife, he says *"Do not cast me away from Your presence and do not take Your Holy Spirit from me." (Psalm 51:11)*

You see, Satan does not have any power to do anything that God does not permit him to do. But God can permit Satan to release an evil spirit against us if we persistently reject the truth.

Then in 2nd Thessalonians 2, this whole chapter is about the coming of the Antichrist and how the way is being prepared and what he is going to do. And it says: *10 and he will come with all the deception of wickedness for those who perish, because they did not receive the love of the truth so as to be saved.* (Is not that frightening? if we do not receive the love of the truth. Then God is going to deal with us and we are going to come under deception). Then it says: *11 For this reason God will send upon them a deluding influence so that they will believe what is false, 12 in order that they all may be judged who did not believe the truth, but took pleasure in wickedness. (2 Thessalonians 2:10-12)*

I believe that is already happening and God is permitting a deluding spirit to come upon various sections of the church which have deliberately rejected the revealed truth of God. Especially upon ministers and leaders who are responsible for these errors. And when that deluding spirit comes upon any person, that person can no longer see the truth. They lose that ability to see the truth.

But Paul is dealing with his own Jewish brothers and he says, that is what happened to my brothers and sisters. Because they had all the prophets, century after century, then they had John the Baptist, then they had the Messiah himself, then they had apostles. And having rejected them, God permitted them to come under a spirit of blindness and stupor. They were not any longer able to see.

That is not just a historical experience of Israel. That is a frightening fact about God's dealings.

11.4 The In-grafted Branches

Rom 11:11 I say then, they did not stumble so as to fall, did they? May it never be! But by their transgression salvation has come to the Gentiles, to make them jealous.

So Paul says, have they fallen forever and the answer is 'May it never be'. Their fall is temporary not permanent. Then Paul goes on and says that through their transgression salvation has come to the Gentiles, to make them jealous.

That is one of the amazing mysteries of God, that through the rejection and crucifixion of the Messiah, the way was opened for salvation to come to the entire Gentile world. We see this illustrated in two passages of Matthew chapter 10. When Jesus sent out his first apostles, he told them only to go to their own people.

These twelve Jesus sent out after instructing them: "Do not go in the way of the Gentiles, and do not enter any city of the Samaritans; but rather go to the lost sheep of the house of Israel. (Matthew 10:5-6)

So in the first Apostolic sending forth in the Ministry of Jesus, they received specific instructions. Only go to the Jews because God had ordained that the Jewish people were to receive the first offer of the gospel.

But after the death and resurrection of Jesus at the end of Matthew's Gospel in Matthew 28, Jesus revised those orders and it says: *And Jesus came up and spoke to them, saying, "All authority has been given to me in heaven and on earth. "Go therefore and make disciples of all the nations, baptizing them in the name of the Father and the Son and the Holy Spirit, (Matthew 28:18, 19)*

All nations means, all the Gentiles. So Israel had the first offer and they refused. Because of their refusal and their rejection of the Messiah, the opportunity for salvation was extended to all other nations. They refused. They lost the kingdom because they rejected the king. They believed the kingdom was for them but they rejected the king.

That is a lesson for the church. If we reject the King, we lose the kingdom. The kingdom will be taken from us. In Matthew 21, the parable of the vine dressers, Jesus said this to the Jewish people: *"Therefore I say to you, the kingdom of God will be taken away from you and given to a people, producing the fruit of it.(Matthew 21:43)*

To qualify for the kingdom, you must produce fruit. Any group that does not produce the fruit forfeits the kingdom. What was the nation to which the kingdom was offered? It was not America, nor Britain, nor Russia. It was the church - a new and a holy nation.

But the church only qualifies to be the custodians of the kingdom as long as we bring forth fruit. If we fail to bring forth the fruit, we do not qualify any longer for the kingdom. The kingdom can be taken away and restored back to the Jewish people. If you look in Acts 1:6 after the resurrection of Jesus, one of the final questions that his disciples asked him was: *So when they had come together, they were asking Him, saying, "Lord, is it at this time You are restoring the kingdom to Israel?"*(Acts 1:6)

Some people say the kingdom will never be restored to Israel. But if that were true, Jesus would have said it will never be restored. But what he said next was that something else has got to happen first. What was the something else?

7He said to them, "It is not for you to know times or epochs which the Father has fixed by His own authority; 8but you will receive power when the Holy Spirit has come upon you; and you shall be My witnesses both in Jerusalem, and in all Judea and Samaria, and even to the remotest part of the earth." (Acts 1:7-8)

So, once the offer of the kingdom had been extended to all nations, it had to reach to all nations and every part of the earth before the age could come to a close.

In Matthew 24:14 Jesus explained: *"this gospel of the kingdom shall be preached in the whole world for a witness to all the nations and then the end shall come.*

So once Israel forfeited the kingdom, the message was sent to all other nations. This age cannot close until all other nations have received the message. So that is what Paul means when he says that, through the fall of the Jewish people, salvation has come to other nations.

Paul emphasizes *"to make them jealous"*. The way that the other nations receive and embrace the gospel, should make the Jews jealous. But contrary to that, the church has indeed done a poor job of making the Jews Jealous.

Rom 11:12 *Now if their transgression is riches for the world and their failure is riches for the Gentiles, how much more will their fulfillment be!*

If all these blessings have come to the other nations, through their transgression, what will come when they are restored? That is what Paul is saying. It is sad if we completely miss the purposes of God. If we do not align ourselves with his plan for the restoration of Israel because the fullness of God's blessing will not come to other nations until Israel is restored.

And then Paul says:

Rom 11:13 *But I am speaking to you who are Gentiles. In as much then as I am an apostle of Gentiles, I magnify my ministry,*

Rom 11:14 *if somehow I might move to jealousy my fellow countrymen and save some of them*

Again Paul wants to bring forth a Gentile church that will also enjoy the blessings of God and demonstrate the presence of God that the Jews will say, we want what they have. But honestly speaking, how often has the church really done anything to make the Jews jealous?

Rom 11:15 For if their rejection is the reconciliation of the world, what will their acceptance be but life from the dead?

Through the rejection of the Jewish people, the Gentiles had the opportunity to be reconciled with God. When the Jews are reconciled, it will bring life from the dead. That is a profound statement.

The restoration of Israel to their Messiah is going to produce cosmic changes for the whole world. I believe that is the hope of the earth. It is important for Gentile Christians to see what is involved in the restoration of the Jewish people because it is in the best interest of the whole world.

I believe that this will give us a picture of what God intended the whole world to be when the Jewish people are restored and are back in a right relationship with the Lord. There is a kind of principle that every nation has its right place and only when nations are in the right place will things go right with the earth. And the first nation that God begins with is always Israel. When Israel is back in their right place and in the right relationship with God, then everything else on earth will get sorted out. Until then, there is going to be confusion.

Then Paul says:

Rom 11:16 If the first piece of dough is holy, the lump is also; and if the root is holy, the branches are too.

That is taken from the ceremonies of the Law of Moses. If you dedicate something to the Lord by offering a little piece of it to the Lord, the whole thing is holy. So if a little first fruit of the Jewish people have been offered to the Lord that means the whole nation is holy.

Then Paul goes in verse 17:

Rom 11:17 But if some of the branches were broken off, and you, being a wild olive, were grafted in among them and became partaker with them of the rich root of the olive tree,

Rom 11:18 do not be arrogant toward the branches; but if you are arrogant, remember that it is not you who supports the root, but the root supports you.

That is so important. This time Paul is writing specifically to believers from a Gentile background. He says; remember that it is not your olive tree. The olive tree is God's people from Abraham, Isaac and Jacob upwards. You did not belong in that olive tree but some of the branches were unbelieving and got broken off. You have been grafted in among them and bear in mind you do not support the tree. The tree supports you. Do not be arrogant toward the Jewish people.

In some parts of the world, the church, has left out that instruction.

The Paul says:

Rom 11:19 You will say then, "Branches were broken off so that I might be grafted in."

They fell because they were unbelieving and "here am I in the tree". Paul then writes that that is true:

Rom 11:20 Quite right, they were broken off for their unbelief, but you stand by your faith. Do not be conceited, but fear;

I hope the church has got that message. Do not be conceited or proud but fear. Why?

Rom11:21 for if God did not spare the natural branches, He will not spare you, either.

Remember that the requirement for the kingdom is fruit. If you do not produce fruit, you forfeit the kingdom. God is no respecter of persons. Israel forfeited the kingdom because they did not bring forth the fruit. Any group of the church that does not bring forth fruit will forfeit the kingdom. The real danger is that, some sections of the church, if they do not begin to produce fruit, will have to forfeit the Kingdom.

Rom 11:22 Behold then the kindness and severity of God; to those who fell, severity, but to you, God's kindness, if you continue in His kindness; otherwise you also will be cut off.

This is very plain language. If you stand by faith and as long as you bring forth the fruit, you will not be cut off. But if you cease to live in faith, then you will fail to bring forth the fruit, and you will be cut off. Just as much as the Jewish branches were cut off.

Then he says consider the kindness and severity of God. There is a great deal of preaching today which speaks only about the kindness of God and does not deal at all with the severity of God. It is like a coin which has two sides. One side is kindness and the other side is severity. If you deface one side of the coin it becomes valueless.

There is this phrase that is wildly used by believers today: "God is good all the time and that is his nature." I would not agree less, but this is conditional. If we present a message of God that speaks only of his kindness and not of his severity, it is like a valueless coin. We have got to be faithful to God.

People need to know that repentance is the key to accessing the Kindness of God. Without repentance, we attract severity. People have to be taught that repentance (180 degree turn from sin, transgression and iniquity) is the condition God has placed to be able to access his blessings.

To simply say come forward and get blessed at the end of a sermon, even if it is done with the best intentions, cannot afford us God's kindness because you cannot keep one foot in Satan's Kingdom and one foot in the kingdom of God and be blessed. You become a split personality. Remember, there are two sides to the coin - God's kindness and God's severity.

Going on,

Rom 11:23 And they also, if they do not continue in their unbelief, will be grafted in, for God is able to graft them in again.

That is a very positive statement. They are not excluded forever. Then he goes on and now addressing the Gentiles, he says:

Rom 11:24 For if you were cut off from what is by nature a wild olive tree, and were grafted contrary to nature into a cultivated olive tree, how much more will these who are the natural branches be grafted into their own olive tree?

That is food for thought. **Grafting**, in horticulture, is the act of placing a portion of one plant (bud or scion) into or on a stem, root, or branch of another (stock) in such a way that a union will be formed and the partners will continue to grow.

In modern horticulture grafting is used for a variety of purposes: to repair injured trees, to produce dwarf trees and shrubs, to strengthen plants' resistance to diseases, to retain varietal characteristics, to adapt varieties to adverse soil or climatic conditions, to ensure pollination, to produce multi-fruited or multi-flowered plants, and to propagate certain species (such as hybrid roses) that can be propagated in no other way.

The principle of grafting in this context involves, taking an uncultivated stock and grafting it in a branch that will produce the desired fruit. The life of the uncultivated stock then flows through the fruitful branch and brings forth fruit.

What Paul is saying is that; what God has done, in getting the Gentiles in, is contrary to nature. Because God has taken an uncultivated stock for a branch and grafted it into a fruitful stock. This is contrary to all principles of grafting.

So we the Gentiles, were unfruitful branches and contrary to nature, God grafted us into, the fruitful olive tree (which is God's historic people going back to Abraham, Isaac and Jacob).

What Paul is saying is that: if God could do that for uncultivated branches, is not it much easier for him to graft the cultivated branches back again. What he is saying should encourage us to pray for Israel to be restored back, into their-own tree.

11.5 God will Again Extend Mercy to Israel

Now we are coming to something very exciting which is God's program to close this age. From verse 25 onwards, Paul outlines very briefly certain things that must take place as this age comes to a close. And he says:

Rom 11:25 *For I do not want you, brethren, to be uninformed of this mystery—so that you will not be wise in your own estimation—that a partial hardening has happened to Israel until the fullness of the Gentiles has come in;*

To be uninformed means to be ignorant. Ignorance is a wall or a darkness that we Christians must fight. God sets no premium on ignorance. I am not talking about education. Education is a two-edged sword. It is partly good and partly not. But ignorance is a terrible evil. You do not have to attend a university to be set free from ignorance.

...of this mystery: A mystery is something that has been kept secret by God. But it is now opened up. So a mystery needs no longer to be mysterious. A mystery is one of God's secrets, which he seemed fit to reveal to us in the church age.

…So that you will not be wise in your own estimation. If you go through this chapter, you will see the number of times God warned and Paul warns against arrogance. Then now here is the mystery:

…that a partial hardening has happened to Israel until the fullness of the Gentiles has come in;

It is never been a total hardening. There are many Jews in every generation who have acknowledged Jesus as their Messiah. It is always been only partial a partial hardening.

This partial hardening is 'until'. Wherever the Bible speaks about God's rejection of Israel, it always follows with the phrase like until. In other words, it is not permanent until the fullness or the full number of the Gentiles has come in. So the full restoration of Israel, will not take place until every Gentile, whom God has foreknown and chosen, has heard and responded to the Gospel.

Israel was the first but they lost their place. So the message was sent out to all other nations. It is only after when all the other nations have responded, when Israel will come back in their fullness. I believe that at this the same time, the Holy Spirit is preparing the hearts of the Jewish people as never before to turn back to their Messiah. This, the gospel of the kingdom is going to be proclaimed to every nation because Jesus said it would. At the same time God is preparing the heart of the Jewish people.

If you listen to the testimonies of Jewish people who have found the Messiah, most of them have come to him by a direct personal revelation. I think Jesus says, I want the privilege of revealing myself to my brothers. From the prophecies in Ezekiel and Hosea, maybe there is going to be a rendezvous between Jesus and the Jewish remnant. He is going to reveal himself to them just as Joseph revealed himself to his brothers.

This is the most beautiful parallel in the story of Joseph. Joseph was alienated from his brothers and abandoned. They thought he died but he was in Egypt and he became totally Egyptian - he dressed like an Egyptian and he spoke like an Egyptian. There was no evidence that he was still Jewish. But in the heart of it all, his brothers had to come to him to fulfill the dream which had made them so angry years before. They bowed down to him as they were talking Hebrew to one another. They did not know that Joseph understood everything they said. He put them through all sorts of things to bring them to the place of total dependence on him. Then it says, he could restrain himself no longer and he sent all the Egyptians out of the house and then he revealed himself. And he said I am Joseph.

See that is what has happened to Jesus. As far as the Jewish people are concerned, he has become totally Gentile. They do not see him as a Jew at all. For most Jewish people, Jesus is a statue or a god that Christians worship in a church and they do not like it. But that is changing and God is softening their hardened hearts and preparing them. A gentle rain of the Holy Spirit is beginning to fall and it is softening that hard soil that has been unresponsive for centuries.

So going on;

Rom 11:26 and so all Israel will be saved (All Israel means the chosen remnant); *just as it is written, The deliverer will come from Zion, he will remove ungodliness from Jacob."*

Rom 11:27 "This is my covenant with them, when I take away their sins."

So God has made a covenant commitment that the Redeemer will come to Israel and take away their sins and the whole nation will be saved.

Rom 11:28 From the standpoint of the gospel they are enemies for your sake, but from the standpoint of God's choice they are beloved for the sake of the fathers;

Rom 11:29 for the gifts and the calling of God are irrevocable.

Rom 11:30 For just as you once were disobedient to God, but now have been shown mercy because of their disobedience,

Rom 11:31 so these also now have been disobedient, that because of the mercy shown to you they also may now be shown mercy.

So the mercy we receive is to bring mercy to Israel. And then he says:

Rom 11:32 For God has shut up all in disobedience so that He may show mercy to all.

Is not that an astonishing statement? That God has got all of us confined in the prison of disobedience - Jews and Gentiles alike. No matter whether you are white or colored or black, we are all dissidents and God has shut us up in order that he might show mercy.

Then we come to this one is a kind of doxology (a short hymn of praises to God) with which we will close section 2 – The destiny of Israel and the Church.

Rom 11:33 Oh, the depth of the riches both of the wisdom and knowledge of God! How unsearchable are His judgments and unfathomable His ways!

Let us not deceive ourselves. We cannot understand all the judgments of God. We do not know all the ways of God. Just accept that fact and trust him. He knows what he is doing even if you do not.

Rom 11:34 For who has known the mind of the lord, or who became his counselor?

Rom 11:35 or who has first given to him that it might be paid back to him again?

And then we close with this glorious statement:

Rom 11:36 For from Him and through Him and to Him are all things. To Him be the glory forever. Amen.

In Revelation 21:6 he says: I am the Alpha and the Omega, the beginning and the end. And when we received this revelation, there is only one thing that is appropriate of us - just to worship Him and to give him all the glory that is due to his name.

PART 3 - HOW TO LIVE WHAT YOU BELIEVE

Romans Chapter 12 - 16

Chapters' 12 through to 16 are where the rubber meets the road. This is where all the doctrines unveiled in Chpaters 1 to 8 and then chapter 9 to 11 are put to the test. Here are the nitty-gritty or down to earth truths on how to live what you believe as you face the mounting pressures of evil in these closing days. You will find that these truth are nothing less than your key to survival.

CHAPTER 12: WORKING OUT YOUR FAITH UNDER PRESSURE

(Romans 12:1 - 12:21)

Most of us who are trying to work out the Christian faith would agree that today we are under all sorts of pressures: social pressures, spiritual pressures, mental pressures, emotional pressures etc. This is where our faith is tested and the question is; will it stand the test?

You can say Amen to all the glorious theology of the first 11 chapters of Romans. But it is in what we are going to unveil now that our faith will be proved or disproved.

The Bible never presents us with abstract truth only. It always presents the truth and then shows us how it relates to the way we live. God is not interested in abstract theology; he is interested in life and the way we live. All the truths of the Bible are designed to make us live a godly, victorious and fruitful life. We may have a lot of knowledge of theology and many degrees, but if we do not have the right result, God's purposes are being frustrated in our lives.

12.1 Our First Practical Response To God's Mercy

Rom 12:1 Therefore, I urge you, brethren, by the mercies of God, to present your bodies a living and holy sacrifice, acceptable to God, which is your spiritual service of worship.

When you find the word 'therefore' in the Bible, you need to find out what it is there for because it always indicates a logical connection with what has gone before.

This therefore in the first verse of Romans 12 is because of all the preceding eleven chapters of Romans. In those eleven chapters, Paul has wonderfully unfolded the divine plan for man to be reckoned righteous with God, to come back into relationship with God and to receive the full provision of the sacrifice of Jesus on the cross. All this has been unfolded by the Holy Spirit through Paul.

However, God does not stop there. Now, the issue is how can we live this out? What does this mean in our day to day lives? That is why the therefore is there because Paul is saying, in the light of all that God has done and provided for us, how should we respond.

And what is delighting is that the response is so simple, practical and down-to-earth. The Holy Spirit is the most practical person. We should all be scared of super spirituality. If it is not practical, it is not spiritual in a true sense.

As we read this first verse, you will see God's requirement. The response he asks from us is very down-to-earth.

I urge you therefore brethren, by the mercies of God to present your bodies a living and Holy sacrifice acceptable to God which is your spiritual (or you may say logical) *service of worship.*

So what is God asking of us, is not something theological or something mystical or intellectually stimulating but he says I want your body. I want that earthen vessel in which you live. That is what I am asking for. And I am not going to be satisfied with anything less. And he said I want you to present your body like a sacrifice on **my altar of service**. He says a **living sacrifice.**

Why does he choose the word living? Because he has in mind the sacrifices of the Old Covenant where the creature to be sacrificed was first killed and then its body was placed on the altar. God is saying, I want you to place your body on the altar of God, but do not kill it. It is not a dead sacrifice but a living sacrifice. The language used here is:

which is your **spiritual service of worship.** These words describe the service of the priests in the temple of the tabernacle.

So we become priests through our faith in Jesus and one of the primary priestly duties that we have to do is to present our bodies on God's altar as a living sacrifice. This is what God is asking from us. It is not complicated. You see, in the Old Covenant, anyone who placed an animal on the altar of God, he no longer owned that animal. From then on, that animal belonged to God, once it touched the altar and the priest took his hands off, then animal was totally set apart to God.

So when you place your body on God's altar, from that time onwards you do not own your body. It belongs to God. You do not have to decide what to eat or what to wear or where to travel. Those are God's decisions. Your body is now his property. He can do what he wants with it.

That is the response that God asks. People who try to be Christians without a response like that just end up with endless problems. They have endless counseling sessions with endless counselors. People who keep their minds fastened on their problems will never come to the end of their problem. Somehow, you have got to get out of yourself. This is God's way. To be out of yourself and your problems is to place your body on his altar and surrender yourself without reservation to God. Then you become his responsibility.

Many of the problems facing Christians today would not exist if they had truly repented and turned away from self-pleasing, self-will or making their own decisions.

As you place your body on God's altar, when he gets your body, he also gets its contents – the soul and the spirit. He gets the whole thing and he is not going to settle for less. You can limp along as a half committed Christian. We have a lot of people like that in the church today. But, you will never know the real satisfaction of the Christian life until you have made that commitment.

Now, as a result of the commitment, Paul then unfolds the consequences that we can look for in our lives. Bear in mind these consequences are not promised to people who have not made the commitment.

There are a number of successive stages that flow out of this initial commitment. Then Paul goes on with a negative:

Rom 12:2 And do not be conformed to this world, but be transformed by the renewing of your mind, so that you may prove what the will of God is, that which is good and acceptable and perfect.

Let us look at the four-fold implication of this scripture.

First: *do not be conformed to this world:*

The actual word is age. Age is a time concept. We are living in a certain age or a period of time. Paul says do not be conformed to this time period. Do not live like the people in this age or time period. In (Galatians 1:4) he tells us that Christ has delivered us from this present evil age. It is an evil age because it has an evil god – Satan (2nd Corinthians 4:5). God is not redeeming this age. God is redeeming us out of this age. Christians who try to live as if they still belong in this age are always in a state of confusion.

God is not going to redeem this age. He is going to close the age and when this age ends, Satan will no longer be a god. That is why he fights with all his might to continue this age as long as he can. But we are not to be conformed to this age. We are not to live like people who belong in time, because we belong to eternity. The writer of Hebrews says we have tasted the powers of the next age through the Holy Spirit (Hebrews 6:4-5).

One reason why God has allowed us to taste the powers of the next age is to spoil our appetite for this age. When you have really tasted what God has to offer you through the Holy Spirit, the things of this age which seem so unpalatable. Why worry about them, why spend your time on them, why get so excited about them because they are all passing away. They are all impermanent, they are all tainted, and they are all corrupted, there is nothing pure and clean in the things of this age. Through the mercy of God, we have been delivered from this age.

Grace to you and peace from God our Father and the Lord Jesus Christ, who gave Himself for our sins so that He might rescue us from this present evil age, according to the will of our God and Father, (Galatians 1:3-4)

Now the word 'this age' is the same word that is used as 'this world' in Romans 12:2.

Many bible translation of Romans 12:2 use the word 'world'. World is another concept. The world is a kind of social system but age is a time concept. We have to be delivered from both. If you go through Galatians it starts with deliverance from this present evil age and ends with deliverance from this present world. The last statement in Galatians is: *God forbid that I should glory except in the Lord Jesus Christ by which the world is crucified to me and I to the world* (Galatians 6:14)

Second: *...but be transformed by the renewing of your mind.*

Notice that God does not change us from outside. He changes us from inside out. He changes the way we think and then that changes the way we live. Religion does the opposite. Religion starts with the outside: what you wear, what you eat, what you drink, the places you go to etc. It tries to make us good by changing the externals but it does not work.

God's method works. He changes us from inside. He changes the way we think and once our way of thinking is changed, we will be changed in the way we live. You cannot think wrong and live right and you cannot think right and live wrong. The way you think determines the way you live.

The essential feature of the people of this age is that they are self-centered. They always face every issue and decision with, what will this do for me? What will I get out of this?

When your mind is renewed, you are God centered. You do not approach situations and decisions like the people of this age. You say what will God get out of this? What is the will of God? What is God's plan? Will this glorify God? That is the change of mind that comes. But that will not come until you have presented your body as a living sacrifice.

God says; do not talk to me about renewing your mind if you have not wholly presented your body as a living sacrifice because that is my basic requirement. You present your body and God will renew your mind. You hold on to your body and God will do nothing for your mind.

Third: *...that you may prove what the will of God is.*

There are millions of Christians who have been born again but have never discovered God's will for their lives. They are just wallowing. They are trying to lead a good life but they have no real motivation. They have no vision. Proverbs 29:18 says: *Where there is no vision, the people cast off restraint;*

Many Christians are undisciplined. They cast off restraint because they do not have a vision.

Paul uses the example of an athlete many times. Why can a man jump higher or run faster than the rest? It is because he had a vision and because of that vision he exercises, he trains himself and submits himself to discipline. Discipline that is much more intense than most Christians will ever contemplate. The thing that motivates him is a vision. No vision no discipline. You are not doing what Paul said he was doing *'pressing toward the mark for the prize of the upward call of God'.*

During crisis, if you do not have a mark, how can you press toward it? The mark only comes when your mind is renewed and God gives you a vision of what he wants to make of you.

Fourth: *It is good, acceptable and perfect*

Paul says three wonderful words about the will of God. It is good, acceptable and perfect. The more you know it, the better it gets.

1.   When you start with God's will it is good. He wants the best for you.

2.   Then it is acceptable i.e. the better you know it, the more you enjoy it and

3.   Finally it is perfect. It covers every area of your personality. It covers every detail of your life. It covers where you sit. It covers the food you eat. It covers the clothes you wear. It covers the people you meet. There is not a detail in your life that is not covered by the will of God. When you have discovered it, it is perfect.

Rom 12:3 For through the grace given to me I say to everyone among you not to think more highly of himself than he ought to think; but to think so as to have sound judgment (to think soberly), *as God has allotted to each a measure of faith.*

That is the next development. You will discover that God is allotted to you a specific measure of faith. God deals with each one of us individually. All of us do not have the same amount of faith. Not all preachers or ministers have the same faith. Some preachers have great faith for healing and some do not. God deals to each of his servant a specific measure of faith.

Then he warns us that faith and pride are incompatible. The two persons whom Jesus praises most for their faith in his earthly ministry were two people who thought themselves totally unworthy. The

Roman centurion who said to Jesus *"I am not worthy that you should come under my roof"* and the Canaanite woman whom Jesus referred to as a dog and she said – *"true Lord I am a little dog but even dogs eat crumbs that fall off their masters table"* and what did Jesus say: *Oh woman your faith is great.* Pride and faith are incompatible.

There is a kind of substitute faith which is very arrogant and boastful. It manifests itself in many Christians including ministers of the word of God. It is characterized by chest thumping and defiant kind of prayers where the participants do not seek the Holy Spirit for guidance. They are carnal kind of prayers which are not under the direction of the Holy Spirit. In Ephesians 6:18 Paul write...*'praying always in the spirit.'*

So God has allotted to each one a specific measure of faith, but it only operates out of an attitude of humility.

The next great truth which is so important is that the measure of faith that God has allotted to us is directly related to our place in the body of Christ. One of the great lessons of this chapter is that you cannot really become an effective Christian until you have found your place in the body of Christ. You cannot be a member of the body floating through the air. You have got to be attached to the body. Just like a finger cannot function on its own if it is not attached to the arm and the arm to the body. There is no room for the person who says "I'll go it alone".

Effective Christian life is about relationships. When you begin to get a little bit self-sufficient, God allows things to happen that will show you that you need your fellow Christians. Part of the plan of God in eternity is interdependence or coexistence between all creations. Isaiah 11:8-9 says: *The infant will play by the cobra's den, and the toddler will reach into the viper's nest. They will neither harm nor destroy on all My holy mountain, for the earth will be full of the knowledge of the LORD as the sea is full of water....*

We need to be functioning as part of the body. Many Christians are frustrated and wonder why it does not go right with them because they have not found their place in the body. You have got faith but you do not know what to do with it.

Let's just read what Paul says there about the body in verse 4 and 5.

Rom 12:4 For just as we have many members in one body and all the members do not have the same function,

Rom 12:5 so we, who are many, are one body in Christ, and individually members one of another.

So, each one of us is designed to be part of a body. We can only function effectively when we have found our place in the body and fulfilling our function. You will find that, the faith that God has allotted to you, is the faith that will enable you to fulfill your function in the body.

Let us take a very simple example. If you are going to be a hand you have to have a hand faith, but if you are going to be a foot and God has given to you a foot faith and you are trying to be a hand, you will be a disaster. Your hand is very effective when it is working as a hand. If you try to walk on your hands, that is another story. Again the cause of much frustration in the body of Christ is that people are trying to play the wrong part. They are trying to fulfill a function for which God has not given them.

Indeed our faith will be tested but basically if you are always struggling for faith, it is almost certain sign that you are not in the right place in the body. Your hand does not have to make a lot of effort to be a hand. It is just a hand without doing a lot of thinking. But if you try to make your hand some other part of the body, then there is a lot of effort and strain involved. There should not be a lot of strain in the Christian life. From time to time we will come under pressure, our strengths may be tested but basically the Christian life should flow as naturally as your hand is doing its job.

Now, that does not mean that your faith will not grow. God intends our faith to grow but it will grow in the place where you should be functioning.

One of the curses of the 'civilized life' is individualism. Individuality is important, but to try to function on your own is a road to disaster and frustration.

If we take into consideration, the average house hold sizes across the world, the world is gravitating towards less than two people living together in a household in many parts of the world. That is not a good picture for the body of Christ. The world is inclined more towards individualism. That is one of the areas where we cannot be conformed to the thinking of this age. We have to learn to be part of a body. We have got to learn to function with other people.

The final stage of this progress is in verses six and following:

Rom 12:6 *Since we have gifts that differ according to the grace given to us, each of us is to exercise them accordingly: if prophecy, according to the proportion of his faith;*

Rom 12:7 *if service, in his serving; or he who teaches, in his teaching;*

Rom 12:8 *or he who exhorts, in his exhortation; he who gives, with liberality; he who leads, with diligence; he who shows mercy, with cheerfulness*

The Greek word for grace is Charis or charisma. This is a derivative of the word for grace. They are grace gifts you cannot earn. So once you have found your place in the body, then God will equip you with the gifts that you need to function in that place. It is really not sensible to pray for gifts in the abstract. Prayers like – Lord, give me this or that gift are not practical. You need to find your place in the body and then you will know what gifts you need. As a matter of fact, God will begin to give them to you. God will not leave you unequipped. Spiritual gifts are not toys but they are tools. We need them to do the job.

This is not a comprehensive list of charisma. You will find another list in 1st Corinthians 12. As for the number of gifts, we should not limit our concept of spiritual gifts. Even celibacy, which Paul says was one of the gifts given to him in 1st Corinthians chapter 7:7, is a gift. It is a very wide range.

Here in Romans 12:6-8, we have seven. Verse six says: since we have gifts that differ according to the grace given to us, let each exercise them accordingly.

1. *If prophecy* according to the proportion of faith. This very important because a lot of people, when they begin to prophesy and see exciting results. Their minds get blown up and they go beyond the proportion of the faith given to them. They start to say things that are not from God and they create in many cases a lot of confusion. The line between prophesy and fortune telling or divination is very thin. Think about the young woman in Philippe (Acts 16:16), when Paul and Silas arrived there with their companions. She went out everywhere saying these men are servants of the Most High God which show us the way of salvation. Every word she spoke was true. She knew it supernaturally but she did not know it by the Holy Spirit. Eventually Paul got so provoked he cast out the divining spirit. In modern day churches, she could have been made a charter member of the church. This is problem that confronts us in the church today. Today there is a great upsurge of prophecy. Thank God for it, but let us have the real thing and let us be cautious that we do not get involved in a counterfeit. So according to the proportion of faith. Do not go beyond your faith. Do not force it, let it come naturally. Let it flow naturally. The Holy Spirit is compared to olive oil. Olive oil flows very smoothly.

2. *If service* or deaconship. A deacon is another word for a servant. The word Deacon is just a translation of the Greek word for a servant. So if you want to be a servant, then specialize in serving. Serving is an art. It involves adjusting your thinking to the thinking of another person and doing it the way the other person wants.

3. He who *teaches*, in his teaching. Note that the Bible says that we should not have too many teachers (James 3:1). Do not be a teacher unless God has called you. Stay out of it because the judgment is stricter. I know God called me to be a teacher. When He called me, I was poorly equipped with the word of the God. I wrote a couple of books using my head knowledge. I plunged myself in and I realized that I did things according to my thinking. God dealt with me strictly and His judgment weighed heavily upon me.

4. He who *exhorts*, in his exhortation. A lot of people have got this wonderful gift of exhorting but it is not teaching. Do not become a teacher when you should exhort. Stick in your profession. There are some wonderful evangelists but when they become teachers, every time they open their mouth, they put the foot in it.

5. If you *give*, give with liberality. Do you realize that there is a Ministry of giving? It is a ministry and it is a gift. Do it with liberality and simplicity. Do not make a big deal of it. Do not give with conditions attached or other ulterior motives. Some people give and try to manipulate the servants of God.

6. He who *leads*, with diligence. It means to apply constant and earnest effort to accomplish what is undertaken; being persistent through the exertion of body or mind.

7. He who shows *mercy*, with cheerfulness. E.g. visiting people in hospital. To some people, it is a chore and there are people who flow when they get to visit sick people in hospital. It is their natural gift and it is a very precious and wonderful gift.

12.2 Fruits That Grow From The Root of Love

The key phrase in this section is 'Let love be without hypocrisy.'

Rom 12:9 Let love be without hypocrisy. Abhor what is evil; cling to what is good.

Sincere love is the root of all Christian service. Is that true of us in the ministry? Is the thing that we are aiming for LOVE? Then Paul goes on to say that if you have got involved in anything else, you are just wasting time. Anything in the church that does not ultimately produce love is a waste of time and is misapplied effort. How much time is wasted in many churches today? So Paul states here that our love should be sincere. Paul is saying that this is how to lead the Christian life. Christianity is not a set of rules but a lifestyle driven by a sincere love. Let us look at 1st Timothy 1:5: *But the goal of our instruction is love from a pure heart and a good conscience and a sincere faith.*

Then Paul outlines a list of 12 things we need to practice to achieve sincere love: *Abhor what is evil; cling to what is good.*

Psalm 45:7 is prophetic scripture about Jesus as Messiah. *Thou hast loved righteousness and hated iniquity, therefore God, thy God has anointed you with the oil of joy above your fellows.* He loved righteousness and hated iniquity. You cannot be neutral about evil. If you love God and love righteousness you will hate evil. (Psalm 97:10) There can be no compromise with evil with those that truly love the Lord.

Rom 12:10 Be devoted to one another in brotherly love; give preference to one another in honor;

Be devoted to one another and prefer one another in honor. Give more honor to other people than you seek for yourself. Paul says those who compare themselves amongst themselves and measure themselves by other people are unwise. There is only one standard and it is Jesus. When you measure yourself by him, it is easy to prefer other people.

Rom 12:11 *not lagging behind in diligence, fervent in spirit, serving the Lord;*

That means – do not be lazy but diligent. If you search the Bible, you will not find one good word said about laziness. Drunkenness is a sin but laziness is a much worse. Laziness is synonymous with wickedness. In the parable of Minas, the master said to the servant who buried his Mina, "you wicked and lazy servant'. (Mathew 25:26). Laziness is much more severely condemned than drunkenness. The strange thing is we will tolerate lazy people in our churches but we do not want drunkards.

In the second part, it says: serving the Lord with passionate dedication. The question is, do you love the Lord passionately? Today, there is very little real passion in the church. We want Jesus to love us passionately yet we do not reciprocate that love.

Rom 12:12 *rejoicing in hope, persevering in tribulation, devoted to prayer,*

In our Christian walk of life, there will be times of great blessing and times of great difficulty. There will be times when you feel full of joy, and there will be times when you feel quite desperate.

Romans 5:3-4 says: *Not only that, but we also rejoice in our sufferings, because we know that suffering produces perseverance; perseverance, character; and character, hope....*

The only thing that we will take with us into eternity is our personality or character. Tribulations are supposed to build up that character. Why should we rejoice when everything seems bleak? It is because we know for certain that God is working in us.

Then we need to devote ourselves to prayer. Prayer maintains a spiritual connection between us and God. When you devote yourself to prayer, God accomplishes his purposes in you. Prayer is a two way communication. We make our request known to God and he gives us back instructions.

Rom 12:13 *contributing to the needs of the saints, practicing hospitality*

This means that we should constantly be sharing with fellow believers. Hospitality in itself is a ministry. Remember what Jesus said. Do not invite the rich in but the poor, the blind and the people who cannot pay you back. He said a wonderful thing that you will be paid back in the resurrection.

Rom 12:14 *Bless those who persecute you; bless and do not curse*

We are to bless those who persecute us. How easy is that? You have to come to the discipline of regularly forgiving people to achieve this.

You say to the people that have been mean and unkind to you, Lord I forgive them. And having forgiven them, bless them in your name.

One of our greatest privileges as Christians is to bless others because it is godly to bless. We have a lot of critics and a lot of people that are against us but our response should be to bless them.

Jesus told his disciples to stop criticizing the woman who anointed him with expensive alabaster oil. "She's done a good work and wherever this gospel is preached, what she has done will be spoken of". So that is the attitude. God blesses those who pour out the perfume. Blessing others is pouring out perfume. When you bless people there is a little area of perfume around you from that time onwards.

Rom 12:15 *Rejoice with those who rejoice, and weep with those who weep*

If there is self-centeredness, you cannot really rejoice with those who rejoice and weep with those who weep. Until you have been delivered from being self-centered, you cannot rejoice or weep with those who weep. One sure recipe for unhappiness is self-centeredness.

Rom 12:16 Be of the same mind toward one another; do not be haughty in mind, but associate with the lowly. Do not be wise in your own estimation

Our mind is the factory of our thoughts. The Lord desires that we regard each other with love in our minds. We should not be self-important or arrogant towards others. We should create time for the lowly and associate with them.

Rom 12:17 Never pay back evil for evil to anyone. Respect what is right in the sight of all men.

Never return evil for evil and maintain a reputation for right dealing.

Rom 12:18 If possible, so far as it depends on you, be at peace with all men

But you cannot have peace with everybody. Some people will not make peace but as far as concerns you, make peace and keep peace with everybody. It will do your whole system good. Strife is poisonous. The word peace in Hebrew is Shalom and it means completeness. It is a beautiful thing when you give out peace because you get peace.

Rom 12:19 Never take your own revenge, beloved, but leave room for the wrath of God, for it is written, "Vengeance is mine, I will repay," says the Lord

If somebody does you wrong, do not revenge yourself. Paul says a very frightening thing. He says make room for the wrath of God. That is a frightening thing. If you do not revenge yourself, God is going to revenge you.

Who would you I rather deal with? Brother Harry's dealing or God's dealing? If Brother Harry avenges himself, I am not afraid, but if God takes over Brother Harry's case, that is rather frightening.

Rom 12:20 "But if your enemy is hungry, feed him, and if he is thirsty, give him a drink; for in so doing you will heap burning coals on his head"

Do not withhold anything good from your enemy. If it is within your power to give, give it. That is God's prescription for dealing with our enemy's. It may seem hard, but regard it as a spiritual prescription. You will be heaping trouble upon his sprit.

Rom 12:21 Do not be overcome by evil, but overcome evil with good.

Respond in the opposite spirit. Here are a few examples:

- Meet hatred with love
- Meet bitterness with sweetness
- Meet anger with gentleness

Never meet a bad person on their on their own level. Overcome evil with good because heaven is made for overcomers.

CHAPTER 13: RELATING TO PERSONAL CONDUCT

(Romans 13:1 - 13:14)

13.1 Submission to Governmental Authorities

The first part of this chapter deals with the issues of relating to secular governmental authority which is extremely important and a very delicate subject to discuss.

There are probably many divergent views among Christians on this point. But I am going to simply focus on what the scripture says and leave it on the Holy Spirit to apply it to our hearts.

Before we begin to read Romans chapter 13, it will be good to take a look at a parallel passage in 1st Peter chapter 2.

It is a significant fact that both Paul and Peter and Paul were executed under the Roman Empire. So we need to bear in mind that whatever they said, they had to live it out. So this is a very sober subject.

13Submit yourselves for the Lord's sake to every human institution, whether to a king as the one in authority, 14or to governors as sent by him for the punishment of evildoers and the praise of those who do right. 15For such is the will of God that by doing right you may silence the ignorance of foolish men. 16Act as free men, and do not use your freedom as a covering for evil, but use it as bond slaves of God. 17Honor all people, love the brotherhood, fear God, honor the king. (1 Peter 2:13-17)

In essence Peter is saying very much the same as Paul says in the first part of chapter 13.

Rom 13:1*Every person is to be in subjection to the governing authorities. For there is no authority except from God, and those which exist are established by God.*

Now, that is a rather breathtaking statement. It was made at the time of the Roman Empire, which had crucified Jesus and later was to execute the author of this epistle that is Paul. But Paul says very categorically that there is no authority except from God and those which exist, both in his time as much as today, are established by God.

Let us just turn to Matthew 28 verse 18 for a moment. This is after the resurrection of Jesus. *And Jesus came up and spoke to them, saying, "All authority has been given to Me in heaven and on earth.* (Matthew 28:18)

And in Colossians 2:10 says: *and in Him you have been made complete, and He is the head over all rule and authority;*

He is the head over all authority. All authority in the universe has been delegated by God the Father to Jesus Christ the Son. Paul wrote these words and Peter wrote the same words that all authority ultimately is in the hands of Jesus.

Rom13:2 *Therefore whoever resists authority has opposed the ordinance of God; and they who have opposed will receive condemnation upon themselves.*

Now, what Paul means is that, the one who resists governmental authority resists the ordinance of God and will receive condemnation. Paul is not talking about resisting righteous authority. He is talking about resisting governmental authority.

Then he goes on:

Rom 13:3 *For rulers are not a cause of fear for good behavior, but for evil. Do you want to have no fear of authority? Do what is good and you will have praise from the same;*

So as long as your conscience is clear and you do what is right, Paul says there is no reason to be afraid. And then he goes on in verse 4:

Rom 13:4 for it is a minister of God to you for good. But if you do what is evil, be afraid; for it does not bear the sword for nothing; for it is a minister of God, an avenger who brings wrath on the one who practices evil.

The word Minister gives us a rather a cloudy impression. We need to use the word servant which is what a minister is. He is not a person but the authority is a minister of God to you for good. So we are not talking about the person that occupies the office. We are talking about the actual office itself and Paul says (about the office) it is a minister of God to you for good but if you do what is evil, be afraid for it (the office) does not bear the sword for nothing. For it is a minister of God or a servant of God, an avenger who brings wrath upon the one who practices evil.

Therefore it is necessary to be in subjection not only because of wrath but also for the sake of conscience. So we are to be subject to the governing authority, not merely because we will be dealt with severely if we are not in subjection, but for the sake of conscience. What Paul and Peter are saying is this: behind that office is God and our relationship to the office ultimately depicts our relationship to God.

What are some hidden lessons in this?

The first lesson from is that we need to pray for those in authority. Christians need to pray for their government. We need intercessors for Governments. 1st Timothy 2:1-2 bear this witness. Bear in mind that 1st Timothy is written to instruct Timothy on how to conduct the affairs of a local church and that is whole message of that epistle.

First of all, then, I urge that entreaties and prayers, petitions and thanksgivings, be made on behalf of all men, for kings and all who are in authority, so that we may lead a tranquil and quiet life in all godliness and dignity. (1st Timothy 2:1-2)

Notice that he starts with the words 'first of all'. In other words, the first thing to focus on in your local church is not preaching but prayer.

There are four different kinds of prayers spoken of there.

- Entreaties would be supplications calling out for mercy
- Prayers would be coming to God
- Petitions would be specific things that we ask for
- Thanksgiving explains itself

On behalf of all men and that should broaden the vision of all Christians. Somebody once said that the average Christians prayer life is: God bless me and my wife, my son John and his wife Amen. What Paul is talking about is a lot more than that. God said that his house will be called a house of prayer for all people. The first group that we are to pray for is not evangelists, our ministry or missionaries or the sick but the kings and all in authority. That is a very significant principle so that we may lead a tranquil and quiet life in all godliness and dignity. Ask yourself this question. Does the government I live under affect the kind of life I live? Yes or no. If yes, then its self-interest to pray for the government is not it? And if we do not pray for the government we deserve what we get.

Many of today's Christians are more prone to criticize their government than to pray for it. Jesus never told us to criticize our governments. In fact when Jesus was confronted with the issue of tax he retorted: *"give unto Cesar what belongs to Cesar"* (Mark 12:17). The Bible tells us to pray for our governments.

Then Paul gives the reason why we should pray for our government. It is not so that we can double our economy or build schools or more infrastructures. The reason is a spiritual one. *This is good and acceptable in the sight of God our Savior, who desires all men to be saved and to come to the knowledge of the truth. (1ˢᵗ Timothy 2:3-4)*

Why does God want good government? It is because good governance promotes peace and opens the door to preach the gospel. That is what God wants and he places a great responsibility upon his church to pray for the government. If we do not pray, we do not have a right to expect the kind of government that will facilitate the preaching of the gospel.

So that is our first responsibility as Christians in relationship to secular Authority. What Paul is saying is governmental officers and authorities are servants of God for the benefit of us.

Rom 13:5 *Therefore it is necessary to be in subjection, not only because of wrath, but also for conscience' sake*

And then Paul goes on to describe the things that government does for us.

Rom13:6 *For because of this you also pay taxes, for rulers are servants of God, devoting themselves to this very thing.*

And so he says fulfill your duties as a citizen.

Rom 13:7 *Render to all what is due them: tax to whom tax is due; custom to whom custom; fear to whom fear; honor to whom honor.*

This is a clear outline of our responsibilities. The question arises. What happens when an ungodly or a wicked man or a persecutor is occupying the position of authority? That is where the rubber meets the road. Let us take the example of Jesus. Jesus is a good pattern.

Let us turn briefly to the Gospel of John chapter 18 and verse 36. Jesus is in front of Pilate and Pilate is questioning him about his claim to be a king, and Jesus answered in verse 36:

Jesus answered, "My kingdom is not of this world. If My kingdom were of this world, then My servants would be fighting so that I would not be handed over to the Jews; but as it is, My kingdom is not of this realm." (John 18:36)

I think that is a very important basic principle. The kingdom of God is never established by carnal weapons. I am not saying we should not use them. But we do not bring in the kingdom of God with carnal weapons. It is not established by physical weapons.

As Christians, we are citizens of the kingdom of God. This Kingdom is not established by fighting physical wars. In Zechariah 4:6 the Lord said to Zerubbabel: *'Not by might not by power, but by my spirit' says the Lord of hosts.*

So it is not by military power nor is it by force of arms. There is only one power that can bring in the kingdom of God - the Spirit of God.

Then in John 19:10-11, again Jesus is in front of Pilate and Pilate says to him in verse 10:

So Pilate said to Him, "You do not speak to me? Do You not know that I have authority to release You, and I have authority to crucify You?" (John 19:10)

Notice the word authority. It was true that Pilate had authority. He certainly did and he was making a true statement. Now listen to what Jesus said:

Jesus answered, "You would have no authority over Me, unless it had been given you from above; for this reason he who delivered Me to you has the greater sin." (John 19:11)

In other words, behind Pilate who was making an unjust decision concerning Jesus, the authority came from God the father. And then he made another remarkable statement. For this reason he who delivered me up to you has the greater sin. I presume that was the Jewish High Priest because he stepped out of the bounds of his authority. He was not operating within his authority. He did something he did not have authority to do.

You can see that Jesus had tremendous respect for secular authority even when it was being used unjustly. *Therefore it is necessary to be in subjection, not only because of wrath, but also for conscience' sake.* (Romans 13:5)

You may say, what if the ruler demands that I do something that I cannot do with a clear conscience as a Christian? The answer is: you refuse to do it. But you submit to the authority and say "I will not do that but you can do whatever you like with me". Do not give up your submission.

There is a very clear example about that in Acts 5:27-29 where the Apostles had been told that they must not preach any more in the name of Jesus.

27When they had brought them, they stood them before the Council. The high priest questioned them, 28saying, "We gave you strict orders not to continue teaching in this name, and yet, you have filled Jerusalem with your teaching and intend to bring this man's blood upon us." 29But Peter and the apostles answered, "We must obey God rather than men. (Acts 5:27-29)

When there is a clear-cut issue, then we have to obey God. If necessary, disobey human authority but let us be very sure that it is really obeying God. In Mark 6:15 Jesus said to his disciples *'go into the entire world and preach the gospel to all creation or every creature'*. So there was a specific command of Jesus which the Apostles were obeying and which the high priests were forbidding them. So the apostles were determined to obey the Lord and not man.

They said we cannot stop. We will not obey you. You can do what you like with us. But on this issue we have to obey God rather than men. The apostles did not start a revolution. They simply submitted to unjust treatment.

Let us just look at something that Paul said a little further on in Romans 16:20. It is a remarkable statement. He said... *The God of peace will soon crush Satan under your feet*. There could be more than one way of interpreting that. But it is the God of peace who is going to crush Satan. How is that fulfilled? One way it was fulfilled was in the subjection of the Roman Empire to Christianity.

Christianity started as a little offbeat movement following the execution of a man who had been a mere carpenter. It had no valid hopes of success but within three centuries, it had brought the Roman Emperor to his knees and God had crushed Satan under the feet of that church – particularly the church at Rome. They did not stage marches, they did not hold protests and they did not have sit-in strikes. What did they do? They prayed, they testified, they preached and they submitted. By their submission they opened the way for God to do for them what they could not do for themselves.

The Christians in the Soviet Union followed in the steps of the early church. They did not staged a revolution or a rebellion neither did they hold protest marches. They went the way of the early church and God has vindicated them. If we submit, we open the way for God to do what he alone can do.

This is an important lesson for every Christian's reflection because you may at one time be confronted with this choice. It is better to be prepared beforehand. Talking about suffering in 1st Peter 4:1, Peter said; *arm yourselves with this mind for Christ also suffered once with sin*. In other words arm yourself with this attitude, that when you are confronted by this difficult choice between obedience to God and obedience to secular Authority, you will be ready to make the sacrifice. I.e. make a decision now and settle it in your minds. Do not go into that situation unarmed. Do not go into the situation assuming nobody will ever ask you to make that sacrifice.

Revelation 12:11, it says: *they overcame him by the blood of the Lamb and by the word of their testimony*. And then it says *they loved not their lives unto the death*.

What it means is that for them it was more important to do the will of God than to stay alive. There must be a degree of commitment on the part of believers. Do not think that Satan is the least bit scared of uncommitted Christians. You can pray all the prayers and Satan laughs in your face. But when you have laid your life on the line, when you make a commitment, he knows that this is a serious business.

13.2 Love fulfills the law

It is so refreshing and beautiful to come back to the theme of love. That is what the main teaching of this section is. Paul says here:

Rom 13:8 *Owe nothing to anyone except to love one another; for he who loves his neighbor has fulfilled the law.*

Rom 13:9 *For this, "You shall not commit adultery, you shall not murder, you shall not steal, you shall not covet," and if there is any other commandment, it is summed up in this saying, "You shall love your neighbor as yourself."*

Rom 13:10 *Love does no wrong to a neighbor; therefore love is the fulfillment of the law.*

So Paul says I do not want you to be in debt. How many of you do not owe anyone anything. You do not owe on your car or you home etc. The Bible says the borrower is a servant to the lender. When we get into debt we become servants of the person that has lent us.

The purpose of Christ's death which is stated in Romans 8:3 and 4 says: *For what the Law could not do, weak as it was through the flesh, God did: sending His own Son in the likeness of sinful flesh and as an offering for sin, He condemned sin in the flesh, (Romans 8:3)*

That happened when Jesus died on the cross

So that the requirement of the Law might be fulfilled in us, who do not walk according to the flesh but according to the Spirit (Romans 8:4)

So we are set free from the Law of Moses and all its ordinances, statutes and regulations and ceremonies, so that the requirement of the law might be fulfilled in us. Another translation says the righteous requirement of the law, which is a better translation because that the word is directly derived from the word for righteous. The same word is used in Revelation 19:8 where it says: *It was given to her to clothe herself in fine linen, bright and clean; **for the fine linen is the righteous acts of the saints.***

So we are set free from the requirements of the Law of Moses in order that the righteous requirement of the law might be worked out in us.

What is the righteous requirement of the law? It is LOVE.

Galatians 5:14 says: *For the whole Law is fulfilled in one word, in the statement, "You shall love your neighbor as yourself."*

Therefore the righteous requirement of the law is love. We are not required to follow all the details of the Law of Moses but we are under obligation to love.

So we do not need to be vague or unclear about how we are supposed to relate to the Law of Moses. We have been set free from all its enactments and requirements but we are required to work out its righteous requirement which is love.

Let's look briefly at what Jesus said in John 13:34: *a new commandment I give you that you love one another even as I have loved you.*

Moses gave them Ten Commandments, Judaism has 613 commandments but Jesus says I will just give you just one commandment because in that one commandment everything is included.

In 1st Timothy 1, Paul says...*But the goal of our instruction is love from a pure heart and a good conscience and a sincere faith.* (He gives three conditions for maintaining love: A pure heart, A good conscience and sincere faith). *For some men, straying from these things, have turned aside to fruitless discussion, wanting to be teachers of the Law, even though they do not understand either what they are saying or the matters about which they make confident assertions.* (1Timothy 1:5-7)

So any kind of teaching or preaching in church that does not produce love is fruitless discussion. It is a waste of words and time. The only goal of all teaching should be love. We need to check ourselves from time to time and ask ourselves…are we really producing love or have we diverted to secondary issues.

There are relatively few congregations that really and specifically make love their primary goal. Somehow many have got themselves diverted into lots of things that, even though are important, are secondary. If we make love our primary goal or motive, everything else falls in place.

Again, look at James 1:25. James says…*But one who looks intently at the perfect law, the law of liberty, and abides by it, not having become a forgetful hearer but an effectual doer, this man will be blessed in what he does.*

James does not specifically state what the perfect law or the law of Liberty is but if you go on to James 2:8, he says…*If, however, you are fulfilling the royal law according to the Scripture, "You shall love your neighbor as yourself," you are doing well.*

So this is the Royal law, the perfect law or the law of Liberty: Love your neighbor as yourself.

That is something to think about. When you are motivated by love, you live like a king and nobody orders you about. Nobody can force you to do anything because you always want to do the right thing. You will never be made to do anything against your will. It is the law of perfection. It is the law of liberty. It is the Royal law and it is kingly.

Why should we waste our time on a lot of other things? The enemy diverts us because he is afraid of Christians who really love one another because they have power, they have authority and furthermore they challenge the world. Jesus said in regard to that commandment we read: by this shall all men know that you are my disciples if you love one another.

13.3 Live in Anticipation of Christ Return

Rom 13:11 Do this (Do all that Paul has been talking about - subjection to authority and love for one another), *knowing the time, that it is already the hour for you to awaken from sleep; for now salvation is nearer to us than when we believed.*

This is my personal understanding to this. That when a true believer dies and passes out of this life he passes into a timeless existence. Eternity is not subject to the laws of time. We no longer have elapsed time. There are no clocks in that world. When he closes his eyes in death, and moves out into a timeless existence, his eyes are not going to open until the resurrection.

To us that is a sort of puzzling statement. In a way the time factor in this age is difficult to comprehend because Paul wrote as if the coming of the Lord was very close.

When he opens those eyes in his resurrected body, the first thing he will see is the Lord coming in. so you are never further from the Lord's coming in time than you are from your point of death because in death there is no time.

A lot of Christians have got the attitude that our aim is to get to heaven. Well, it is a tremendous privilege to believe that you are going to go to heaven when you die but that wasn't Paul's aim. Look for a moment at this scripture in Philippians 3: **8***More than that, I count all things to be loss in view of the surpassing value of knowing Christ Jesus my Lord, for whom I have suffered the loss of all things, and count them but rubbish so that I may gain Christ, and may be found in Him,* **9** *not having a righteousness of my own derived from the Law, but that which is through faith in Christ, the righteousness which comes from God on the basis of faith,* **10** *that I may know Him and the power of His resurrection and the fellowship of His sufferings, being conformed to His death; 11in order that I may attain to the resurrection from the dead.* (Philippians 3:8-11)

In verse 11, did Paul say in order that I may get to heaven? No, he says in order that I may attain to the resurrection from the dead. The resurrection is our goal and not heaven.

When we are in heaven, our spirits will be there but our bodies will be decomposed. That is not the end of salvation. Jesus has purchased spirit, soul and body and Paul says I pray that your whole spirit soul and body may be preserved blameless at the coming of our Lord Jesus Christ.

Going on:

Rom 13:12 *The night is almost gone, and the day is near. Therefore let us lay aside the deeds of darkness and put on the armor of light*

Rom 13:13 *Let us behave properly as in the day, not in carousing and drunkenness, not in sexual promiscuity and sensuality, not in strife and jealousy*

Rom 13:14 *But put on the Lord Jesus Christ, and make no provision for the flesh in regard to its lusts.*

That is a picture of people who are living in excited anticipation of the Lord's return. The motivation for holy living is not a set of rules. It is the fact we are going to meet Jesus and we need to be ready and we are going to stand before his judgment seat and he is going to weigh every word we have spoken, every thought that is passed through our minds and every action - with those eyes that penetrate to the very core of our being.

You will be able to hide nothing in that day. Everything will be transparent in the eyes of the Lord Jesus. That is the main motivation for holiness in the New Testament church.

Titus 2 from verse 11 and following, it says: **11** *For the grace of God has appeared, bringing salvation to all men,* **12** *instructing us to deny ungodliness and worldly desires and to live sensibly, righteously and godly in the present age,* **13** *looking for the blessed hope and the appearing of the glory of our great God and Savior, Christ Jesus,* **14** *who gave Himself for us to redeem us from every lawless deed, and to purify for Himself a people for His own possession, zealous for good deeds. (Titus 2:11-14)*

Therefore, the real motivation for Holy living is anticipating the Lord's return. A minister of God's word once said that in the modern day church, there is lack or very little excitement about the Lord's return.

When you have been away from your child for a couple of days, when he hears you knocking on the door, he or she really gets excited that daddy or mommy is home. If you did not receive that expectant reception, you will be really disappointed. Jesus is excited. He loves us passionately and he wants to be loved passionately.

Thanks be to God who gives us the victory through our Lord Jesus Christ.

CHAPTER 14: DON'T BE GUIDED BY RELIGIOUS RULES

(Romans 14:1 - 14:23)

14.1 Religious Rules about Diet and Holidays

(Romans 14:1 - 14:12)

This theme is very relevant today than it was a couple of years back. The issue of diet and holidays is a very current issue and somewhat controversial. More and more people are becoming concerned about issues of diet and observance of days e.g. observing Sabbath on Saturday.

The real theme of this scripture is acceptance and harmony. God is more concerned with harmony in the body of Christ than he is with the exact observance of certain set rules.

Let us begin by reading the first three verses of Romans chapter 14.

Rom 14:1 Now accept the one who is weak in faith, but not for the purpose of passing judgment on his opinions.

The key word is 'accepting one another'. Accept the one who is weak in faith. Do not to criticize him. Do not tear his opinions apart. Do not point out to him how incomplete his understanding is, because that is not a truly spiritual attitude. It may prove how clever you are but it does not build the body of Christ. So the two things which Paul is emphasizing are our acceptance and building the body.

Then Paul gives this example: the first example deals with food and the next one deal with observing certain days.

Rom 14:2 One person has faith that he may eat all things, but he who is weak eats vegetables only.

Why does he eat vegetables only? Is it because he is a vegetarian? No. It is because he wants to eat Kosher. Kosher means the way that Orthodox Jews prepare and choose and serve their food. It has to be done very exactly i.e. everything served on a special kind of plate. It has to be prepared in a special way and you must not mix milk with meat or meat products with milk products. If you have consumed milk you have to wait for five hours before you can consume meat and all sorts of foods are excluded. Part of this is based on the Law of Moses. For most people, it is not a burning issue but it is a very current issue in Israel for Jewish believers today.

Romans 14:3 The one who eats is not to regard with contempt the one who does not eat, and the one who does not eat is not to judge the one who eats, for God has accepted him.

There are two wrong attitudes here: first of all, there is the brother who has been liberated. "I am not under the law brother. That is all in the past. I eat anything I like and you do not understand. You are still in bondage". That is the one who regards with contempt the one who does not eat.

But it is not a one-way relationship because the one who does not eat criticizes the one who eats and he says; "he is not a real Jew any longer. He is not keeping kosher". For the Jewish people, one of the burning issues is maintaining Israel as a separate identity because when the laws of kosher and the observance of Sabbath are broken, the Jews very quickly mingle and lose their national identity. So it is really an important issue.

Closer home, there are those Christians who do not eat pork and they regard anyone who eats pork with contempt. It is more important to maintain harmony and build up the body of Christ than prove yourself right by the rules you observe. You can prove yourself right and damage the body of Christ.

Again, the issue of women covering their hair in 1st Corinthians 11… *every woman when praying or prophesying with a head uncovered dishonors her head*. There are lots of serious committed Christians who do not understand it that way. So we leave others free to do what they believe.

In some places, every woman has to wear a hat or she would not be accepted as a Christian. The key thing here is to fellowship with perfect harmony. Remember harmony is the goal.

Then Paul goes on:

Rom 14:4 *Who are you to judge the servant of another? To his own master he stands or falls; and he will stand, for the Lord is able to make him stand.*

So the real sin is not eating or observing or not observing the Sabbath. The real sin is criticizing your fellow believers. That is something that people are very prone to do.

Verses 5 and 6 brings us to the next question which is observing certain days and the particular day that is perhaps the most controversial is the day called the Sabbath or Saturday. Bear in mind that it is not Saturday because the Jewish Sabbath begins on Friday evening at sunset and ends on Saturday evening at sunset. So we are not talking about just Saturday. It is a different concept of measuring the days of the week. It goes back to creation where it was the evening and the morning that was day 1. God's Day does not begin with dawn, it begins with sunset. That is a remarkable thing and we will not go into that now.

Rom 14:5 *one person regards one day above another, another regards every day alike. Each person must be fully convinced in his own mind.*

I think it implies that we should stop trying to convince other people.

Rom 14:6 He who observes the day, observes it for the Lord, and he who eats, does so for the Lord, for he gives thanks to God; and he who eats not, for the Lord he does not eat, and gives thanks to God.

Each one is doing what he believes is right on the side of the law.

That is a matter for each person to decide for themselves. It is necessary to look at other passages particularly Colossians 2:13-16 which deals with what was accomplished by the sacrificial death of Jesus on the cross.

And you, being dead in your sins and the uncircumcision of your flesh, hath he quickened together with him, having forgiven you all trespasses; (Colossians 2:13)

What that Paul is teaching here is that Jesus by his death on the cross took away from Satan every weapon that he could use against us and his primary weapon is guilt. As long as he can make us feel guilty he has us where he wants us. But by his death on the cross, Jesus made provision for us to be set free from guilt. He made provision for all our past sinful acts to be forgiven.

But in order to carter for the future, Jesus had to set aside the Law of Moses as the requirement for achieving righteousness with God.

14Blotting out the handwriting of ordinances that was against us, which was contrary to us, and took it out of the way, nailing it to his cross; 15And having spoiled principalities and powers, he made a shew of them openly, triumphing over them in it. (Colossians 2:14, 15)

So once you come to the cross in faith, the law is finished. It has no more claims over you. You are no longer subject to the law through the death of Jesus. You have been delivered from the demands of the law. The law has dominion over a born again man as long as he lives. But when the law has put you to death that is the last thing it can do to you. And we, in Jesus were put to death and have come back to life beyond the cross free from the demands of the law.

Then Paul goes on and this is a very important verse

16 *Let no man therefore judge you in meat, or in drink, or in respect of any holyday, or of the new moon, or of the Sabbath days: (Colossians 2:16)*

Paul does not say "do not observe them" but he says "do not let anybody judge you" about whether you observe them or not because we have been set free from the requirements of the law.

So again the warning is against judging. Do not judge others and do not let anybody judge you. Everybody has got to decide for himself or herself how he understands God's will in his life.

Going back to Romans chapter 14:

Rom 14:7 *For not one of us lives for himself, and not one dies for himself;*

Rom 14:8 *for if we live, we live for the Lord, or if we die, we die for the Lord; therefore whether we live or die, we are the Lord's.*

Rom 14:9 *For to this end Christ died and lived again, that He might be Lord both of the dead and of the living.*

So what Paul is saying is this: what matters is our personal relationship with the Lord. Once we belong to the Lord, he is never going to leave us. We are his for time and for eternity. Whether we live, we are living for the Lord and whether we die, we die for the Lord. The Lord is the one to whom we are finally responsible to.

There is this pastor's whose wife who was very supportive to him and his ministry to the point that she did everything for him. But the Lord began showing her that her relationship with him comes first not her relationship with her husband. That is true of every one of us.

You may have a wonderful marriage partner but your first relationship is with the Lord. There is a time coming when all the other relationships will drop when you pass out of time into eternity. The one relationship that will not change is the relationship with Jesus. We need to live our lives now in the light of that awareness. That the one thing that is ultimately is decisive in time and eternity is your personal relationship with Jesus. When you go through the gates of time and into eternity, there is only one person who will go with you and that is Jesus.

There was a lady who said to her husband by his deathbed "this is a place where I cannot go with you. You have got to go on your own". Paul is really reminding us that we better be aware of that fact.

Further in Romans 14, we come to a very important issue which is a warning against judging our fellow believers. This is more needed today than in those days. Many Christians suffer all sorts of problems in their lives because they sin by judging. There is only one judge and that is God.

Consider this for a moment: You are part of the people attending a hearing in a court. Up on the raised dais, is the seat for the judge but it is vacant because the judge has not yet walked in yet. What would happen to you if you got out of your seat and walk up on that platform and sit in the judge's chair. How long would you be allowed to sit there? You will be thrown out and that is just because of taking the place of a human judge. How dare we take the place of God and occupy his chair. What condemnation we bring on ourselves when we judge our fellow believers.

Now, there are certain areas in which we have to exercise judgment. A father has to exercise judgment in respect to his family. A pastor has to exercise judgment in respect to his congregation. Consider this simple principle: where you have responsibility, you have authority to judge but if you are not responsible do not judge. You are not responsible for your fellow believer's life or his family. Do not judge him.

Rom 14:10 but you, why do you judge your brother? Or you again, why do you regard your brother with contempt? For we will all stand before the judgment seat of God.

The word translated judgment seat there in Greek is Baima and we have two judgment scenes.

- One before the great white throne. The great white throne judgment is still quite a long way off. That is the judgment of all the resurrected dead.
- One before the Bema or the Baima. The bema judgment is the judgment in which Christ judges his people. It is very important to remember that there is no condemnation for those who are in Christ. This is not a judgment to determine whether you are saved or lost but it is a judgment to assess your service for Jesus in this life. There every Christian is going to have to stand directly and personally before the Lord Jesus and answer for everything we have done.

Paul says, if you realize that, you would be so busy preparing yourself and you would not have time to judge other people. The people who are judging others are almost certainly not preparing themselves for the judgment seat of Jesus. And then Paul quotes from Isaiah:

Rom 14:11 for it is written, "As I live, says the lord, every knee shall bow to me, and every tongue shall give praise to god."

When we come to the Bema judgment, were going to kneel before Jesus and every tongue shall confess to God. Confess out of the bottom of your heart. There is nothing that is going to be held back. There will be no secrets. There will be no covering up corners of your life. The whole truth is going to come out before Jesus. I suppose he may ask each one of us some pretty pertinent questions.

Why did you criticize that preacher?

Why did you take communion with that lady and then go out immediately and start criticizing her?

One of the reasons why believers have unbelieving children is because they spend so much time at home criticizing other believers and the children listen and think well, if that is what Christianity is why should I be one?

The principal is, never talk against the members of the body of Christ in front of your children. If you want your children to respect God and His people, you better not do it in front of them.

So Paul sums it up.

Romans 14:12 *So then each one of us will give an account of himself to God.*

For whom am I going to give account of? Myself

Let us look for a moment in a parallel passage. Paul is speaking about the motivation of his life and ministry: *9 Wherefore we labour, that, whether present or absent, we may be accepted of him. 10 For we must all appear before the judgment seat of Christ; that every one may receive the things done in his body, according to that he hath done, whether it be good or bad. (2 Corinthians 5:9, 10)*

That is an appointment none of us is going to miss. You may miss a lot of appointments and turn up late for a lot of situations but you are going to be there on time for this appointment. We must all appear before the judgment seat of Christ that each one may be recompense deeds done in the body. We are going to have to answer for everything we have done in this life according to what he has done whether good or bad. There are only two categories good or bad. There is nothing neutral.

Everything that is done for the glory of God and according to the will of God and the Word of God is good and everything else is not good. The devil always wants to persuade us that there is some kind of spiritual neutrality and we are in a grey zone. It is neither black nor white. That is a plain lie.

Jesus said very plainly: He that is not with me is against me. He that does not gather with me is scattering. There are only two kinds of activity in this life as a believer. You are either gathering you or you are scattering. You are either being fruitful or you are wasting your time. (What about all the hours you have sat in front of a silly television set when you could have been praying or reading your Bible or fellowship with believers or edifying your own family).

If we truly repent and confess and ask for forgiveness, we do not have to answer for those things.

14.2 Be Guided By Love and Not Religious Rules

We are familiar with a number of addictions: tobacco, alcohol, drugs, television etc. Another addiction is criticizing people. If you are going to stop, you are going to need God's supernatural grace to stop because you are addicted. It is a destructive addiction. It destroys you and it destroys the people you criticize and it disrupts the body of Christ.

Live your life in view the fact that you are going to have to account for everything you say and do to Jesus. Ask the Holy Spirit to reveal the things that you need to confess and repent.

God gives us the opportunity to judge ourselves. Check our behavior against the Word of God and once we say, I was guilty, I did wrong, Lord I am sorry, I repent forgive me, it is erased. We do not have to answer for that.

When you come to the Lord Jesus the first time as a sinner he uses his bulky eraser to erase everything you have ever done that was evil. But as you go along you may say and do things that are wrong and it is all right if you confess and repent. Jesus just erases that little piece of tape.

You never need the whole bulk eraser again but you do need to keep the tape clean.

Rom 14:13 *Therefore let us not judge one another anymore, but rather determine this—not to put an obstacle or a stumbling block in a brother's way*

All through these chapters of Romans, the guiding principle is love and from time to time Paul goes back and points out that love is what guides you to do the right thing. So he says here:

Rom 14:14 *I know and am convinced in the Lord Jesus that nothing is unclean in itself; but to him who thinks anything to be unclean, to him it is unclean.*

Paul says there is no food that in itself is unclean but if a person thinks something is unclean and eats it or consumes it on that basis it is unclean to him. It defiles him. This is very important and we need to look at two scriptures:

In Mark 7, Jesus is talking about the question of what we eat and he says there is nothing outside the man which going into him can defile him, but the things which proceed out of the man are what defile the man. The disciples did not understand that and so they questioned him verse 17:

17When he had left the crowd and entered the house, His disciples questioned Him about the parable.18And He said to them, "Are you so lacking in understanding also? Do you not understand that whatever goes into the man from outside cannot defile him, 19because it does not go into his heart, but into his stomach, and is eliminated?" (Thus He declared all foods clean.) (Mark 7:17-19)

That is a very important statement. From that time onwards, with the authority of Jesus there is no such thing as an unclean food in itself. But subjectively a food may be unclean.

Danes eat eels, Chinese eat frogs, dogs, snakes etc., some Africans eat snakes, apes, and snails etc. and consider them a delicacy.

Paul writing to Timothy says;

1But the Spirit explicitly says that in later times some will fall away from the faith, paying attention to deceitful spirits and doctrines of demons, 2by means of the hypocrisy of liars seared in their own conscience as with a branding iron, 3men who forbid marriage and advocate abstaining from foods which God has created to be gratefully shared in by those who believe and know the truth. 4For everything created by God is good, and nothing is to be rejected if it is received with gratitude; 5for it is sanctified by means of the word of God and prayer. (1st Timothy 4:1-5)

Paul is talking about certain errors that will creep into the church. He talks about men who forbid marriage and advocate abstaining from foods which God has created to be gratefully shared in by those who believe and know the truth. You have to believe, and know the truth, for everything created by God is good and nothing is to be rejected if it is received with gratitude.

Paul is talking about food and says that nothing is to be rejected for it is sanctified by the Word of God and prayer. When you pray over your food, it is not a mere formality because you do not know what you are eating. But if you have the faith that it can be sanctified by your prayer, it is already sanctified by the Word of God. When your prayer is in faith, it will stop you from getting all sorts of food poisoning. You better be sure you have the faith.

Rom 14:15 *For if because of food your brother is hurt, you are no longer walking according to love. Do not destroy with your food him for whom Christ died.*

The central principle is love. You do not abstain from food because you feel it is forbidden. But if in a certain sense you were to eat in front of your brother, you would offend him, then do not eat e.g. for an

Orthodox Jew, there are some kinds of food which absolutely appalled them. You should never eat bacon in front of an Orthodox Jew believer. Not because there is anything wrong with bacon, but because he thinks there is something wrong with bacon.

You see, Paul looked out at all humanity, whether it was Jewish or Gentile. He saw people for whom Jesus died. That is the way he looked to people and his whole dealing with people was on that basis. We need to have the same vision. Then in verse 16:

Rom 14:16 Therefore do not let what is for you a good thing be spoken of as evil;

Do not expose yourself to unnecessary criticism. When you are criticized, negative forces are released against you. Why should you expose yourself to those forces unnecessarily?

Rom 14:17 For the kingdom of God is not eating and drinking, but righteousness and peace and joy in the Holy Spirit.

This is a wonderful verse. So being in the kingdom of God is not a question of what we eat or drink. There are three things that essentially define the kingdom of God: righteousness, peace and joy.

In this age in which we live in, the kingdom of God is only a reality where the Holy Spirit is at work. The boundaries of the kingdom on earth at this time are determined by the area where the Holy Spirit operates. Outside of the Holy Spirit all you have is laws and rules and religion. It takes the Holy Spirit to bring the kingdom of God into a life or a situation and when the Holy Spirit moves in and is allowed to have his way, he will produce three results: righteousness, peace and joy. Notice that the first result is righteousness, second peace and third Joy.

Now Jesus said in Matthew 5:6: *"Blessed are those who hunger and thirst for righteousness, for they shall be satisfied.*

Jesus did not say blessed are those who hunger for peace or after Joy or after healing or after prosperity but after righteousness.

If you look around, you will see many Christians who hunger and thirst after healing or prosperity, but you will not meet very many that are hungry and thirsty for righteousness. The blessing is on those who hunger and thirst for righteousness. Once you have entered into righteousness, peace and joy will follow as natural consequences. Do not go for peace and do not go for joy but make righteousness your aim.

Today, there is a terrific talk in the world about the need for peace which is very valid, but this cry for peace is going to become a means of deception and the manipulation of the saints because the world is going to seek for peace and maybe even claim it has achieved peace without righteousness. That is a deception. There is no true or permanent peace without righteousness.

Let us look at two passages. In Isaiah 48:22, it says…*"There is no peace for the wicked," says the LORD.* As long as we tolerate wickedness, there is no possibility of permanent peace. Exactly the same words are found at the end of Isaiah 57 in verse 21: *"There is no peace," says my God, "for the wicked."*

So the essential and primary condition for peace is righteousness. And that is what the kingdom of God is. Its righteousness, then peace and joy in the Holy Spirit.

The question you need to ask yourself privately is: Are you in the kingdom of God right now? Are you enjoying righteousness, peace and joy in the Holy Spirit? If not, you may have religion. You may be charismatic, you may be Pentecostal, you may be Baptist, Methodist, Presbyterian or whatever, but you are not in the kingdom of God because those are the boundaries of the kingdom of God: Righteousness, peace and joy in the Holy Spirit.

And then verse 18 is very real:

Rom 14:18 *For he who in this way serves Christ is acceptable to God and approved by men.*

In what way?; In the way of righteousness, peace and joy.

If you serve God in righteousness, peace and joy, in any set up or situation you find yourself in, you are not only acceptable to God but also approved by men. In the long run the ungodly know how, a Christian should act.

Rom 14:19 *So then we pursue the things which make for peace and the building up of one another.*

If all you do is to say to people, "I am a born again Christian", but your actions are not just (righteous) to those around you, God will not accept you. Jesus said: *You are the salt of the earth. But if the salt loses its savor, how can it be made salty again? It is no longer good for anything, except to be thrown out and trampled by men.* (Matthew 5:13)

Going on to Romans 14:20, we are now getting to the application.

Rom 14:20 *Do not tear down the work of God for the sake of food. All things indeed are clean, but they are evil for the man who eats and gives offense.*

Paul was more concerned with the work of God and building the body of Christ. Let us always build up the body even if it means personal sacrifice. All things indeed are clean but they are evil for the man who eats and gives offense. So I am perfectly free to eat bacon, but if I eat bacon in front of a new Jewish believer who does not know these things, I will offend him. They are evil to him and I will be guilty of evil.

Rom 14:21 *It is good not to eat meat or to drink wine, or to do anything by which your brother stumbles.*

The issue is, are you building up your brother or are you breaking him down? What Paul is saying is this, I am perfectly free myself to do all the things listed in that verse but I would not do them in front of people who would be offended by them.

Rom 14:22 *The faith which you have, have as your own conviction before God:*

Do not get into arguments about these things. Whether you are convinced about it or not, let it be between you and God.

Happy is he who does not condemn himself in what he approves: That is a searching statement. You can approve things which are perfectly legitimate, but in approving them, you condemn yourself because of the effect you have on your fellow believers. Then Paul goes on:

Rom 14:23 *But he who doubts is condemned if he eats, because his eating is not from faith; and whatever is not from faith is sin.*

There is only one basis for righteous which is living in faith. If you are not doing it out of faith, do not do it. Whatever is not based on faith is sin.

CHAPTER 15: SELF-DENIAL ON BEHALF OF OTHERS

(Romans 15:1 - 15:33)

15.1 The Marks of True Spiritual Strength

Paul is talking in relationship to the previous passage.

Rom 15:1 *Now we who are strong ought to bear the weaknesses of those without strength and not just please ourselves.*

The true measure of spiritual strength is not how much you can do but it is how much you can bear. Strength in this sense is being able to lift others up. Your strength is not holding people down. It is lifting people up. In Revelation 21:14, it says about the New Jerusalem: *The wall of the city had twelve foundations bearing the names of the twelve apostles of the Lamb.* The Apostles are in the foundation.

So spiritual strength is not holding everybody down and dictating to everybody. It is being able to hold up those who are not as strong.

Then Paul goes on:

Rom 15:2 *Each of us is to please his neighbor for his good, to his edification.*

The key word there is edification.

Rom 15:3 *For even Christ did not please Himself; but as it is written, "The reproaches of those who reproached you fell on me."*

Jesus brought upon himself the reproaches of those who hated God because he was living for God. We have to be prepared to bring reproach upon ourselves when we live for God. Then he says,

Rom 15:4 For whatever was written in earlier times was written for our instruction, so that through perseverance and the encouragement of the Scriptures we might have hope.

This is very important. Whatever is in the scriptures is there for our benefit and to instruct us.

It is wonderful to be encouraged but remember that the scripture encourages only those who persevere. It is not enough to believe. You have to keep on believing that your faith will be tested. You will go through trials. The scripture will bless you if you persevere. It says of Abraham, *'after he had patiently endured he received the promise'* (Hebrews 6:15). Abraham's faith was tested for something like 25 years. He patiently endured having the promise of a son who would be his heir.

People say that faith is all you need. That is not true. You need faith and patience. These two together, are undefeatable.

Rom 15:5 Now may the God who gives perseverance and encouragement grant you to be of the same mind with one another according to Christ Jesus,

Rom 15:6 so that with one accord you may with one voice glorify the God and Father of our Lord Jesus Christ.

What is Paul aiming at is harmony. He's not writing simply to produce individual believers. But his aim is to produce a body that can function in unity and harmony. Harmony between believers, so that regardless of their personal differences, they may focus on the Lord, in His goodness and together in harmony glorify and praise the Lord Jesus Christ. That is the positive goal of all this teaching and Paul takes us through various areas which would hinder that and warns us against them. But remember that the positive goal is a harmonizing a group of believers who praise God together with one accord and in one voice.

Some of the lessons that we looked at in our previous lesson emphasized the need for us to put the interests of the body before our own personal opinions and convictions at times.

That is what the church should be. A body of people who have one purpose which is to glorify the God and father of our Lord Jesus Christ. All preaching and all teaching and all church activity should always have that as its goal. Then Paul goes on:

Rom 15:7 Therefore, accept one another, just as Christ also accepted us to the glory of God.

So there is another example of a practical application. Accept one another just as Christ accepted us to the glory of God. That is a challenging statement because Jesus did not wait for us to get straightened out and really cleaned off before he accepted us. He accepted us just the way we were and then he began to change us.

There are so many people, and especially in the body of Christ, whose problem is rejection and the only solution is acceptance. You cannot say to them "well once you get straightened out, I will acknowledge you as a fellow believer". You have to take people the way they are just as God took us the way we were. So it is a challenging statement, accept one another just as Christ accepted you. Do not expect everybody to be perfect. Everybody has problems, even preachers, even pastor, even the leaders of the work of God. Do not expect perfect leaders. Accept them the way they are if you believe that God put them in that place. If there is one place where people should find acceptance, it is the body of Christ.

15.2 How the Gospel Affects the Jews And Gentiles

Now we are going on from that point of acceptance and we come to a point that we covered in a previous section. That is, God's plan for Israel and the church. Paul goes back for a moment and he reiterates the difference in the approach of God to the Jewish people and to the Gentiles. It is good in a way to recapitulate this at this point and he says in verse 8:

Rom 15:8 For I say that Christ has become a servant to the circumcision (That is the Jewish people) *on behalf of the truth of God to confirm the promises given to the fathers,*

Rom 15:9 and for the Gentiles to glorify God for His mercy; as it is written, "Therefore I will give praise to you among the Gentiles, and I will sing to your name"

So Jesus came first and foremost as a servant to the Jewish people to confirm all the promises that had been made, over the centuries, to the Jewish people. He also came to bring mercy to the Gentiles who had no promises and who had no prior history of God's covenant's and dealings. So there is always this difference.

In Galatians Paul speaks about the gospel of the circumcision i.e. the gospel for the Jewish people and the gospel of the un-circumcision i.e. the gospel for the Gentiles. It is not a different gospel. It all centers in the person of the Lord Jesus Christ - His death, his resurrection and his ascension. But the difference is in approach.

You just start with the fact we are all sinners and that we all need a Savior which is true with both Jewish and Gentile believers. But with the Jewish people, you have to explain to them that this is the outworking of the history that they have had from Abraham onwards, taking them back to Abraham through Moses.

It is very important for Gentiles to know the origin of the gospel too i.e. the origin of our faith but for the Jewish people it is essential because Jesus was a servant of the circumcision to confirm and fulfill the promises that God had made to them. But for the Gentiles, we did not have any background in the promises of God, except as a nominal Christian, which is quite different and all we needed was mercy.

So, in essence, the Jewish people are like a field that had been plowed and cultivated over many centuries. When Jesus sent the disciples out to his own people, he said you are entering into the labors of men who labored long before you (John 4:38). So it was the continuing of a process that had begun way back. But the Gentiles were an uncultivated field. They had never been cultivated and the gospel just came to them without any background in the history of their ancestors. So, as more and more Jewish people are coming to believe in the Messiah, we need to know how to approach them.

Then Paul does not have to take a lot of time to prove that Jesus came to the Jews. He has to take a lot of time to prove that the Gentiles can come in. This was nineteen centuries ago. Now the boot is on the other foot. Let's just look very quickly at these promises which he refers to.

The first is in Psalm 18:49. This is a great triumphant song of David after God had given him victory over all his enemies and is also predictive of the Messiah.

Therefore I will give thanks to you among the nations, O LORD, And I will sing praises to Your name. (Psalm 18:49)

When you read the word nations in most translations, you need to say to yourself Gentiles. There are two main terms: there is people and nations. People, in the Hebrew, are those who have a covenant relationship with God. Nations or Gentiles (goyim) in Hebrew are those who have no relationship with God.

You remember what Jesus said to the Canaanite woman when she came for the healing? He said you are just a little dog. You do not have any relationship with God. You are unclean, you are outside the covenant. Many people have wondered why Jesus spoke to her in such in a way using such a harsh term. In the Middle East, to call anyone a dog is another matter.

I hope you can see it. There is only one way that you can relate with God, when you have a covenant with God. God does not relate on any other basis, except through a covenant. So we who were Gentiles and who have trusted Jesus for salvation and believed in his atoning death and resurrection, we have become a people also.

So the New Testament tells us as believers that we are a people because we have a covenant relationship with God. God has two peoples in the earth:

1. The Jewish people, who even though they are outside the grace of God at the moment, are still a people because of an unbreakable covenant that God has made with them. and;

2. The Gentiles who used to be dogs. We are no longer dogs, we who have a relationship through the New Covenant in Jesus Christ.

Rom 15:10 *Again he says, "Rejoice, O Gentiles, with His people."*

This is in Deuteronomy 32:43: *"Rejoice, O nations, with His people;*

Do you see the use of both words there? Because now you have become a people, you can come into a covenant relationship with God.

Rom 15:11 *And again, "Praise the Lord all you Gentiles, and let all the peoples praise Him."*

This is in Psalm 117:1 *"Praise the LORD, all nations; Laud Him, all peoples!*

What Paul is doing is that he is addressing it primarily to Jewish people. He said look our own scriptures said that God was going to send mercy to the other nations. What angered the Jewish people most in Paul's ministry is that he was taking the message to the Gentiles. The Jews at that time regarded this as their exclusive right that no other nation had access to.

Rom15:12 *Again Isaiah says, "there shall come the root of Jesse, and He who arises to rule over the Gentiles, in him shall the gentiles hope."*

This scripture comes from Isaiah 11:10: *Then in that day, the nations will resort to the root of Jesse, (Jesus) who will stand as a signal for the peoples; and His resting place will be glorious.*

So Paul is saying, it was predicted by our great prophet Isaiah that the nations, the 'goyim' will resort to the root of Jesse or the son of Jesse.

Another scripture in Isaiah 42:4: *"He will not be disheartened or crushed Until He has established justice in the earth; and the coastlands will wait expectantly for His law."*

Coastlands are all those parts of the earth that border on the ocean. All continents are going to wait expectantly for the law of the Messiah.

Rom 15:13 *Now may the God of hope fill you with all joy and peace in believing, so that you will abound in hope by the power of the Holy Spirit.*

Again we come to the purpose of this teaching. Let me point out to you how important hope is. Paul says in 1st Corinthians 13:13 … *But now faith, hope, love, abide these three; but the greatest of these is love.*

Hope is one of the three abiding realities. But you can only abound in hope by the power of the Holy Spirit. The Holy Spirit is the greatest optimist. When he comes in you, you may have been the worst pessimist but you begin to become an optimist.

15.3 Principles and Accomplishments of Paul's Ministry

Paul was pretty forthright but he was also tactful and he is writing to a church he has never visited. Although he knows a lot of the people in the church and he had been giving them a lot of teaching some of which is pretty strict, and so he kind of apologizes for being a teacher to them. But at the same time reminds them that he is the apostle of the Gentiles and that this is his job.

Rom 15:14 And concerning you, my brethren, I myself also am convinced that you yourselves are full of goodness, filled with all knowledge and able also to admonish one another.

In other words, Paul is telling them that they really hardly need teaching (remembering that he has written to them this long letter with 15 chapters of teaching). He is really sweetening the pill at this point.

Rom 15:15 But I have written very boldly to you on some points so as to remind you again, because of the grace that was given me from God,

That is the grace of Apostleship to the Gentiles

Rom 15:16 to be a minister of Christ Jesus to the Gentiles, ministering as a priest the gospel of God, so that my offering of the Gentiles may become acceptable, sanctified by the Holy Spirit.

What a view of his ministry. He said I am like a priest in the Old Covenant. I have got a sacrifice to offer up to God. But it has to be sanctified. What was the sacrifice? It is the Gentile Church. He said 'my sacrifice' a little later on and in this epistle he says my gospel.

What a sense of responsibility. God has committed this task to me. To make everybody know that the message of the gospel, includes not merely the Jewish people, but the Gentiles too. And he said; I am offering this up, as a priest in the Old Testament would offer up a sacrifice. Every sacrifice, you know had to meet certain conditions. It had to be anointed with oil and it had to have other things that accompanied it.

So Paul envisions himself as a priest offering up, not just a little land or even a bullock, but offering up the whole Gentile Church to God. And his concern is that it will be sanctified. That it will be holy. In a way, one main thrust of Romans is to produce a holy church. He says forgive me that I have written such a long letter and I know that you really know much of these things but this is my job. This is what God called me to do.

Now we come to something very important. Something we should all be conscious of.

Rom 15:17 Therefore in Christ Jesus I have found reason for boasting in things pertaining to God.

It is legitimate to boast provided you boast about the right thing. Not about yourself, but about the things that pertain to God. Then he goes on to explain what he means:

Rom 15:18 For I will not presume to speak of anything except what Christ has accomplished through me, resulting in the obedience of the Gentiles by word and deed,

The ultimate purpose of his ministry was to bring the Gentiles, through faith, into obedience to the Word of God. How did he do it?

Rom 15:19 in the power of signs and wonders, in the power of the Spirit; so that from Jerusalem and round about as far as Illyricum I have fully preached the gospel of Christ

That is the full gospel. Paul says, I just did not preach the word but my word has been attested by supernatural signs and miracles. I fully preached the gospel and the purpose of it was to make the Gentiles obedient. Not just nominal believers, not just head believers, but committed from the heart to the Lord Jesus Christ and the truth of his word.

The emphasis is this: when you are a Christian, you should be better than you were before. If you were a teacher before, you should be a better teacher than you were before. If you were a nurse you should be a better nurse than you were before. The fact that you have been saved, does not mean that you can get away with sloppiness. It means you are going to be much more efficient than you were before.

What Paul is trying to convey here is that you can get head acceptance by teaching people's heads but there is only one power that can reach people's hearts and that is the Holy Spirit. When he comes in sovereign power, there will be miracles and there will be signs and wonders. It is not the signs that convince people. The signs get their attention but it is the power of the Holy Spirit that brings the signs and that also convinces and they become obedient from the heart.

There is a lot of difference between obeying from the head, which can be perfectly sincere and genuine, and obeying from the heart. One of the effects of obeying from the heart is that people get a burden for others.

Paul knew what he was talking about. If you want heart faith and heart obedience, it comes only by the supernatural power and presence of the Holy Spirit and miracles will accompany it.

Let us turn our attention for a moment to the words of Paul in 1st Corinthians 2:1-5 and what he is writing about when he came to Corinth:

1And when I came to you, brethren, I did not come with superiority of speech or of wisdom, proclaiming to you the testimony of God. 2 For I determined to know nothing among you except Jesus Christ, and Him crucified. (That is the most unusual decision. That is, to make up your mind to know nothing except one thing –Jesus Christ.)

3 I was with you in weakness and in fear and in much trembling, 4 and my message and my preaching were not in persuasive words of wisdom, (Which was the whole essence of Greek culture. The highest accomplishment amongst the Greeks was to be an orator and to be able to persuade people with words) *but in demonstration of the Spirit and of power,* (The Holy Spirit is invisible but his presence can be demonstrated by what he'd done) 5 *so that your faith would not rest on the wisdom of men, but on the power of God.*

It is good, not to have your faith resting on the wisdom of men because it changes with every generation. The Word of God and the power of God never change. You need to consider Paul's experience sometimes because he had been to Athens before he went to Corinth and Athens was the intellectual center of the Greek world. He had preached a rather intellectual sermon which he actually quoted from Greek poets and the results were meager. Then when he was going on to Corinth, which was a large wicked seaport with all the vices and the wickedness of a seaport, somewhere between Athens and Corinth he made up his mind. I am not going to know anything among these people but Jesus Christ crucified and the city was turned upside down.

Historians estimated that the early church in Corinth grew to 25,000 people out of what Jesus Christ crucified and the power of the Holy Spirit that will not bear witness supernaturally to anything but Jesus Christ crucified. We can have all sorts of elegant sermons and programs but if you want the power of the Holy Spirit, you better focus on Jesus Christ on the cross.

One of the disasters in the modern church in so many places is that, the cross has been displaced from the center and all sorts of publicity stunts have been put in its place. But the Holy Spirit is not interested in gimmicks.

Rom 15:20 *And thus I aspired to preach the gospel, not where Christ was already named, so that I would not build on another man's foundation;*

Rom 15:21 *but as it is written, "they who had no news of him shall see, and they who have not heard shall understand."*

That is apostolic motivation. The key word for every apostle is 'go and preach the gospel'. Go into every nation. An apostle is not a pastor circulating among established churches. He is a man with a vision for the unreached and that is where God bears supernatural testimony. When you arrive among a group of people that have never heard the name of Jesus and you tell them that there was a son of God and he came to earth, died and rose again. What is going to make them believe? It is the supernatural testimony of the Holy Spirit.

Corrie Ten Boom and her famous little admonition to preachers said: KISS (keep it simple stupid). We have got too sophisticated and too elaborate. We need to come back to the poor and reach the unreached.

Abandon your sophistication and your clever methods and your personal ambition and be prepared to exalt Jesus and focus on the cross. God has no favorites. He will do as much for us if we meet the conditions. In fact, he will do more because we are living in the harvest hour and I believe God is prepared to perform amazing miracles to reap the harvest.

15.4 Paul's Projected itinerary

Rom 15:22 For this reason I have often been prevented from coming to you;

Rom 15:23 *but now, with no further place for me in these regions,* (I have reached everybody between Jerusalem and Rome and the next step is Rome), *and since I have had for many years a longing to come to you*

Rom 15:24 *whenever I go to Spain—for I hope to see you in passing, and to be helped on my way there by you, when I have first enjoyed your company for a while—*

Rom 15:25 *but now, I am going to Jerusalem serving the saints.*

Rom 15:26 *For Macedonia and Achaia* (That is the Christians in those places) *have been pleased to make a contribution for the poor among the saints in Jerusalem.*

Rom 15:27 Yes, they were pleased to do so, and they are indebted to them. For if the Gentiles have shared in their spiritual things, they are indebted to minister to them also in material things.

Rom 15:28 Therefore, when I have finished this, and have put my seal on this fruit of theirs, I will go on by way of you to Spain.

So he said that presently, I am in Corinth which was where this epistle was written. I am going to Jerusalem to deliver up the money that they have offered and make sure the right people get the money and then I am going to go to Spain. But on the way to Spain, I will stop over and see you in Rome.

Then he says;

Rom 15:29 I know that when I come to you, I will come in the fullness of the blessing of Christ.

So here is Paul saying he will come in fullness of blessing. But he came as a prisoner in chains having had a pretty harrowing journey in which they had been in a storm for 14 days without seeing the Sun or the Moon. They landed on an island after being wrecked. Then the first thing that happened as Paul was out there gathering wood (he did not stand around and say I am the apostle, you people need to get the wood together. He was out there gathering wood) a viper fastened itself on his hand. But Paul just shook it off in the fire continued. The people who stood by expected to see him drop dead because they said that this man must be a murderer. He escaped the Vengeance of the sea but God has got him through the Viper but when he did not die. They said well this man is different and the whole island came together and they had a revival on the island of Malta.

He did come in the fullness of the blessing of God, but he did not come as a super apostle. He came as a very humble servant of Jesus Christ. He had prayed, in Romans chapter 1:10, for a prosperous journey. He went as a prisoner in chains through a 14 day storm on a shipwreck. But it was a prosperous journey, because God's purposes were accomplished. 278 persons on that ship saw the miracle-working power of God. They saw a God who answers the prayer of a man and they knew that they were alive because of that man. It is very interesting because at the beginning of that journey, the Roman centurion and the captain of the ship where the people that gave the orders. But by the end, it was Paul who gave the orders. That is what is called promotion God's Way.

When God puts you through humiliating situations, just recognize this is the pathway to promotion.

15.5 Personal Request for Prayer

Rom 15:30 Now I urge you, brethren, by our Lord Jesus Christ and by the love of the Spirit, to strive together with me in your prayers to God for me,

Rom 15:31 that I may be rescued from those who are disobedient (or unbelieving) *in Judea, and that my service for Jerusalem may prove acceptable to the saints;*

Rom 15:32 so that I may come to you in joy by the will of God and find refreshing rest in your company.

I want to pick out one particular phrase there in verse 30: *"that you will strive together with me in your prayers to God for me"*

The word strive, is the word from which we get agonizing in modern English. It is the word that is used of a contest in the Olympic Games. This is a challenge to intercessors. Do you know what it is to strive, to agonize, to go through a conflict on behalf of a servant of God? The success of a ministry depends mainly on the intercessors who uphold the servant of God through prayer.

And this is dramatic in Paul's case because he prayed that he might be preserved from the disobedient in Jerusalem. If you read acts 21 through to 28, it is the story of how he had to be preserved two or three times with specific attempts to kill him. He was subject to mob violence; he was rescued at the last minute by a Roman centurion. The difference between life and death for Paul depended on the prayers of God's people. If they had not done what he said and striven together, he would never have made it to Rome.

There is no higher ministry than that of intercession. The problem is that many people who are called to be intercessors do not feel they are doing enough because they are not out in front. Because they are not on a platform, they give up on the ministry. Do not do that, God needs you. The servants of God in the ministry need you to be willing to strive together to fight to wrestle with the powers that seek to destroy men in ministry. The ultimate victory cannot be won without intercession.

Then we get that beautiful phrase at the end of this chapter:

Rom 15:33 Now the God of peace be with you all. Amen

What a wonderful ending to a somewhat stormy chapter. There are seven places in the New Testament where God is called the God of peace. (Romans 16:20, 2nd Corinthians 13:11, Phil 4:9, 1st Thessalonians 5:23, 2nd Thessalonians 3:16, Hebrews 13:20)

Shalom is Hebrew word for peace. It is the Hebrew greeting, but it is much more than what we understand by piece in English. It is related to a word that means completeness or perfection.

Peace (Shalom) = Harmony, wholeness, completeness, every account settled. The verb that is formed from it means to pay in full.

CHAPTER 16: GREETINGS & FINAL INSTRUCTIONS

(Romans 16:1 - 16:27)

This is a chapter mainly of personal greetings. Some people have questioned whether it really should be part of Romans. It is totally part of Romans because God does not just give us lectures and leave out personal relationships. He demonstrates so after all this wonderful theology that personal acknowledgements are important. Paul spends one chapter practically just greeting people by name. That is a much more vivid way of saying personal relationships matter. It is not all just up there in the theoretical realm of doctrine. It is got to be lived out and worked out in personal relationships.

We are not just dealing with humanity en mass or even the church but there are intimate valuable personal relationships which are built in the body of Christ and which are of great value in the sight of God. None of us is just a number with God. When you joined school, they probably gave you a number but God does not do that with you. You are not a just a number with God when you came to salvation. He knows you personally and he wants us to know one another personally. He attaches great importance to personal relationships.

There were 36 individuals in this chapter that Paul mentions and all but two of them by name those who were associated with Paul in ministry.

16.1 Personal Greetings

Rom 16:1 I commend to you our sister Phoebe, who is a servant of the church which is at Cenchrea;

Rom 16:2 that you receive her in the Lord in a manner worthy of the saints, and that you help her in whatever matter she may have need of you; for she herself has also been a helper of many, and of myself as well.

Phoebe was the sister that carried the letter to Rome. She was a servant of the church a Deaconess of the church in Corinth. That is in the in the Peloponnese. If Phoebe had not been faithful, we would never have the Epistle to the Romans. God trusted one little woman with the supreme task of getting this letter to the church in Rome. There were no public postal services at the time. Every letter demanded a person to take it. Think of how many letters there were in the New Testament and see how much importance they attach to communication with one another.

Today, there is very little writing between Christians and especially the shepherds to the flocks. If the New Testament Christians had not been better letter writers, we would never have had the old and the New Testament.

Some good and encouraging manners to Christians today: Never receive anything by way of encouragement or contribution from people without it being acknowledged. Never receive anything from anybody, never visit a home without writing a personal letter of thank you. That builds personal relationships. It takes time and it takes thoroughness to build personal relationships. It is the little things that build the relationships.

Rom 16:3 Greet Prisca and Aquila, my fellow workers in Christ Jesus,

Rom 16:4 who for my life risked their own necks, to whom not only do I give thanks, but also all the churches of the Gentiles;

Prisca and Aquila were two of Pauls' longtime friends, who have been in all sorts of trouble with him. There is something about being in trouble with people. It builds a relationship.

Rom 16:5 also greet the church that is in their house. Greet Epaenetus, my beloved, who is the first convert to Christ from Asia.

Rom 16:6 Greet Mary, who has worked hard for you.

Rom 16:7 Greet Andronicus and Junias, my kinsmen and my fellow prisoners, who are outstanding among the apostles, who also were in Christ before me.

Rom 16:8 Greet Ampliatus, my beloved in the Lord.

Rom 16:9 Greet Urbanus, our fellow worker in Christ, and Stachys my beloved.

Rom 16:10 Greet Apelles, the approved in Christ. Greet those who are of the household of Aristobulus.

Rom 16:11 Greet Herodion, my kinsman. Greet those of the household of Narcissus, who are in the Lord.

Rom 16:12 Greet Tryphaena and Tryphosa, workers in the Lord. Greet Persis the beloved, who has worked hard in the Lord.

Rom 16:13 Greet Rufus, a choice man in the Lord, also his mother and mine.

Rom 16:14 Greet Asyncritus, Phlegon, Hermes, Patrobas, Hermas and the brethren with them.

Rom 16:15 Greet Philologus and Julia, Nereus and his sister, and Olympas, and all the saints who are with them.

Rom 16:16 *Greet one another with a holy kiss. All the churches of Christ greet you.*

There were relatives of Paul, heads of households and two people picked out as hard workers. That was just typical of Paul. He could remember the women who worked hard. Then the list of the people referred to elsewhere.

16.2 Warning against Divisions

Then in verses 17 through 19: A warning against those who peddle false teaching for the sake of personal gain.

Rom 16:17 *Now I urge you, brethren, keep your eye on those who cause dissensions and hindrances contrary to the teaching which you learned, and turn away from them.*

Paul warns us to be vigilant that there will be some among us who will cause disagreements and hindrances and his advice is: turn away from such. The goal of Christian living is to have righteousness, Peace and Joy. However, for some reasons, there will be other people who will want to cause divisions and from such, turn away. In the next verse, Paul gives us an insight of these kinds of men;

Rom 16:18 *For such men are slaves, not of our Lord Christ but of their own appetites; and by their smooth and flattering speech they deceive the hearts of the unsuspecting.*

Paul singles out selfishness as the root of those who cause strife. He calls them slaves to their own desires and they even use flattery to deceive the unsuspecting. Their intention is to cause divisions, in-fighting, disharmony, conflict, tension, bitterness, animosity etc. and they are not of Christ.

Then Paul commends the church in Rome;

Rom 16:19 For the report of your obedience has reached to all; therefore I am rejoicing over you, but I want you to be wise in what is good and innocent in what is evil.

And then this remarkable promise in Romans 16:20

Rom 16:20 The God of peace will soon crush Satan under your feet. The grace of our Lord Jesus be with you.

We looked at the fact that the Roman Church in three centuries defeated the Roman Empire without use of any physical weapon or modern technology in media and propaganda. They just dethroned one of the most powerful empires in human history. I believe that this is a promise also to the end time Church. Satan is going to be crushed beneath the feet of the Church of Jesus Christ.

16.3 The Eternal Purpose and Power of the Gospel

And then there is this wonderful closing in a way doxology in verses 25 and 26:

Rom 16:25 Now to Him who is able to establish you according to my gospel and the preaching of Jesus Christ, according to the revelation of the mystery which has been kept secret for long ages past,

Isn't that exciting? That God lets us into a secret that previous ages and generations have never been allowed to know.

Rom 16:26 but now is manifested, and by the Scriptures of the prophets, according to the commandment of the eternal God, has been made known to all the nations, leading to obedience of faith;

Rom 16:27 to the only wise God, through Jesus Christ, be the glory forever. Amen.

That is the message we have. What a privilege to receive it and what a privilege to proclaim it you.

Amen